The Handbook of Literacy Assessment and Evaluation

Second Edition

The Handbook of
Literacy Assessment and Evaluation

Second Edition

Bill Harp

University of Massachusetts Lowell

Christopher-Gordon Publishers, Inc.
Norwood, Massachusetts

Credits

Figures from Gambrell, Linda B., Palmer, Barbara Martin, Codling, Rose Marie, & Mazzoni, Susan Anders. (1996, April). Assessing motivation to read. *The Reading Teacher,* 49 (7), 518-533. Used by permission of the International Reading Association.

Appendix & excerpt from Schmitt, Maribeth Cassidy. (1990, March). A questionnaire to measure children's awareness of strategic reading processes. *The Reading Teacher,* 43 (7), 454-461. Used with permission of the International Reading Association.

Appendix A, B, C, & D from Bottomly, Diane M., Henk, William A., & Melnick, Steven A. (Dec. 1997/ Jan 1998). Assessing children's views about themselves as writers using the Writer Self-Perception Scale. *The Reading Teacher,* 51 (4), 286-291. Used by permission of the International Reading Association.

Appendix A, B, C, & D from Henk, William A., & Melnick, Steven A. (March 1995). The reader self-perception scale (RSPS): A new tool for measuring how children feel about themselves as readers. *The Reading Teacher,* 48(6), 470-482. Used with permission of the International Reading Association.

Christopher-Gordon Publishers, Inc.
1502 Providence Highway
Norwood, Massachusetts
(800) 934-8322

Printed in the United States of America

10 9 8 7 6 5 4 3 2 1   03 02 01 00

ISBN: 1-929024-11-8
Library of Congress Catalogue Number: 99076808

Dedication

Dedicated to

Cassi, Hillary and Nathan—
my constant reminders of the importance of superb literacy teaching and learning.

Short Contents

Section 1
Teacher-Made Assessment and Evaluation Tools

Section 2
Published Assessment and Evaluation Tools

Expanded Contents

Section 1
Teacher-Made Assessment and Evaluation Tools

Section 2
Published Assessment and Evaluation Tools

Conceptual Contents

Attitude, Motivation, Self-Perception Assessment Tools

Comprehension and Metacomprehension Assessment Tools

Developmental Assessment Tools

Emergent Literacy Assessment Tools

Informal Reading Inventories

Miscue Analysis Tools

Norm-referenced Assessment Tools

Observational Assessment Tools

Writing Assessment Tools

Reproducible Teacher-made Tools

Preface

The purpose of this handbook is to give the classroom teacher, reading specialist, administrator, or student concise, up-to-date information on the most popular assessment and evaluation tools in literacy. This second edition retains many of the tools reviewed in the first edition and adds twelve new tools.

We asked persons who had used the first edition to review it critically and offer suggestions for the second edition. We also sent a questionnaire to users of the first edition asking them which tools should be retained in the new edition and which ones should be added. The contents of the second edition reflect their thinking. In addition, many of the tools are now accompanied by black-line masters of the tool itself. You can easily make copies and try the tool out with your learners. My hope is, however, that when you try a tool that I have designed you will modify it in ways that make it more useful to you and your learners. The real value of this book lies in the information it provides you in making important assessment and evaluation decisions.

Assessment is the collection of data on a student's performance. *Evaluation* is the interpretation of that data—looking at a learner's strengths and identifying the learner's next learning goals. Assessment and evaluation go hand in hand. One should not be done without the other. Because assessment and evaluation should always inform instruction, you will find a section in each review that addresses ways in which that particular tool informs instruction.

The *Handbook* is divided into two sections. The first section reviews tools that are teacher-made. Some tools are an actual assessment device and others are strategies that teachers use to collect data that informs instruction. The second section of the *Handbook* reviews published assessment and evaluation tools. The publisher of the tool is always indicated in the "Where do I get more information" section at the end of the review.

Each review consists of the following features:

- What is it? This section describes the nature of the assessment and evaluation tool.

- How does this tool inform instruction? This section details the ways you can use the tool to inform your instruction. Some of these discussions include the insights of teachers who use the tool.
- What are the advantages of the tool?
- What are the disadvantages of the tool?
- Where can I get more information about the tool?

Advice of the reviewers on how the *Handbook* should be organized was very mixed. Some recommended retaining the alphabetical listing in the Table of Contents. Others recommended a conceptual organization in which like-tools would be grouped together. I have decided to retain the alphabetical listing in the Table of Contents, but I have provided a second, conceptual Table of Contents. This is not proof that I am indecisive! It is an attempt to make the book more useful to you.

My sincere thanks go to all of you who enjoyed the first edition and those who gave me invaluable feedback on ways to improve the second edition. I wish especially to thank the reviewers who carefully read the first draft of the second edition and contributed greatly to the quality of the finished manuscript. They are Jack W. Humphrey, Director of Middle Grades Reading Network, University of Evansville, IN, and Marie Jordan-Whitney, Language Arts Coordinator, Fairfield Public Schools, CT.

It is my sincere hope that if you are seeking answers to difficult questions about assessment and evaluation in literacy that you will find this book extremely helpful. I have tried to offer unbiased, critical reviews of the tools. Tools were selected for inclusion on the basis of their popularity, not on the basis of my philosophical orientation. I wish you the greatest success in bringing learners to literacy.

—B. H.

Section 1

Teacher-Made Assessment and Evaluation Tools

Analytic Trait Writing Assessment

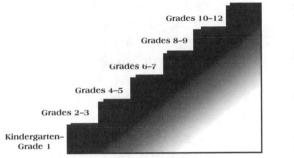

Level:

Primary

through

High School

What Is It?

Analytic Trait Writing Assessment is a way to set very specific criteria for evaluating student writing. The name comes from the fact that you identify the "traits" that you wish to look for in the writing, and then analyze writing samples for those traits. Some state testing systems have incorporated Analytic Trait Writing Assessment. If your state assessment doesn't include it, perhaps your school system will create a district-wide assessment. At minimum, it works best if the faculty of a school agrees on the traits to be evaluated at the school level.

As teachers have moved into teaching writing as a process, it has become necessary to rethink how writing is evaluated. The traditional practice of giving a letter grade to a piece of writing, or giving one grade for content and one grade for mechanics has proven to be relatively unhelpful to students. Furthermore, such grading practices ignore what students learn about the writing process when they are engaged in process writing.

Through Analytic Trait evaluation you and your students are able to see exactly how a piece could be improved or how the developing writer has grown. Generally, the desired traits are identified for various genre of writing such as personal experience narrative, historical fiction, poetry, persuasive pieces, informative pieces and so on.

The process begins with the teacher asking students to write a piece within an identified genre to a known audience. The audience might be a classmate, the teacher, the building principal, or some other member of the school community. It works best when the writer knows the audience and is writing about a topic or issue that is important to him or her. The writing typically extends over a three-day period.

On the first day—once the audience, purpose and form of the writing are determined—students engage in some discussion of the topic and write rough drafts. On the second day, students are encouraged to revise their writing. In some schools they are given criteria for revising the genre in which they are writing. For example, if they are writing a personal experience narrative, the criteria might be:

- I checked to make sure I wrote about something that happened to me.

- I checked to see that I put in details.

- I checked the beginning, the middle and the end of the story to make sure that I wrote about everything that happened.

- I checked to make sure I connected the parts of the story in ways that make sense.

- I checked the whole piece for spelling errors.

- I checked the whole piece for capitalization and punctuation errors.

Frequently these criteria are part of the on-going writing process in classrooms and so are familiar to students at the time of the writing assessment. As you introduce your students to a genre, you might create a large wall-chart displaying the traits that will be evaluated for the genre. In this way Analytic Trait Writing Assessment becomes a teaching tool as well as an assessment and evaluation tool.

On the third day, students are encouraged to do any final editing and to make a neat last copy. The writing samples are then collected and scored. Scoring is handled in a variety of ways. Some states have reduced the amount of norm-referenced testing required in order to use financial resources to train persons to score writing samples and to pay for the time required for scoring. In some schools, teachers are trained to score and teachers exchange writing samples for scoring. In rare instances, volunteers have been trained to do the scoring.

The criteria used in analytic trait scoring is often determined at the dis-

trict level by a committee of teachers, specialists, administrators and, sometimes, parents. This determination is guided by considering "what do we value" in an emerging writer, a developing writer, and a fluent writer. Writing pieces are evaluated on the following: ideas and content, organization, voice, word choice, sentence structure, and writing conventions. When the paper is read, each category is assigned an overall rating of 1 through 4, 5, or 6. The highest rating varies across schools.

Benchmarks or models are selected from children's writing samples. For example, actual pieces of writing that merit 1's, 2's, 3's, 4's (or higher) on "ideas and content" become the benchmarks that raters compare other pieces against in determining the rating for "ideas and content." Figure 1 illustrates the criteria for a 5, 3, or 1 rating for ideas and content as used in one public school system. Figure 1 illustrates the point that, as one moves to increasingly higher ratings on a piece, the writing is incrementally more sophisticated.

How Does Analytic Trait Writing Assessment Inform Instruction?

Many teachers find it useful to schedule a writing assignment that is to be scored every other week. When a piece is assigned, the students prepare a rough draft during one or two writing periods and then type or word process their work. You would then collect the pieces and make transparencies of one or more of them and the class evaluates them together, using the identified Analytic Trait criteria. For example, students looking at samples on the

Figure 1   Ideas and Content Criteria

5 Paper

The paper is clear and holds the reader's attention all the way through.

- The writer seems to know the topic well, and chooses details that help make the subject clear and interesting.

- The writer is in control of the topic and has focused the topic well.

- Important ideas stand out. The writer uses the right amount of detail (not too much or too little) to make the important ideas clear.

3 Paper

The reader can figure out what the writer is trying to say, but the paper may not hold the reader's attention all the way through.

- The writer has some things to say, but doesn't seem to know quite enough about the main idea(s).

- Some ideas may be clear, while others may be fuzzy or may not seem to fit.

- The writer may spend too much time on minor details and/or not enough time on main ideas.

1 Paper

The paper is unclear and seems to have no purpose.

- The writer has not thoughtfully explored or presented ideas; he or she may not seem to know the topic very well.

- Ideas seem very limited or seem to go off in several directions. It seems as if the writer wrote just to get something down on paper.

- Ideas are not developed. The paper may just restate the assignment.

overhead might discuss the introductions, elaborations, transitions, or other writing skills as identified.

The students are then asked to work with a partner and evaluate each other's paper, writing the feedback on the back of the paper. This process is repeated two or three times. The students then use the feedback to revise their work. Seeing the good examples on the overhead and carefully considering the Analytic Trait criteria helps the students understand what makes an essay stronger and what can be changed in a weaker essay to make it stronger.

Many teachers feel that having the standards set down in an Analytic Trait system encourages careful instructional attention to the criteria and that this has had positive results in terms of students' increased writing ability.

When a student has completed an essay and it has been scored, then instruction can be individualized for each child. If you frequently make copies of the essays for your records, you will find that clear patterns emerge in the scoring of the essays. From your analysis of the essays, you can determine what will be taught or demonstrated during mini-lessons for the class or for individual students. Teachers have found it helpful to make copies of the traits for each genre and give those to students to keep in their writing folders. The lists then become a tool for focusing attention on the traits during writing conferences.

What Are the Advantages of Analytic Trait Writing Assessment?

The greatest advantage of Analytic Trait Writing Assessment is the meaningful evaluation of writing performance. The process not only offers specific feedback to the writer, but also provides clear criteria for ways in which writing can be improved. When an author's work is rated 3 in "word choice," one need only look at the criteria for a higher rating to understand how to improve the piece (use fewer general or ordinary words, eliminate new words that do not fit, eliminate "big" words that were used to impress, reduce the use of slang). Another advantage is that a school or school system can develop the criteria in ways that specifically tie assessment and evaluation in writing to the curriculum and values of the district. Finally, if done early in the year, Analytic Trait Writing Assessment can give both you and your children (who engage in self-evaluation) direction for improving writing throughout the year.

What Are the Disadvantages of Analytic Trait Writing Assessment?

The disadvantages of Analytic Trait Writing Assessment are that it is time consuming and requires careful training of raters. These features can make this kind of assessment expensive.

Where Do I Get More Information About Analytic Trait Writing Assessment?

Martinez, R. D. (1998). *Assessment development guidebook for teachers of English language learners.* Portland, OR: Northwest Regional Educational Laboratory.

Oregon Department of Education, Publications Sales Office, Salem, OR 97310-0290. *Oregon Statewide Writing Assessment.* ED366960.

Stoneberg, B. (1988). *Analytic trait writing assessment.* Albany, OR: Greater Albany Public School District. ED299567.

Anecdotal Records

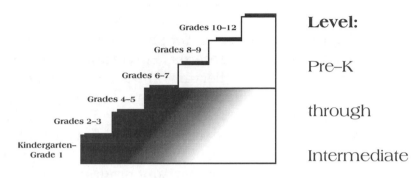

Level:

Pre–K

through

Intermediate

What Are They?

Think of the number of times in your busy day that you see one of your students do something that you want to remember. It might be a first attempt at something, or it might be a milestone in growth. Anecdotal records are the written records a teacher keeps of his or her observations of children. Increasingly teachers have realized that, while testing and collecting work samples is helpful, their knowledgeable observations of children at work add another level of understanding that can be missed with tests and work samples.

Anecdotes, defined in the dictionary as short narratives of interesting or amusing biographical incidents, has become the name for such teacher-made records. When the term is applied to teaching and learning, it is used to describe important observations made of children's work that have implications for noting progress or defining future instruction.

As teachers make use of observation to inform their instruction, they find it necessary to record these observations for later reference. A variety of systems for recording anecdotes have emerged. Some teachers use three-ring binders with a section for each child in which they record the anecdotes on 8½ × 11 paper. Other teachers prefer to record observations "on the run" and use post-it notes or blank name badges (carried in pockets or aprons or left on shelves, bookcases, etc.) to write notes and later attach those to sheets in a binder. Other teachers have created file systems in which anecdotal records are kept. Still others make use of the computer to keep notes. However they are collected, anecdotal records serve a variety of useful purposes.

The major purpose of anecdotal records is to record the teacher's (and sometimes the child's) discoveries of what the child can do. When teachers put the child at the center of instructional planning (rather than tests or texts), they become keen observers of children's strengths. They then use these understandings of a child's strengths to identify what their next learning goals should be. For example, a first grade teacher wrote:

10/22—For the first time today, Shelley miscued and noticed it did not make sense. She reread and corrected her mistake. Hooray! I need to reinforce this with her during our next reading conference.

10/24—Today I shared a running record with Shelley. Each time I asked her why she made a self-correction she told me that what she read did not make sense. I will use her next guided reading session to reinforce the questions: Does it look right? Does it sound right? Does it make sense?

Another purpose of anecdotal records is to track changes in attitude or behavior. A second grade teacher wrote: "Jim balked at writing time. After I typed his story he settled down and illustrated it. Jim scribbled on his desk and refused to wipe it off. In some ways he is acting apprehensive and afraid of writing." A few weeks later the teacher recorded: "Jim was the first to finish writing his book. He seemed proud to read it to the class."

Teachers find it useful to create a schedule that notes which children they should be sure to observe during a day or across a week. You cannot take notes on every observation of each child. Scheduling a segment of the class to observe each day or week is helpful. When a deliberate attempt is made to make anecdotal notes across time, they become very useful tools for reflecting on children's progress within a given time span. For example, knowing that you have recorded observations of each child across a four-week period, you can review those notes and write summary statements about accomplishments and next learning goals. These summaries can then be used in preparing report cards, as well

as parent-teacher or parent-teacher-child conferences. When the records are accessible to learners, children can use them in self-evaluation activities.

Yet another purpose of anecdotal records is program evaluation. By reflecting on the records made over a semester or over a year, you can see trends in children's accomplishments, attitudes, and behavior that will inform your evaluation of the reading and writing program.

Some teachers have found anecdotal records useful in analyzing data for their own research. For instance, teacher Nancy Lord used anecdotal records as data collection in a project that sought to increase the reading levels of students who came from homes where reading was not valued or modeled. The students were read to by adults two to three times each day for six weeks. In addition to pre- and post-testing, anecdotal records were kept. Lord discovered that the one-to-one reading resulted in relationship building between the adult and the student. Where such relationships were established, greater reading gain occurred, and students who showed the greatest interest in reading also made the greatest gains in vocabulary and oral expression. These students were less disruptive during whole group story time. Much of the data in this project were from anecdotal records.

How Do Anecdotal Records Inform Instruction?

In order to get the maximum results from this tool, you must be very well organized. Many teachers have found it useful to use a three-ring notebook with each child's name written on a divider, with several pages between each divider. Each page is divided into three columns: one for the date, another for the particular anecdote, and a third column for writing how you plan to act on the information that the anecdote provides.

You might also have a chart in the front of the notebook where you record the date and time of your last anecdotal record taken on each student. This way you can easily keep track of who you have taken notes on (and who you may have overlooked). You can set increasingly challenging goals for yourself as to the frequency with which you record notes on each of your learners. Reading and writing workshops during which you schedule conferences with children will be a particularly fruitful time to take records. Be sure to plan both time for you to roam the class and observe children, as well as time to hold one-on-one conferences.

Your records may include observations of both academic and social development. In looking at behavioral issues related to literacy skills, you might record how you observe a student choosing a book, how that student interacts with the book, etc. For example: Is she just flipping through looking at pictures? Or, is she actively engaged with the print? Does she just grab any book off the shelf? Or, does she carefully choose?

Such careful observations will allow you to develop individual lesson plans for each student. In any one class, there is such a wide range of literacy levels among the students that it is necessary to develop individualized plans for each one. For example, you may notice that a particular student is using context to understand the meaning of a word. You will make a note of that accomplishment and plan to reinforce this strategy in a guided reading lesson or conference. Or, you might observe that a student is struggling with a sound/symbol relationship and you make a note to revisit that phonic element during a reading conference or in a focus lesson.

You will also find it helpful to review all of the individual anecdotal notes and look for trends in the class. For example, you may note that several of your learners are returning to the same genre during choice reading time. You may decide to take steps to broaden their reading choices by introducing them to new genre. You might see that several children are making few self-corrections when they read aloud. You may decide to talk with them about the importance of asking if their reading is making sense to them. Your careful analysis of your anecdotal records will be a valuable resource for planning instructional grouping and specific lessons. In addition, it will be helpful to look at patterns that develop with each student over time to see what both their short-term and long-term challenges will be.

Anecdotal records, like almost any assessment/evaluation tool, become more and more useful after you have had practice with it. The most important aspect of becoming proficient at taking anecdotal records is to know what you are looking for and what to record. You find that the more you do it, the better the quality of the records. You are able to record information that becomes more and more pertinent and valuable.

What Are the Advantages of Anecdotal Records?

The advantage of anecdotal records is that they reflect the immediate observations and understandings about learners as you engage with them. Such records are immediate and highly relevant. If you develop the habit of observing carefully, you will have much information that is useful for planning and for sharing with parents. Teachers who begin taking anecdotal records report that their observations of children's attitudes, understandings, and behavior become more keen. One study investigated the match between teacher assessment of children and the children's performance on tests. The teacher assessments were found to be very accurate predictors of children's performance on tests (Stoner and Purcell, 1985). Finally, anecdotal records may be used for a variety of important purposes as outlined above.

What Are the Disadvantages of Anecdotal Records?

The "disadvantages" of anecdotal records are really challenges. The greatest challenge is organizing the data in such a way that it is maximally useful to the teacher and to the learner. The process of recording observations and organizing them in an effective way is time consuming. Furthermore, when we select a child to observe, we always do so with a bias (positive or negative) that may color our observations and interpretations. We need to be aware of our biases and challenge ourselves to develop interpretations that are as objective as possible.

Where Do I Get More Information About Anecdotal Records?

Johnson, N. J. (1993). *Celebrating growth over time: Classroom-based assessment in language arts.* Literacy improvement series for elementary educators. Portland, OR: Northwest Regional Educational Lab. ERIC RF358436.

Lord, N. (1993). *How to increase reading level of students who come from homes where reading is not modeled.* ERIC ED3711346.

McLain, K., Mayer, V., & Heaston, A. (1994). *Informal literacy assessment: An organized meld of evaluative information.* EDRS Opinion Papers, ERIC ED366936.

Perks, C. A. (1996). Write 'em up! *Teaching - PreK - 8,* 27, 1, 74–75.

Rhodes, L. K. (1992). Anecdotal records: A powerful tool for ongoing literacy assessment. *The Reading Teacher,* 45, 7, 502–509.

Schleper, D. R. (1996). Write that one down!: Using anecdotal records to inform our teaching. *Volta Review,* 98, 1, 201–208.

Smith, L. M. Et al (1993). *Assessment for student learning in early childhood education.* Columbia, SC: South Carolina Center for Excellence in the Assessment of Student Learning, College of Education, University of South Carolina.

Wheeler, P. H. (1993). *Methods for assessing performance.* EREAPA publication series no. 93–6. Livermore, CA: EREAPA Associates.

Wylie, C., & Smith, L. (1992). *Assessment and reporting practices in the first three years of school. Junior school study. Interim report to the ministry of education.* Wellington: New Zealand Council for Educational Research. ERIC ED344694.

Assessing Background Knowledge

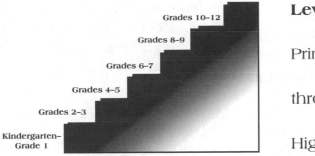

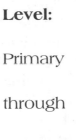

Level:

Primary

through

High School

What Is It?

We have come to understand that reading is a meaning-making process in which there is a transaction between the thought and language of the author and the background knowledge of the reader. Assessing background knowledge is determining the understandings, attitudes, biases, and beliefs a reader brings about a topic to the reading act.

As a reader, what comes to mind when you read *fast food restaurant*? Images probably include drive-throughs, waiting in lines, ordering from a menu board, fries, burgers, sodas, uniforms, a counter with registers, and speedy service. Why didn't you think of a *matre de*, linen table cloths, silver, and gourmet sauces? You didn't think of these things because your mental structures (background knowledge) about fast food restaurants does not include these things. These mental structures have come to be known as *schemata*.

Reading comprehension is enhanced when the reader's background knowledge is relevant to the text being read. We understand that, in writing,

children write far better about topics for which they have a good deal of background knowledge. Because background knowledge plays such an important role in both reading and writing, it is necessary for both you and your students to assess your learners' background knowledge as you approach new topics.

Teachers often focus on background knowledge in doing guided reading activities. Before a selection is read, students are asked a series of questions that help bring their background knowledge to consciousness. The following set of steps is helpful:

1. Inform readers of the topic or theme of the selection. Probe their background experiences and knowledge about the topic or theme.

2. Ask them to think about three questions:

    a. What do I know about the topic?

    b. What experiences have I had with the topic?

    c. What will I need to remember from my experience as I read?

The use of background knowledge in reading extends beyond knowledge of the topic. It also includes knowledge of text structures, genre, and authors. For example, prior to reading a piece of historical fiction, children could be asked to recall what they know about historical fiction, what piece(s) of historical fiction they have read, and what they think they should remember about historical fiction while reading the piece under consideration.

Similarly, children could be asked to recall, for example, what they understand about a major idea/supporting details text structure in which the author states the major idea or conclusion and then offers the evidence to support it. The discussion would end with asking the children how they will use their knowledge of this text structure in reading the selection.

Background knowledge also includes one's understanding of an author and that author's work. For example, children who have read Chris Van Allsburg's books might be lead to discuss what they know about the surprise twist in many of his stories and what they would predict in an unfamiliar story.

Background knowledge also applies to writing. Teachers often help students assess their background knowledge prior to beginning a writing project either as a group or one-on-one in a writing conference. Both the teacher and the writer can assess background knowledge by dealing with the following questions:

1. What might the topic be of your next writing piece?

2. Who will be the audience for your writing?

3. What do you know about the topic and about the audience?

4. What information will you need to learn, and how will you go about learning it?

5. How will you organize your information in ways that will make it useful to you in your writing?

How Does Assessing Background Knowledge Inform Instruction?

In gathering background knowledge, teachers can use many different strategies, such as anecdotal records, observations of oral language, conferences, and interviews. Reading inventories that ask children about what kind of television programs they watch and what they do when they are not in school are also helpful.

As you observe individual children making choices such as selecting a book to read, ask about why they selected that particular book and try to find out their experience with that topic. Teachers who know about the background knowledge of their students will be much more likely to select material (or help learners select material) that the children will at least try to read. Children who have difficulty and are struggling readers need to have materials that interest them personally if they are going to make the effort to read them.

Knowledge about the child's academic strengths and weaknesses is important, but so is knowledge about their emotional experience. By coming to deeper understandings of your learners emotionally, you can often guide them toward or away from certain titles as you deem necessary and helpful. One teacher shared the story of a fifth-grader who was not reading very well and was working on a simple text with the pattern of "just like daddy." She thought that the student began to cry because he was unable to read the text well. She offered comfort and support about the reading, only to have the child reveal that he was not crying about the reading; he was crying because his dad had died and the text reminded him of his father. Background knowledge can provide clear information about the appropriate content of texts.

The interest and experience of the child may be more important than the level, since many teachers have had the experience of having a child read material of interest at a higher level than would have been expected. In addition to choosing material that is interesting to children, background knowledge can help you know which parts of a text or which tasks will be new and which might be more difficult for a given child.

Child-centered instruction (meaning instruction that is firmly based on the children's own needs and interests) is not possible without knowing the children well. Background knowledge can help teachers plan for individual and small group instruction in areas where help is needed and help the teacher match the content of the curriculum to the interests of the children. If three children are interested in the garter snake in the terrarium, then those three can choose research about snakes, books about snakes and their habits, and other projects related to snakes. Other children might not be at all interested in snakes and would

need to be involved in other studies that did interest them.

In today's classroom, with its many levels and its diversity, one of the most critical things you may need to know is what will motivate a child and what materials are relevant and interesting. If the children are involved in interesting projects, that allows you to take time for individual instruction. Choosing materials that interest the children is also an excellent management tool in the sense that children will behave so much better when they are not bored or frustrated with their school tasks. Knowledge of children's backgrounds can help the teacher provide wide choices and then allow individuals to select specific pieces that fit their schema and/or interests.

Many teachers use anecdotal records, dialogue journals, current events reports on activities outside school, talking to parents, email, classroom web pages, and other means of keeping informed about children's ongoing or new interests.

What Are the Advantages of Assessing Background Knowledge?

The advantages of background assessment in either reading or writing are the enhanced comprehension in reading and the enhanced richness of writing. When teachers help children think about their background knowledge, they are modeling ways in which readers and writers approach their tasks independently. One of the greatest advantages of assessing background knowledge is simply getting to know your students, and their parents, community and culture.

As our classrooms become increasingly more multi-cultural, the advantages of assessing background knowledge are amplified. As you tap into the background knowledge of your students, you will become more aware of and sensitive to the cultural differences that exist. Celebrating these differences will make all learners feel more a part of the learning community, and you will gain some important understandings about the cultural differences as they apply to literacy learning. For example, not all cultures read and write in our Western linear fashion. Knowing these differences will help you support learners as they meet the challenges of coming to literacy in English.

What Are the Disadvantages of Assessing Background Knowledge?

The disadvantage in assessing background knowledge is that it depends on a self-report by the learner. Therefore, the assessment is only as valid as the student's report. Further, in both reading and writing, the questions we ask to bring background knowledge to consciousness are only good to the extent that they spark lively, enthusiastic discussion that in turn enriches reading and writing.

Where Do I Get More Information About Assessing Background Knowledge?

Cote, N. (1995). *Children's use of prior knowledge and experience in making sense of informational text.* Paper presented at the Annual Meeting of the American Educational Research Association, San Francisco, CA, April 18–22, 1995. EDRS ED385395

McAloon, N. (1994). Prereading and background knowledge. *Journal of Reading, 38,* 2, 142–145.

Meade, A., & Cubey, P. (1996). *Thinking children: Learning about schemas.* Wellington, NZ: New Zealand Council for Educational Research.

Moore, S. R. (1996). *Collaboration and the reading-writing relationship: Implications for building schemata for expository text.* Paper presented at the Annual Meeting of the American Educational Research Association, NY, April 8-12, 1996. EDRS ED395303.

Mustapha, Z. (1995). *Schemata as a reading strategy.* EDRS ED415497.

Rosenblatt, L. M. (1991). Literature—S.O.S.! *Language Arts, 68*(6), 444–448.

Rumelhart, D. E. (1982). Schemata: The building blocks of cognition. In J. Guthrie (Ed.), *Comprehension and teaching: Research reviews.* Newark, DE: International Reading Association.

Rumelhart, D. E. (1984). Understanding understanding. In J. Flood (Ed.), *Understanding reading comprehension* (pp. 1–23). Newark, DE: International Reading Association.

Assessing Metacomprehension

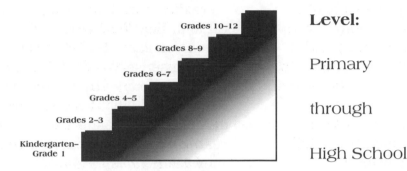

Grades 10–12
Grades 8–9
Grades 6–7
Grades 4–5
Grades 2–3
Kindergarten–
Grade 1

Level:

Primary

through

High School

What Is It?

When your students are reading are they asking themselves three critically important questions about their reading? Are they asking, "Does it look right? Does it sound right? Does it make sense?" If they are asking these questions, they are engaged in metacomprehension. Metacognition is a term used to describe our thinking about our own thinking. When this concept is applied to reading, it is often called metacomprehension. Metacomprehension means thinking about my own comprehension. We know that one of the important things that sets good readers apart from poor readers is that good readers know reading is a meaning-making process. They monitor this process, and can take corrective action when the process fails. Poor readers do not know this (Lapp and Flood, 1984).

Assessing metacomprehension is measuring the extent to which a reader can monitor his or her own creation of meaning when reading and take corrective action when meaning-making fails. In writing, it is looking at how a writer thinks about his or her use of

the writing process, evaluates the unfolding piece, and can take action to improve the writing.

Teachers essentially use three avenues to assess metacomprehension in reading and writing: written questionnaires; discussions in guided reading, reading and writing conferences; and interviews. The questions used in written questionnaires and in interviews could be the same. Please refer to Interviews (p. 79) for an extensive discussion of the role interviewing plays in assessment and evaluation. Here we will consider the assessment of metacomprehension in guided reading, as well as reading and writing conferences. For additional information, please see the Retrospective Miscue Analysis, Running Records, Reading Conferences and Writing Conferences reviews in this book.

Guided Reading

Guided reading is an instructional strategy in which you work with a small group of children, all of whom have copies of the instructional level text in hand. You guide children through the text with careful consideration of how they are using the reading process and what strategies they are able to employ. Readers focus on their behavior as readers. Guided reading situations are ideal opportunities to assess metacomprehension ability. As readers mature, their ability to describe their reading behaviors increases. Harp and Brewer (1996) have recommended the Guided Metacomprehension Strategy (GMS) as a way to assess and teach metacomprehension ability.

The Guided Metacomprehension Strategy begins with schemata awareness. Here you ask readers to consider what they know about the topic of the reading before they begin to read. Their background knowledge is assessed as you listen to their self-reports. Next, readers are asked to think about their purposes for reading the text—for information, for entertainment, or to be persuaded, for example. This discussion allows you to assess what they know about purposes for reading.

The next phase of the GMS is prediction making (if it is an unknown text). After showing readers the title, a picture, a sentence, a paragraph or an incident in the story you ask, "What do you think this story will be about?" The way in which readers offer predictions and the nature of the predictions will permit you to assess how they engage with a text. After a section has been read, further predictions can be made by asking, "What do you think will happen next?"

Following a period of silent reading, the discussion focuses on the predictions that were made and then asks readers to think about their use of the reading process and story structure.

Their use of the process may be assessed by asking: How did you learn from the story? What parts of the story were easy to read? Why? What parts were difficult? Why? How did you overcome difficulties? What did you do when you came to a part that was not making sense? What did you do when you came to a word you did not know? You can talk about the reading strategies that good readers use before they read, during their reading, and after they read.

You can assess students' understanding of story structure through such questions as: Where are we in the plot? Who are the central characters? What is the conflict? Where does the story take place?

We can further tap into metacomprehension of a text by asking readers about their responses to the text. Here we ask: Did anything particularly interest you? Frighten you? Surprise you? Make you think? What information do you want to be sure to remember from this text? How has your thinking changed as a result of reading this text? How did you respond to the work of the author? In addition to assessing metacomprehension as suggested above in guided reading, we can assess it in reading conferences.

Reading Conferences

Reading conferences are usually done one-on-one between the teacher and child. This affords you an opportunity to talk in some depth with a child about his or her reading. Teachers often use this time to review a running record (see Running Records review on p. 25) and to talk about the child's use of the reading process. Asking about self-corrections and why the reader made them is an excellent way to focus on the reading process. It permits you to assess the degree to which readers are asking themselves as they read: Does this look right? Does this sound right? Does this make sense? What did you do when the word in the text wasn't the word you predicted? When you come to a word that doesn't make sense, what do you do?

Writing Conferences

Questions may be used during one-on-one writing conferences to assess the extent to which a writer is monitoring his or her use of the process. Illustrative questions include (but are not limited to):

- Do you think you are a good writer? Why or why not?
- What things are you doing well as a writer? How do you know?
- What things would you like to be doing better as a writer? How will you accomplish them?
- How do you decide what topics you will choose as a writer?
- How do you select your audience?
- How do you get and organize information you will need as a writer?
- How well do you do these things listed above?

You can further tap into a writer's thinking about his or her own writing by asking: When you write something, what questions do you ask yourself about your writing? How do you look at a piece of your writing and think of ways to make it better?

Guided reading activities, interviews, and conferences all provide opportunities for assessment of metacomprehension.

How Does Assessment of Metacomprehension Inform Instruction?

There was a time in reading education when we believed that if we could teach children 150 discrete reading skills, we would make readers of them. Amazingly, that worked for many children. Skills are still important. But our knowledge of the reading process has progressed to the point that we now understand that readers' abilities to use reading strategies are equally as important as their ability to use skills. Assessing metacomprehension is really assessing strategy use.

Careful observation of your learners during guided reading, shared reading, the taking of running records and the debriefing of running records will give you insight into their strategy use. Think of strategies in three categories: before-reading strategies, during-reading strategies, and after reading strategies. The strategies to look for in each of these categories are listed in Figure 2.

What Are the Advantages of Assessing Metacomprehension?

The greatest advantage in assessing metacomprehension ability is the understanding you gain of how the reader views the reading process and makes use of the strategies of a self-monitoring reader. You will be able to define specific instructional goals based on your assessment of metacomprehension abilities.

Figure 2   Before-reading, During-reading and After-reading Strategies

Before-Reading	During-Reading	After-Reading
Previewing	Making inferences	Reviewing & reflecting on my reading
Using background knowledge	Question-Answer Relationships	Summarizing
K-W-L	Self-questioning	Repeated reading
Prediction making	Self-monitoring	Miscue analysis
	Looking ahead & back	

The observation of increased metacomprehension awareness across time is useful documentation of the effectiveness of a reading program. If your anecdotal record summaries indicate increased evidence of your learners' abilities to monitor their own creation of meaning, this surely will document the effectiveness of your reading program. Likewise, anecdotal summaries that record increasing instances of children revising writing in light of their own questions about their writing will document program effectiveness. An increase in the self-correction ratio on a running record is another good way to demonstrate increased metacomprehension ability.

What Are the Disadvantages in Assessing Metacomprehension Ability?

The greatest weakness in assessing metacomprehension ability is that such assessment is frequently based on students' self-reports. It is possible that students will say they are using certain strategies just to please you. Or they may report doing more than they actually do in order to get approval. Some children will need extra assistance in learning to use the language of metacomprehension. Young children may have difficulty accurately discussing their use of the reading process. Baker and Brown (1984) report that it is very difficult for children in primary grades to explain why they are having trouble understanding something they have read.

Where Do I Get More Information About Assessing Metacomprehension Ability?

Baker L., & Brown, A. L. (1984). Cognitive monitoring in reading. In J. Flood (Ed.), *Understanding reading comprehension* (pp. 21–24). Newark, DE: International Reading Association.

Cambourne, Brian. (1988). *The whole story: Natural learning and the acquisition of literacy in the classroom.* New York: Scholastic, Inc.

Garner, R. (1986). *Metacognition and reading comprehension.* Norwood, NJ: Ablex.

Harp, B., & Brewer, J. A. (1996). *Reading and writing: Teaching for the connections.* Fort Worth, TX: Harcourt, Brace College Publishers.

Lapp, D., & Flood, J. (1984). Promoting reading comprehension: Instruction which insures continuous reader growth. In J. Flood (Ed.), *Promoting reading comprehension* (pp. 273–288). Newark, DE: International Reading Association.

Myers, S. S. (1991). Performance reading comprehension—product or process. *Educational Review, 43,* 3, 257–273.

Rhodes, L. K., & Shanklin, N. (1993). *Windows into literacy: Assessing learners K–8.* Portsmouth, NH: Heinemann.

Schmitt, M. C. (1990). A questionnaire to measure children's awareness of strategic reading processes. *The Reading Teacher, 43,* 7, 454–462.

Tice, T. N. (1991). Metacomprehension. *Education Digest, 56,* 6,50.

Attitude Assessment

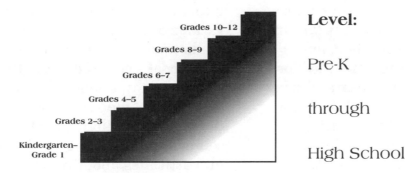

Grades 10–12

Grades 8–9

Grades 6–7

Grades 4–5

Grades 2–3

Kindergarten–
Grade 1

Level:

Pre-K

through

High School

What Is It?

We are experiencing a growing awareness among literacy educators that attitude has a great deal to do with success in learning to read and write. Attitude assessment is determining a child's general perceptions of reading and writing, such as whether or not the child enjoys reading and writing, and the child's feelings about engaging in reading and writing activities. Attitude assessment may involve asking the child to respond to a questionnaire in which the responses are written by the child or transcribed by the teacher. Some teachers assess attitude through asking questions orally. This verbal exchange permits you to probe the child's attitudes and may permit you to gain insight into the causes of the attitudes. Observation of children's literacy behavior is sometimes used to infer attitudes toward reading and writing.

Teachers appreciate the relationship between attitude and success in reading and writing, because children with more positive attitudes usually are more successful. They are also more willing to engage in reading and writing activities. For these reasons, it is important to understand the attitudes your students hold toward reading and writing.

Attitude surveys are sets of questions used by teachers to assess attitude. A number of attitude surveys have been published. Some are listed at the end of this section. One, McKenna and Kear's, is norm-referenced. Surveys that assess attitude typically make statements to which children respond on a Likert-type scale marking words or cartoon faces with various degrees of frowns or smiles. Statements on a reading survey typically include: I like to read at home; Reading is fun at school; I like reading more than watching TV; I enjoy going to the library. Statements on writing attitude surveys typically include: I am a good writer; I like to write; I like it when other people read my writing; I like to get help when I am writing; I like to write at home. Some surveys make negative statements such as "writing is boring" or "I don't like to read." Other surveys contain open-ended questions such as: How do you feel about reading? What kinds of writing do you like to do?

John Daly and Michael Miller (1975) developed an instrument for assessing attitude toward writing which has been used in research. It is known as the Daly Writing Apprehension Scale. The scale has been modified for use as part of the Illinois State Writing Assessment. The Modified Daly Scale contains statements about writing to which students respond on a five-point scale from "strongly agree" to "strongly disagree." Statements include: I enjoy writing. I worry when my teacher says my class is going to take a writing test. I like to have my friends read what I have written. I don't think I write as well as other students. I don't like to have my teacher grade my writing. The remaining statements are similar to those described above.

Teachers, especially those who doubt the validity of information they get from surveys, use observations of children's reading and writing behaviors to infer attitudes. Such observations are sometime guided by a checklist. Observation checklists in reading typically contain items such as: Spends time in the reading corner; Chooses to read during choice time; Volunteers to use books to seek out information; Is engaged with the activities during guided reading; Rereads favorite stories and books; Willingly engages in book discussions; Actively participates in buddy reading.

Observation checklists in writing typically contain items such as: Willingly engages in writing activities; Uses writing for a variety of purposes; Uses aspects of process writing effectively; Brings in writing done at home;

Chooses to write beyond that which is "assigned."

Observations of children's reading and writing behaviors may be entered into anecdotal records. Making observations of the number of books a child reads within a time frame, the nature of the books checked out of the library, the way a child approaches a reading or writing conference, and the degree to which the child is able to engage in self-evaluation may give you insight into attitudes about reading and writing.

You may find it helpful to use a combination of surveys, observations, and discussions to assess attitudes among your students. For example, if you suspect that the responses you got on a survey may reflect more accurately what the child thinks you want to hear than actual attitudes, you can combine observations to confirm the responses on the survey. A discussion could then follow about ways in which your observations confirm attitudes, or you could ask a child about discrepancies you see between statements and behavior. For example, "You told me you really like to read, but I don't see you choosing to read during choice time. What does that mean?" Or you might say, "I understood that you don't like to write, but I see you writing during choice time. Have you changed your attitude about writing? What made you change your attitude?"

Some teachers have used questionnaires for parents in an effort to assess children's attitudes. These surveys are used to tap into parent's perceptions of their children's attitudes. Parental questionnaires typically contain questions such as, What does your child tell you about his or her reading or writing? How do you see your child using reading and writing at home? How does your child approach homework assignments that involve reading or writing? How often do you see your child voluntarily reading or writing at home?

How Does Attitude Assessment Inform Instruction?

Teachers often use this tool at the very beginning of the school year and then use it on an ongoing basis throughout the school year to monitor changes in students' attitudes. With young children you will probably want to conduct the assessment in a one-on-one interview recording the child's responses. With older children you can assess large groups at one time with their written responses. The questions you ask at the beginning of the year may be quite open-ended regarding, for example, favorite books. This question might be repeated from time to time throughout the year as choices change and mature.

It is wise to get parents involved in this process. Since asking children about their "attitudes" is a controversial topic in some places, parents may be asked to first sign a release form before we can ask the children such questions. You will probably find that the majority of parents are happy to participate.

The information you learn from an attitude assessment can result in information that will help you guide children to certain kinds of books, certain authors, or certain genres. The information may guide you in helping chil-

dren select topics on which to write or audiences for writing. Attitude assessment can lead to you making decisions about the topic of themes or units of study.

It is helpful to compare notes with colleagues teaching at the same grade level and to share resources if you have children who want to explore particular themes. For example, you may see at the beginning of the school year that many students have been reading fairy tales at home, so this might be a good starting point. Sometimes it is a sports theme that draws in students, or it may be a theme related to current events.

Teachers have found that one of the reasons this tool works well is that the student monitors how his or her attitudes change over time. They often have group discussions in which students discuss their own attitudes toward reading and writing and how they have changed. Sometimes these open discussions of attitudes can have positive influences on children. For example, if one student talks about how his attitudes changed for the better, this often will encourage others to think about changing their own attitudes. Students begin to understand that they can control and/or change their attitudes and that is an empowering notion. These discussions are very helpful for the growth of the students and can give you insights that you might not otherwise have.

The following pages contain a Reading Attitude Assessment and a Writing Attitude Assessment. Please feel free to use them as they are written or to modify them in ways that will best serve the needs of your learners.

Reading Attitude Assessment

Name_____ Date _____

1. How do you feel when you think about your reading? _____
_____
_____

2. How do you feel about reading books at home? How often do you read at home?
_____
_____

3. How do you feel about using the library? How often do you go there?_____
_____
_____

4. How do you feel when it is time for reading time in class? _____
_____
_____

5. How do you feel when you are asked to read aloud in class? _____
_____
_____

6. How do you feel when the teacher reads to you? _____
_____
_____

7. What do you do best as a reader? _____
_____
_____

8. What do you need to learn to do better as a reader? _____
_____
_____

9. What are your favorite things to read about? _____
_____
_____

10. What do you read on the Internet? _____
_____
_____

11. How do your parents feel about your reading? _____
_____
_____

Writing Attitude Assessment

Name_____ Date_____

1. How do you feel when you think about your writing? _____
   _____

2. How do you feel about writing at home? What do you write at home?_____
   _____

3. How often do you write at home? _____
   _____

4. How do you feel when it is time for writing in class?_____
   _____

5. What do you like when we work on writing? _____
   _____

6. Is there anything you would change about the way we work on writing in class? ___
   _____

7. How do you feel when you are asked to read your own writing in class? _____
   _____

8. How do you feel when other students read their writing in class?_____
   _____

9. What do you do best as a writer? _____
   _____

10. What do you need to learn to do better as a writer? _____
    _____

11. What is your favorite kind of writing? What do you like to write about? _____
    _____

12. In what ways to you use the computer for writing (word processing, email)? _____
    _____

13. How do your parents feel about your writing? _____
    _____

What Are the Advantages of Attitude Assessment?

Attitude assessment permits you to better understand how a child feels about reading and writing. If we know the causes of attitudes, we can sometimes change conditions and foster more positive attitudes as a result. Negative attitudes, if accurately assessed, may contribute to a child's reduced performance as a reader or writer. Such assessment permits you to consider the child's likes or dislikes, and fears or joys as you plan instruction. Attitude assessment is another way to get to know your students. Parent questionnaires may be used to open a dialogue with parents about their perceptions of their children's attitudes. This can result in improved home/school communication. Having parents complete a survey before a parent/teacher or parent/teacher/student conference can give you direction for structuring the conference.

What Are the Disadvantages of Attitude Assessment?

The greatest disadvantage of attitude assessment is that it is primarily dependent on self-report. Children may tell you what they think you want to hear rather than sharing their real attitudes. Another disadvantage is that when we move beyond self-report, attitudes must be inferred—by the teacher or parent—based on the behavior or statements of the child. There is a very real risk that we may interpret the signals incorrectly.

Where Do I Get More Information About Attitude Assessment?

Atwell, N. (1987). *In the middle.* Portsmouth, NJ: Boynton Cook.

Dale, J., & Radell, K. (1995). *Effects of instruction on time spent reading and reading attitudes.* EDRS EED385817.

Daly, J. A., & Miller, M. D. (1975). The development of a measure of writing apprehension. *Research in the teaching of English, 9,* 242–249.

Emig, J., & King, B. (1985). Emig-King writing attitude scale for students. In W. T. Fagan, J. M. Jensen, & C. R. Cooper (Eds.), *Measures for research and evaluation in the English language arts,* Vol. 2, pp. 173–174. Urbana, IL: National Council of Teachers of English.

Gettys, C. M., & Fowler, F. (1996). *The relationship of academic and recreational reading attitudes school wide: A beginning study.* A Paper presented at the Annual Meeting of the Mid-south Regional Education Association, Tuscaloosa, Al. ED 402586

Heathington, B. S., & Alexander, J. E. (1978). A child-based observation checklist to assess attitudes toward reading. *The Reading Teacher, 31* (7), 769–771.

Hill, B. C., & Ruptic, C. (1994). *Practical aspects of authentic assessment: Putting the pieces together.* Norwood, MA: Christopher-Gordon Publishers, Inc.

Kush, J. C. (1995). One-year stability of the Elementary Reading Attitude Survey. *Mid-western Educational Researcher, 8,* 132–134.

McKenna, M. C., & Kear, D. J. (1990). Measuring attitude toward reading: A new tool for teachers. *The Reading Teacher, 43* (9), 626–639.

McKenna, E. (1997). *Gender differences in reading attitudes.* M.A. Project, Kean College of New Jersey.

Usen, M. I. (1999). *The effects of knowing student perceptions and feelings about reading in combination with teacher views in order to increase motivation.* M.A. Research Project. Kean University. EDRS ED427306

Weaver, C. (Ed.) (1998). *Reconsidering a balanced approach to reading.* Urbana, IL: National Council of Teachers of English.

Book Handling Tasks

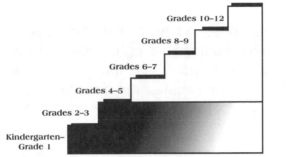

Level:

Pre–K

and

Primary Grades

What Is It?

If you are working with pre-schoolers or emergent readers, one of the things you will want to learn early is whether or not these children know how to handle books. Do these children know how to hold a book for reading? Do they know about turning pages? What concepts about books do they have? You can easily create your own book handling assessment or you may elect to use more formal, published ones. (See *An Observation Survey of Early Literacy Achievement* and *Test of Early Reading Ability—2* reviews in Section Two of this book)

Teachers use book handling tasks to assess children's understandings about books. These understandings include knowing which parts of the book are the front, back, top and bottom. Concepts about books further include knowing which parts are print and which parts are pictures, how and when the pages are turned, and where to begin reading. More sophisticated book handling knowledge includes the concepts of title, author and illustrator, and even copyright and publisher.

Teachers assess book handling knowledge through casual observation, as well as more structured situations. It may be possible to assess your learners' book handling knowledge by observing children at the library corner and during "free reading" time when you record your observations as anecdotal records. If you wish to make more structured observations you may find the checklist on the next page helpful. Please feel free to modify it in ways that will make it more useful to you and your learners.

Recognize that cultural differences may play a significant part in a child's performance on this task. For example, books printed in Japanese open just opposite to the way books printed in English open. If you suspect that cultural understandings are affecting performance on the task, you should engage the child in conversation about books they have at home or books written in their first language. It would indeed be unfortunate to conclude that a child did not know how to handle a book simply because the book was different from the ones he or she knows well!

Book Handling Checklist

Name_____ Date _____

Select a book that you think the child has not seen before. Turn the book upside down and hand it to the child with the spine of the book on the right. Indicate that you are going to ask some questions about how to use this book. Ask the questions below, either checking correct responses or recording responses after the question. Ask only the questions you deem appropriate for the age of the child and the responses you are getting.

_____ 1. Show me how to hold this book so that I can read it.

_____ 2. Where is the front cover?

_____ 3. Where is the back cover?

_____ 4. How would I begin reading this book?

_____ 5. Where do I start?

_____ 6. What parts of the book are print? (Or point to a word and say, "What do we call this?")

_____ 7. What parts of the book are pictures?

_____ 8. When I have finished this page, what do I do?

_____ 9. Where do I read now?

_____ 10. How can I tell who wrote this book?

_____ 11. How can I tell you drew the pictures for this book?

How Do Book Handling Tasks Inform Instruction?

The knowledge gained from using the book handling task is a useful starting point when planning instruction. Since book handling tasks need to done in a one-on-one situation, you will need to arrange work with one child while the other children are engaged in activities such as choice time, looking at books, playing with blocks, and so on.

Once you know which children focus on the print in a book, understand where the reader begins, understand directionality of print, and so on, then plans can be made for instruction. For example, with a small group that does not know it is the print that is being read, you might use a big book and make a point of emphasizing the print by pointing to it with a pointer, or running a hand under the print as it is being read. If children know about the print in general, then the emphasis would be on some element of the print that they do not yet know, such as upper case letters/lower case letters or periods.

The information you gain from structured book handling tasks can be verified through your observation of children in "natural" situations. In other words, when children are looking at books on their own, playing the teacher, or any other situation in which books are a part of the experience, they demonstrate their knowledge. Observations are valid assessments and can effectively be used in conjunction with the more formal checklist.

What Are the Advantages of Book Handling Tasks?

Children's performance on book handling tasks can give you insight into both what the child knows about books and, by inference, insight into how much the child has been read to and talked to about books. Children who do not have concepts about books need to develop this knowledge as part of your reading to them and shared reading experiences.

The one-on-one book handling assessment provides you with opportunities to know individual children better and to probe their understanding. In this way you can get more information than you might get from observations alone.

What Are the Disadvantages of Book Handling Tasks?

The time it takes to make the observations or conduct the assessment one-on-one may be seen as a disadvantage. However, most teachers want to know as much as possible about their emergent readers, and consider the time well spent.

Where Do I Get More Information About Book Handling Tasks?

Clay, M. M. (1993). Concepts about print in *An observation survey of early literacy achievement*. Portsmouth, NH: Heinemann.

Hood, W. J. (1995). I Do Teach and the Kids Do Learn. *Primary Voices K–6, 3,* 16–22.

Morrow, L. M. (1993). *Literacy development in the early years: Helping children read and write.* Needham Heights, MA: Allyn and Bacon.

Otto, B. (1991). *Informal Assessment of Emergent Reading Behaviors through Observations of Assisted and Independent Storybook Interactions.* Paper presented at the Annual International Reading Conference (36th, Las Vegas, NV, May 6–10). ERIC: ED353074.

Cloze Procedure

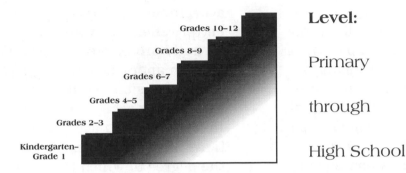

Level:

Primary

through

High School

What Is It?

We have come to clear understandings that readers draw on their knowledge about language and how it works to make meaning when they read. Using language cues as a reader means drawing on one's knowledge of semantics and syntactics in order to monitor the creation of meaning. The cloze procedure is a measure of reading comprehension based on the assumption that reading is an interactive process in which the reader interacts with the ideas and language of the writer. In the process of this interaction, the reader is calling on semantic and syntactic knowledge (as well as background knowledge) to make predictions about what the author will say. Part of this prediction activity is making predictions about words. In a cloze procedure, words have been left out of the text so that the reader may use the semantic, syntactic and schematic cueing systems to predict the missing words.

To experience how a cloze procedure operates, predict the words that would appropriately occupy each blank in the example on this page.

The teacher must know for whom a text is too difficult. Not every child in a

(1) _____ can read the social (2) _____ or science text with

(3) _____ and understanding. For example, (4) _____ fact that a

child (5) _____ in fourth grade does (6) _____ mean he or she

(7) _____ read the fourth grade (8) _____ studies text. The

fourth (9) _____ text will contain a (10) _____ range of diffi-

culty, perhaps (11) _____ third to eighth or (12) _____ grade.

The range of (13) _____ achievement levels in a (14) _____ fourth

grade class stretches (15) _____ first to sixth or higher. As we move up

through the grades, the ranges become even broader.

The exact replacements are: (1) class (2) studies (3) ease (4) the (5) is (6) not (7) can (8) social (9) grade (10) considerable (11) from (12) ninth (13) reading (14) typical.

Many teachers, especially from third grade on, find that expository texts are frequently too difficult for many learners. The cloze procedure provides a quick and easy way to assess for which of your learner's expository texts are too difficult. To create a cloze procedure, select a passage of about 350–400 words. Type the selection, leaving the first and last sentences intact but omitting every fifth or seventh word in the rest of the text. Insert a blank line of about 15 spaces where each word is omitted. Proper nouns are not omitted. To ensure reliability, a passage should incorporate a minimum of 50 blanks.

To score a cloze exercise, count the number of blanks in which the student replaced the *exact* word that had been omitted. If the student exactly replaces 45% to 59% of the words, the selection is probably at the student's instructional reading level; if 60% or more, at the independent reading level. If the correct replacements amount to less than 45%, the text is at the reader's frustration level (Bormuth, 1968). Teachers have expressed frustration or concern over having to count only exact replacements. The exact replacements are used because that is the way the original formulas were calculated in order to relate performance on a cloze with the traditional functional reading levels. If you are not interested in equating performance on a cloze with the functional reading levels, you may modify your scoring in a variety of ways.

We understand that even the most fluent readers make miscues. This understanding leads to the notion that counting synonyms or meaningfully acceptable substitutions in a cloze may better reflect the way in which readers actually process text. You could still gain an appreciation for the degree of comprehension exhibited in the cloze by counting acceptable replacements. In fact, counting acceptable substitutions would result in an assessment of the degree to which the reader uses semantic and syntactic cues, you just wouldn't be able to equate your scoring to the traditional functional reading levels.

Keep (1987) has suggested creating blanks on selected parts of speech rather than with every fifth word, and accepting replacements that are not exact. He suggests that if not exact replacements are counted, that the criterion of 70–80% acceptable replacements equates to the instructional level. Kemp suggests that a replacement percentage of 85 equates to an independent level. Acceptable replacements of 70% or less would indicate very limited comprehension.

Another variation on the cloze procedure has come to be known as a "modified cloze."

In a modified cloze, selected words are removed rather than removing every fifth or seventh word. Typically function words, those that carry the most meaning, are selected for removal. You can then ask students to predict the words that would fill the blanks and then ask them to discuss why they made their predictions. In this way you can assess their degree of understanding of the semantic and syntactic cueing systems. If you indicate the first letter of the removed word at the beginning of the blank space, students can also rely some on their knowledge of the graphophonic cueing system in make predictions.

Teachers often find modified cloze activities valuable assessment and teaching tools. For example, Grant (1991) discovered that educational gains result when English-as-a-Second-Language students work in cooperative groups to complete modified cloze procedures.

Another variation on the traditional cloze procedure is computer-administered cloze tests. Clariana (1991) reported the results of a study of 101 students in grades four through eight indicated that computer-mediated cloze reading tests adequately account for a student's reading ability and may be used to select reading materials for individualization of instruction.

How Does the Cloze Procedure Inform Instruction?

The first week of school, explain to your students that you are going to have them do a reading activity that requires them to make predictions. You might talk about the role of prediction in reading if you think this is a new concept for them. Explain that this activity will help you know how to help them use textbooks such as the science and social studies texts.

Once you know which of your learners are frustrated by reading these texts, you can plan alternative ways of having them learn important information. Sometimes you may engage children with the challenging texts through shared reading. Other times you may have students engage with the text by reading with a buddy. Sometimes you may read the selection aloud for the whole class. You might ask volunteers at a senior citizens center to make audio tapes of selected reading from challenging texts so that children can listen and follow along at a listening center.

What Are the Advantages of the Cloze Procedure?

The cloze procedure is a quick and efficient way to assess the number of children in a classroom for whom a text is too difficult (or too easy). The cloze procedure is further helpful in assessing children's abilities to draw on semantic and syntactic (and possibly graphophonic) cues in making predictions about word replacements. The modified cloze has utility as an instructional device to focus on talking about words, sentence structure, parts of speech, alternative word choices and developing metacomprehension ability.

What Are the Disadvantages of the Cloze Procedure?

While performance on a cloze procedure has been shown to correlate well with reading comprehension, it measures only narrow aspects of comprehension. While drawing on semantic and syntactic cues is critical to reading, the extent to which readers draw on background information or read critically cannot be easily assessed by the cloze procedure.

Some students, especially those who can see multiple possible replacements, find completion of the cloze very frustrating. Students who rely heavily on the graphophonic cueing system may also be frustrated in doing a cloze procedure.

Where Do I Get More Information About the Cloze Procedure?

Abraham, R. G., & Chapelle, C. A., (1992). The meaning of cloze test scores: An item difficulty perspective. *Modern Language Journal, 76,* 468–479.

Allison, Stan et al (1996). *Using the "cloze" procedure to assess reading material for alternative/adult education students.* Michigan Adult Education Practitioner Inquiry Project. ERIC: ED403422.

Bormuth, J. R. (1968). The cloze readability procedure. *Elementary English, 45,* 429–436.

Clariana, R. B. (1991). A computer administered CLOZE placement test and a standardized reading test. *Journal of Computers in Mathematics and Science Teaching, 10,* 107–113.

Grant, J. (1991). *Individual and cooperative completion of cloze.* EDRS ED341259.

McKenna, M. C., & Layton, K. (1990). Concurrent validity of cloze as a measure of intersentential comprehension. *Journal of Educational Psychology, 82,* 372–377.

Developmental Checklists in Reading

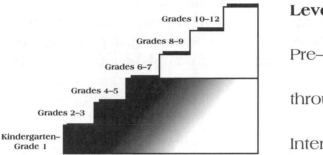

Grades 10–12

Grades 8–9

Grades 6–7

Grades 4–5

Grades 2–3

Kindergarten–
Grade 1

Level:

Pre–K

through

Intermediate

What Are They?

We all want to become increasingly better observers of our learners' work and growth. But with 25 or more learners in a classroom, it is very difficult to make the kinds of careful observations we need to make without some well-organized system for doing that.

Developmental checklists in reading are observation guides that can add the necessary structure to our observations that some of us need. Our observations are usually recorded with either anecdotal notes or with checklists. Some teachers use a combination of both. There are many reading checklists in the literature, and teachers sometimes prefer to create their own. Whether you use a published one or create your own, the first consideration is the extent to which you can accurately describe your learners as readers by using the checklist.

How do we assure a fit between the reading checklist and our curriculum? The best way is to devise the checklist by asking what we value in emergent readers, developing readers, and fluent readers. This may be done

as a faculty, in collaboration with other school personnel and parents. Creating a checklist especially designed to monitor what is valued in a school is clearly the best way to assure "fit" with the curriculum.

Another consideration in selecting or devising checklists is the depth of understanding about the reading process held by teachers. In order to be analytical observers of readers, we must develop deep understandings of the reading process, the cueing systems, and miscue analysis. Checklists designed by experts in reading may be helpful to teachers whose understandings of the reading process are emerging.

Reading checklists, though varied, tend to be organized in one of two ways. One pattern of organization is developmental. The attitudes, understandings, and behaviors of readers at developmental stages are described. Another way to organize our observations of readers is to think of the behaviors we want to see in children before they read, while they read, and after they read. The following pages (pp. 41–43) present sample checklists organized by developmental stages.

They are offered as an example in the hope that they will give you some ideas for developing your own checklists. For example, you may want to add items from Clay's *An Observation Survey of Early Literacy Achievement* to the emergent and developing lists or you may wish to add information from running records or retellings to the developing and fluent lists.

The second way in which reading checklists are typically organized is in terms of activities to do before, after, and during reading. "Before Reading" activities include using text features and drawing on background knowledge to make predictions. "During Reading" activities include monitoring one's own creation of meaning, using strategies when reading fails, adjusting use of the cueing systems depending on the demands of the text, and being able to point out difficulties experienced with the reading. "After Reading" activities include responding to reading with writing, drama, art or movement; ability to recall, to summarize, and to identify plot and setting, characters, theme, author's purpose, tone or mood; the ability to share personal reactions and relating reading to other texts and past experiences.

Hill and Ruptic (1994) worked with teachers on Bainbridge Island, WA, who wanted to bring congruence between philosophy, curriculum and evaluation. They met in grade level groups to ask themselves what reading skills most children develop by the end of any grade. From these discussions they developed benchmarks that could be used for evaluation. A reading continuum grew from these benchmarks.

The Bainbridge Island Reading Continuum is more detailed than those checklists that view development in three stages (emergent, developing, fluent). The Bainbridge Island Continuum views readers in nine developmental stages. These stages are: preconventional, emergent, developing, beginning, expanding, fluent, proficient and independent. A description of these stages, the reading continuum, and the reading continuum checklist will be found in Appendix A.

As you seek to develop or find a reading checklist, it is important to keep one other thing in mind. No checklist is static. As our understandings of the reading process develop and deepen, we will need to change the checklist. As our learners teach us more, we will see ways to improve the checklist.

How Do Developmental Checklists in Reading Inform Instruction?

The developmental checklist in reading provides a frame of reference for the anecdotal information that you record. By referring to the checklist frequently, you will be reminded of the kinds of things you want to be sure to observe in your learners. The developmental checklist is a tool that will help you develop instructional goals and objectives for the students as we progress throughout the school year.

The combined use of anecdotal records and the developmental checklist can play a key role in informing your instruction. At virtually any grade level, you will have students coming in at widely differing levels of reading development. By creating an observation schedule by which you regularly mark the checklist, you will be able to

Reading Development Checklist

Emergent Readers

Name_____

In the space to the left, record the date of your observation. Use the space under each item to write comments.

_____ Enjoys listening to stories, rhymes, songs and poems.

_____ Is eager to participate in group stories, rhymes, songs and poems.

_____ Approaches books with enthusiasm.

_____ Revisits some books.

_____ Knows that his/her language can be written and then read.

_____ Understands how to handle books for reading.

_____ Is able to make predictions and follow plot.

_____ Knows some print conventions (period, question mark).

_____ Knows some book conventions (front cover, back cover, title page).

_____ Uses reading in play activities.

_____ Uses pictures to help create meaning.

_____ Is developing finger, print, voice match.

_____ Identifies some words.

_____ Is beginning to use graphophonic cues.

_____ Is beginning to develop strategies to use when meaning fails.

Reading Development Checklist

Developing Readers

Name _____

In the space to the left, record the date of your observation. Use the space under each item to write comments.

_____ Is eager to attend to long books in reading and listening.

_____ Shows an interest in meeting challenges of texts.

_____ Displays confidence as a reader. Is willing to take risks and make predictions.

_____ Is eager to share ideas with others.

_____ Has increasing knowledge of book and print conventions.

_____ Understands how background knowledge contributes to meaning.

_____ Appreciates the value of predicting, confirming and integrating.

_____ Has several strategies to invoke when meaning fails.

_____ Increasingly makes more accurate predictions.

_____ Reads increasingly more complicated texts across a range of genre.

_____ Chooses to read independently.

Reading Development Checklist

Fluent Readers

Name _____

In the space to the left, record the date of your observation. Use the space under each item to write comments.

_____ Expects books to offer a variety of meanings, some satisfying, some not.

_____ Is confident as a reader.

_____ Eagerly participates in book discussions, author studies, and other forms of response to literature.

_____ Appreciates the power of reading.

_____ Uses the cueing systems to best meet reading needs and demands of the text.

_____ Understands the role of purpose in reading.

_____ Knows how to use the library to get information and meet needs.

_____ Knows how to use electronic media to get information and meet needs.

_____ Demonstrates increasing sophistication in prediction, sampling, confirming and integrating as a reader.

_____ Is developing study skills and can use textbook features.

_____ Is able to summarize, outline, and retell in detail.

identify the individual, small group, or whole class instruction your learners need.

The information you obtain using the checklist can also be used in reading conferences. For example, if you see that a child is having problems making predictions, you may decide to focus on that ability in your next reading conference. Referring to the checklist lets you see where to plan you next instruction for the child.

You may find a checklist to be very helpful in dealing with parents who want to know how their children are progressing. You can be very concrete and use specific examples in letting parents know where their child's strengths are and what areas need more work. This is helpful in opening a dialogue with parents on how they might work with the child at home on these challenging areas. Also, when you speak to a parent of a child who is having great difficulty in reading, it is important that there is something positive to say about what the child has accomplished. The checklist can be a tool for showing the parent the things the child has accomplished.

list is designed by you, or you and colleagues, there is a very close match between the curriculum and what teachers in your school value in readers.

Checklists, well done, can be helpful to the teacher who is an emerging student of the reading process. A checklist divided by developmental level can, for example, be very helpful to the inexperienced teacher in terms of what to look for in emergent readers. For example, a checklist containing items such as "uses literature as a basis for dramatic play" or "reads back short experience stories written by the teacher" will be a useful guide to the teacher for observing children. Teachers who have had only a skills perspective on reading can learn to take a more developmental, strategy-oriented perspective using checklists. In addition to helping teachers observe that children can decode short vowel sounds and use ending punctuation, a developmental checklist will guide the teacher to observe the ways in which developing readers use all of the cueing systems or make meaningful substitutions when reading.

What Are the Advantages of Developmental Checklists in Reading?

Developmental checklists in reading are an exceptionally useful tool to guide our observations of children using the reading process. They provide a framework that helps you make the same observations from child to child. They help us keep a developmental perspective on our assessment and evaluation of readers. When the check-

What Are the Disadvantages of Developmental Checklists in Reading?

The inherent disadvantage in checklists is that they are static. Children change and grow as readers on almost a daily basis. No one checklist can capture that growth across time. Checklists, which guide our observations, may result in a more limited understanding of children as readers when compared to what we may learn in conference with those children. Checklists work best when combined with other sources of information.

How Do I Get More Information About Developmental Checklists in Reading?

Hill, B. C., & Ruptic, C. (1994). *Practical aspects of authentic assessment: Putting the pieces together.* Norwood, MA: Christopher-Gordon Publishers.

Hornsby, D., & Sukarna, D. (1986). *Read on: A conference approach to reading.* Portsmouth, NH: Heinemann.

Irwin, J., & Baker, I. (1989). *Promoting active reading comprehension strategies.* Englewood Cliffs, NJ: Prentice Hall.

Manning, M., & Manning, G. (1996). Assessment and evaluation. *Teaching PreK–8, 27,* 6, 86–88.

Manning, M., & Manning, G. (1997). Self-evaluation. *Teaching PreK–8, 27,* 92–95.

Mooney, M. (1988). *Developing life-long readers.* Katonah, NY: Richard C. Owen Publishers.

Wood, K. (1988). Techniques for assessing students' potential for learning. *The Reading Teacher, 41,* 440–447.

Developmental Checklists in Writing

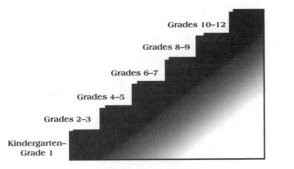

Level:

Pre–K

through

High School

What Are They?

Developmental checklists in writing are tools that guide our observations of children's work as writers. They, like reading checklists, may be organized along a developmental sequence or continuum, or they may be organized to examine the child's use of stages of the writing process.

For a more detailed discussion of development or selection of checklists, please refer to the previous selection on developmental checklists in reading (see pp. 39–45).

Some writing checklists are organized to guide the observation of children's attitudes, understandings, and behaviors as writers at the emergent stage, the developing stage, and the fluent stage. The following pages present sample checklists organized by developmental stages. They are offered here as examples in the hope that it will give you some ideas for developing your own checklists.

When writing checklists are not organized around developmental stages, they are often organized around aspects of the writing process. These checklists may be divided into sections

with labels such as the following: Selecting Audience and Form, Selecting and Ordering Information, Rough Drafting, Getting Responses, Editing, Polishing, and Publishing. Key learning outcomes for each of the sections listed above, including spelling, are discussed in detail in *Dancing with the Pen: The Learner as a Writer,* found in the reference list at the end of this section. The key learning outcomes for writing can be found in Appendix B.

White (1992) offers a process checklist for writing that includes: writes during designated time, uses constructive strategies for getting started, takes conference period seriously (is willing to help classmates by listening to their drafts, realizes other children may have meaningful suggestions), shows growth in understanding of the difference between revising and editing, uses support systems in the classroom, views revision as part of a healthy writing process, and actively participates during sharing. White includes helpful suggestions for several forms, editing questions, and evaluation criteria.

Hill and Ruptic (1994) worked with teachers on Bainbridge Island,

Writing Development Checklist

Emergent Writers

Name _____

In the space to the left, record the date of your observation. Use the space under each item to write comments.

_____   Is eager to use writing in play activities.

_____   Is willing to put writing on paper.

_____   Draws pictures and makes scribbles to express ideas.

_____   Knows how to place paper and pencil for writing.

_____   Is able to use the keyboard in writing.

_____   Has knowledge of directionality, word, and space.

_____   Has begun using simple sentence structures.

_____   Understands that writing communicates meaning.

_____   Knows that what he or she says can be written, and that what can be written can be read by self and others.

_____   Understands that certain conventions must be met in order to enable others to read writing.

_____   Is beginning to make corrections in writing.

_____   Can select writing pieces for publication.

Writing Development Checklist

Developing Writers

Name _____

In the space to the left, record the date of your observation. Use the space under each item to write comments.

_____ Is interested in writing on a variety of topics.

_____ Shows confidence in writing ability.

_____ Has begun to more accurately use print conventions.

_____ Understands the stages in the writing process.

_____ Is able to identify audience, purpose, and form.

_____ Is able to write on a wide range of self-selected topics.

_____ Is developing an understanding of text structures.

_____ Is able to use a variety of text structures in writing.

_____ Is able to edit and revise writing in response to feedback from others.

_____ Is developing skill in handwriting.

_____ Is able to use key features of the word processor.

Writing Development Checklist

Fluent Writers

Name _____

In the space to the left, record the date of your observation. Use the space under each item to write comments.

_____ Is pleased to be able to write across a range of genres.

_____ Writes with the reader in mind.

_____ Is skillful in using most print conventions.

_____ Is skillful in using a variety of text structures in writing.

_____ Expects to polish writing that is to be read by others.

_____ Is able to research and organize information prior to and during writing.

_____ Uses literature as models for writing.

_____ Writing demonstrates understanding of plot, setting, theme, characterization, and purpose.

_____ Is able to skillfully use the word processor.

WA, who wanted to bring congruence between philosophy, curriculum and evaluation. They met in grade level groups to ask themselves what writing skills most children develop by the end of any grade. From these discussions they developed benchmarks that could be used for evaluation. A writing continuum grew from these benchmarks.

The Bainbridge Island Writing Continuum is more detailed than those checklists that view development in three stages (emergent, developing, fluent). The Bainbridge Island continuum views writers in nine developmental stages. These stages are:

1. Preconventional
2. Emergent
3. Developing
4. Beginning
5. Expanding
6. Bridging
7. Fluent
8. Proficient
9. Independent

A description of these stages, the writing continuum, and the writing continuum checklist is in Appendix A.

The same point that was made about reading checklists applies to writing checklists: they should never be viewed as permanent. Children's abilities as writers change rapidly and our understandings of the writing process deepen. Therefore, checklists need to be reviewed and changed regularly.

How Do Developmental Writing Checklists Inform Instruction?

Writing checklists work best when they are frequently reviewed by you and your students. A good way to

achieve this is to attach the checklist to the students' writing folders. It serves as a reference for them when writing. It makes them aware of what is expected of them and where they need to focus their attention.

Another effective way to keep the checklist in mind is to conference with students as often as you can using the developmental checklist. Teachers often schedule time to work on the writing process three times a week. During this time, they are able to schedule four to five conferences a day. It usually takes two weeks to complete the conferences.

Figure 3 is a sample of writing from Cecilia. Her teacher, Frank LoCoco, uses the Critique Sheet in Figure 4. Frank fills out a critique sheet when he reads the piece and asks students to fill out their own sheet. They both bring the sheets to a writing conference. As you can see, the instructional goals for Cecilia as a writer might well be working on making sentences relate to the theme or topic better with better flow from sentence to sentence. Using a critique sheet might also result in Cecilia setting the goal of improving her conclusions as she writes.

The developmental checklist provides a framework to help you identify whether additional instruction is needed on a specific writing skill. For instance, you might notice there were two or three students who were having difficulty with punctuation. They were not using quotation marks appropriately. You could group these learners together for instruction.

By sharing the checklist with parents during parent conference time you can show them how successful their

Figure 3   Cecilia Fleming's Writing Sample

Cecilia Fleming   December 19   1

<u>**My Brother**</u>   2L

→ My brother can sometimes be soooo annoying. This is a true story. In front of other people he maybe a sweet little angel, but infront of his family, he is not such a sweet little angel at all! He does what even you tell him not to do. He's altoalot of bother if you were to meet him, or try to do your homework. If you were to meet him for like a little hour you would go: Ugh! UGh! UGH!

P.S.

He may be nice sometimes with his family though not very y! likey! at all!!!

Figure 4   Critique Sheet—Grades 1 & 2

```
+ = Excellent                        ✓ Narrative
✓ = Adequate                         ___ Expository
- = Weakness                         ___ Persuasive
0 = Non-Existent                     ___ Poetry
```

<u>CRITIQUE SHEET - GRADES 1 & 2</u>

Student *Cecilia Fleming*   School *Lincoln*

Title *My Brother*   Teacher *Frank LoLoco*

✓ Format is appropriate to the purpose of the writing

+ Average communication unit greater than eight words

✓ Sentence patterns vary

✓- Sentences relate to theme or topic; ideas flow from sentence to sentence; a point is communicated

+ Writing sounds like natural speech

+ Feelings expressed by the writer

+ Adjectives used; some attempt to use figurative language; images are fresh and new

✓ Word choice precise, not general

✓- Attempt at introduction and <u>conclusion</u> *weak*

✓ Verb tense consistent

✓ Punctuation, capitalization, spelling generally correct

* * * * * * *

✓ Original thought (trite expressions, situations, structure avoided)

✓ Consistent structure (rhythm, rhyme pattern, form; character action, situation

✓ Clear communication of thought; the reader derives meaning

✓ Appropriate use of the writing process (Rough draft, conferencing, editing, (final) draft)

child has been with the writing process and what more the student needs to learn. It affords you the opportunity to open a dialogue with them about specific writing skills to reinforce at home.

What Are the Advantages of Developmental Writing Checklists?

Developmental writing checklists are useful tools in bringing assessment and evaluation of writing development into line with the curriculum. Data from the checklists can be used in program evaluation, as well as in planning next learning steps for children.

Such checklists can also be helpful in our efforts to have a more developmental perspective on children's writing. When a group of teachers and other interested persons collaborate in the creation of the checklists, a dialogue is opened which may help all of us focus on the important aspects of writing instruction.

Teachers who are new to process writing may find it helpful to use checklists developed by more experienced teachers. However, it is important to remember that evaluating a child's writing behavior using a checklist is very much like taking a snapshot of that writer. It represents that student on one day on one writing task. Seen from a broader perspective, performance and achievement in writing are both very fluid.

What Are the Disadvantages of Developmental Checklists in Writing?

The inherent disadvantage in checklists is that they are static. Children change and grow as writers on almost a daily basis. No one checklist can capture that growth across time. Checklists, which guide our observations, may result in a more limited understanding of children as writers when compared to what we may learn in conference with those children.

Where Do I Get More Information About Developmental Writing Checklists?

Gregory, C. (1994). The tool you need for assessing writing. *Instructor, 104,* 52–54.

Manning, M., & Manning, G. (1996). Assessment & evaluation. *Teaching PreK–8, 27,* 86–88.

Manning, M., & Manning, G. (1997). Self-evaluation. *Teaching PreK–8, 27,* 92–95.

Morrow, L. M. (1993). *Literacy development in the early years: Helping children read and write.* Needham Heights, MA: Allyn and Bacon.

New Zealand Ministry of Education. (1992). *Dancing with the pen: The learner as a writer.* Katonah, NY: Richard C. Owen.

Scheideman, S. N. (1995). Writing checklists: Empowering students to succeed. *Teaching & Change, 2, n.pag.*

Schwartz, S., & Pollishuke, M. (1991). *Creating the child-centered classroom.* Katonah, NY: Richard C. Owen.

White, M. C. (1992). Schoolwide writing process and assessment. In K. S. Goodman, L. B. Bird, & Y. M. Goodman (Eds.). *The whole language catalog: Supplement on authentic assessment* (pp. 158–159). New York: SRA Macmillan/McGraw-Hill.

Dialogue Journals

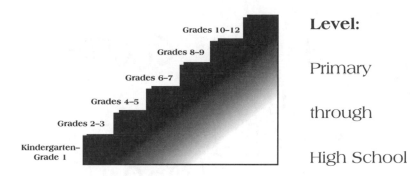

Level:

Primary

through

High School

What Are They?

Have you often wished you had time to have a conversation with each of your students on a frequent basis? Dialogue journals can approximate such conversations. Dialogue journals are journals written by students, with you as the intended audience. You read the entries and write a response, thus opening a "dialogue" with the student. In some classrooms the dialogue is between students, but typically the respondent is the teacher.

In these exchanges between you and your learners, you are able to make honest responses to what the writer says, not necessarily to teach, but to converse. Like any good conversation, this dialogue builds upon what each participant says—sometimes questioning, sometimes confirming, sometimes extending or challenging. Dialogue journals are seen by teachers who use them as a way to listen to students. Figures 5, 6, and 7 contain examples from the dialogue journals of Mary McGovern, Andres Hendricksen, and Joey Mastrangelo, third-graders in New Jersey. Please note that, in addi-

tion to a response from the teacher, there are also responses from parents. Teachers often find it greatly enriches the journal experience if students take them home for parents or care givers to write responses to what the child and teacher have written.

Some teachers feel strongly that the dialogue journal should be seen as nothing more than that—a dialogue. In their view, using the dialogue journal as an assessment tool is inappropriate. Others view the dialogue journal as a rich source of information about the student as writer (each entry is a first draft) and argue that it would be unfortunate to let all of that data go unused.

If the dialogue journal is used as an assessment tool, you may want to take an organized look at the nature of the writing. The questions we ask ourselves about journal writing are necessarily different than questions we ask about other kinds of writing. In journal writing the writing process is not followed. Each journal entry is at once a first draft and a last draft. When you are using journal entries to assess writing, you might look at fluency, topic choice, voice, and conventions.

Figure 5   Excerpt from Mary McGovern's Dialogue Journal

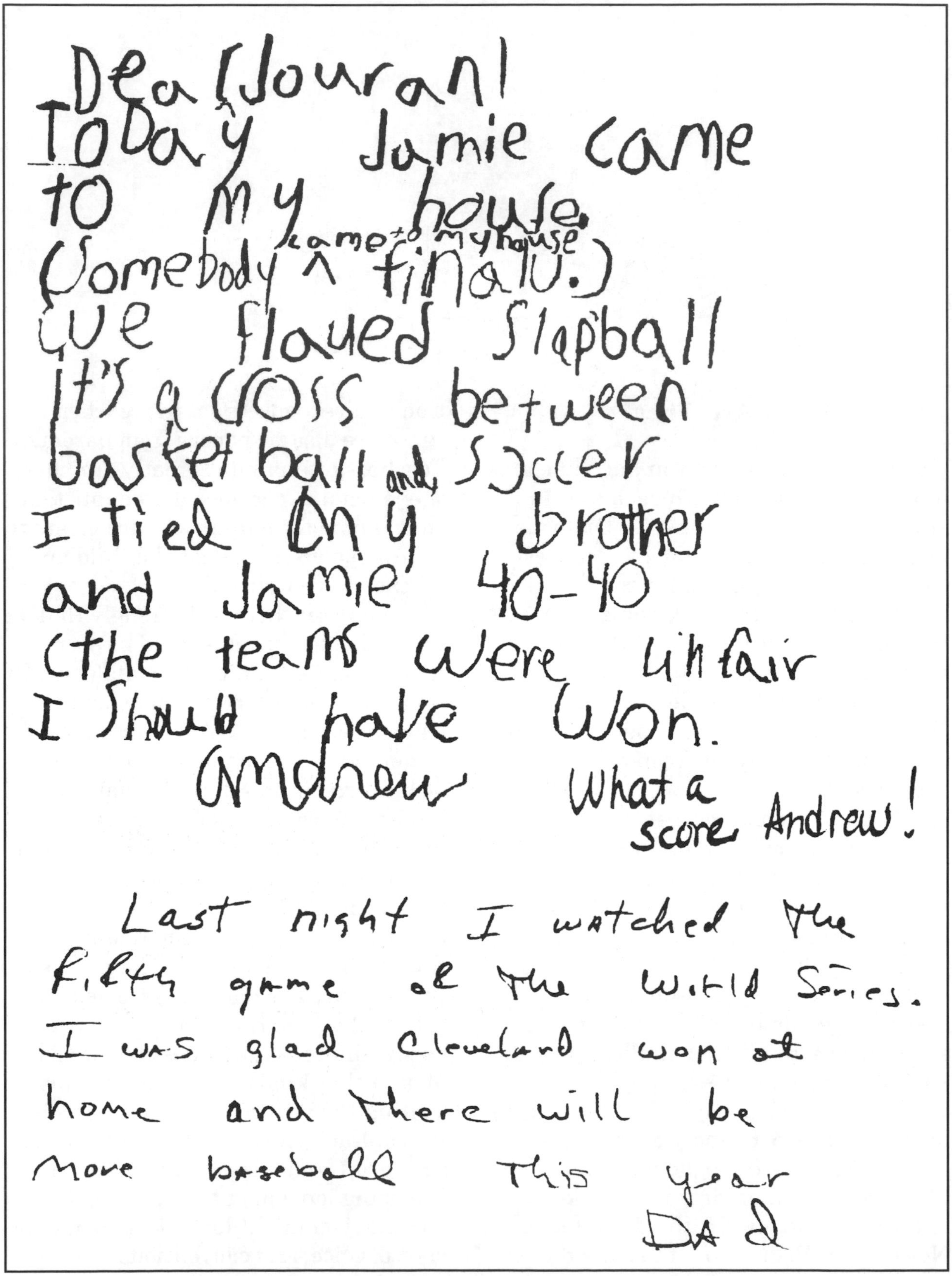

Dear Jouranl
Today Jamie came
to my house.
(Somebody ^came to my house finaly.)
We flaued slapball
It's a cross between
basket ball and sоссеr
I tied my brother
and Jamie 40-40
(the teams were unfair
I should have Won.
                Andrew   What a
                              score Andrew!

    Last night I watched the
fifth game of the World Series.
I was glad Cleveland won at
home and there will be
more baseball this year
                              Dad

Figure 6   Excerpt from Andres Hendrickson's Dialogue Journal

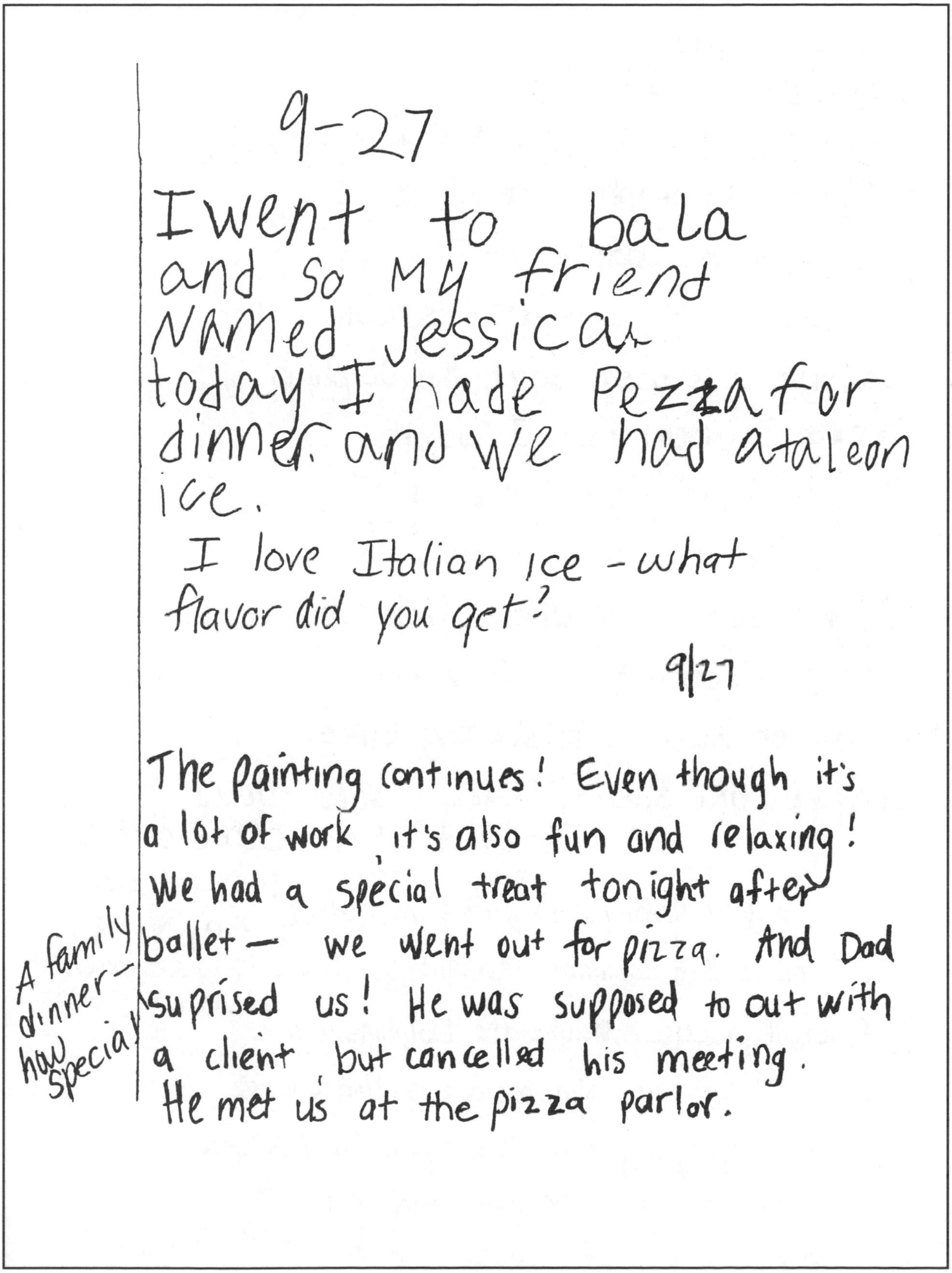

9-27

I went to bala
and so my friend
Named Jessica
today I hade Pezza for
dinner. and we had ataleon
ice.

I love Italian ice - what
flavor did you get?

9/27

The painting continues! Even though it's
a lot of work, it's also fun and relaxing!
We had a special treat tonight after
ballet — we went out for pizza. And Dad
suprised us! He was supposed to out with
a client, but cancelled his meeting.
He met us at the pizza parlor.

*A family
dinner —
how
special*

Figure 7   Excerpt from Joey Mastrangelo's Dialogue Journal

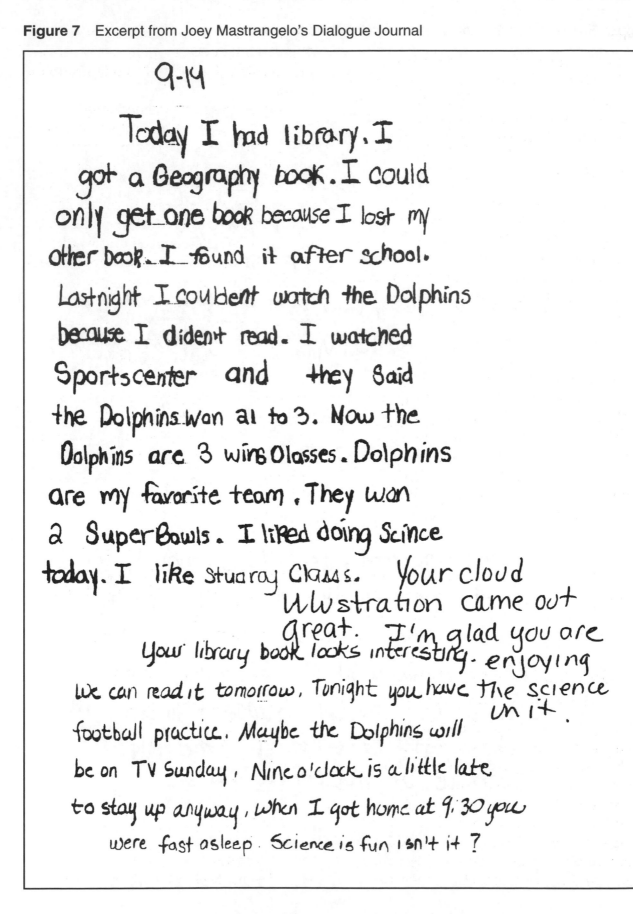

9-14

Today I had library. I got a Geography book. I could only get one book because I lost my other book. I found it after school. Lastnight I couldent watch the Dolphins because I dident read. I watched Sportscenter and they said the Dolphins won 21 to 3. Now the Dolphins are 3 wins 0 losses. Dolphins are my favorite team. They won 2 SuperBowls. I liked doing Scince today. I like stuary Class.

Your cloud illustration came out great. I'm glad you are enjoying Your library book looks interesting. We can read it tomorrow. Tonight you have the science football practice. Maybe the Dolphins will be on TV Sunday. Nine o'clock is a little late to stay up anyway. when I got home at 9:30 you were fast asleep. Science is fun isn't it? unit.

Fluency

Is there evidence that the writer is finding it easy to write? Usually easy to express ideas? Sometimes difficult to express ideas? Are there instructional implications here regarding fluency?

Topic Choice

When choosing topics, is the writer showing a wide range of interests, a narrow range of interests, or is the writer obviously not exhibiting variety in topic choice? Are there instructional implications here regarding topic choice?

Voice

Is the writer letting his or her own "voice" come through easily? From time to time? Seldom? Never? Do you see a transition across time from tentative writing to writing that is clearly expressing self? Are there instructional implications here regarding voice?

Conventions

Is the writer using good sentence structure? Varied sentence structure? What can I learn about this writer as a speller? Are there instructional implications here for punctuation?

How Do Dialogue Journals Inform Instruction?

When you implement dialogue journal writing, you need to think very carefully about the schedule because responding to journals is time consuming. Teachers have found it useful to have everyone write at the beginning of the year. This is valuable, as you can quickly get to know your students and they can start to feel comfortable in writing to you. It will probably become necessary, however, to begin to limit the journal to one group at a time.

Once you have formed smaller groups of dialogue journal writers you will be able to find out more about their language arts skills. You can get a sense of the prior knowledge, previous experience, and special interests of each of your learners. You will be able to assess their strengths and weaknesses in such areas as sentence structure, syntax, grammar, punctuation and writing conventions.

By asking students to write in their journals about a particular story the group has read together, you can get a sense of their comprehension ability and their skills in vocabulary, summarizing and paraphrasing. You can also assess their abilities to form opinions, extend ideas and provide transitions. Most importantly, through the dialogue, you can motivate, support and challenge each student.

The following is a journal entry made by Michael after his teacher asked him to tell her what he thought of a book he was reading about Helen Keller:

> I liked the book about Hellen Kellers she was a very brave woman her teacher was really good. Helen became very famous and wanted to help other people who were deaf and blind. When I read the book I covered my ears and closed my eyes for a while I wanted to know what it was like for her. When I see a blind person now with a stick or a dog I think about Hellen Kellers. I wonder if they read her book or if they had some-

*one read it to them. I'm glad
that Hellen Kellers had a good
life but I'm glad too that I can
hear and see, but maybe I'd
like to be blind and deaf like
her for just an hour.*

Of this journal entry, Michael's teacher said, "I am encouraged to note that Michael has done more than just retell the book; he has extended his thinking, so I want to encourage more of this. He is trying to deepen his awareness of what Helen Keller's experience was, so I want him to continue probing. In my response I ask him to compare what it would be like being deaf to being blind—the advantages and disadvantages of each situation or I may ask him to write to me describing a day in his life if he were deaf or blind. I also wrote: 'This book about Helen Keller seems to have stimulated your interest in the experience of people who are blind and/or deaf. I saw a book in the library about a man named Louis Braille who developed a system for the blind to read. You may want to check this book out. Let me know what you think.'

This example illustrates the richness of response you can make to the things your students say and how you can use journal entries to drive the curriculum.

You will find that the journals are rich sources of data to use in planning instruction. You will probably not only want to write responses to what your learners write, but you will often want to make additions to your anecdotal records as a result of reading the journals. For example, after reading Michael's response about the Helen Keller book, his teacher noted in her

record book that he needs some work on his sentence structure, particularly with run-on sentences. Other entries she has made in her notebook include: "Mark is communicating well but still doesn't have a good sense of what a sentence is"; "Priscilla is writing in short, choppy sentences and I need to make her aware of this and show her various methods of combining sentences"; "Lee is reading with great ease. I need to help her find some chapter books that will challenge her."

Dialogue journal entries can become useful points of discussion in one-on-one conferences with your students. You might schedule a conference every few weeks with each student who has been writing a journal. Here you can analyze the flow of dialogue that has taken place and reflect on what you have shared and learned from each other.

What Are the Advantages of Dialogue Journals?

Dialogue journals provide the writer with the opportunity to write on any topic with the clear understanding that the teacher is going to carefully read it and react to it. The assessment and evaluation advantage in dialogue journals is that they give you repeated examples over time of the writer's evolving skill in creating what are essentially "first drafts." Here you have frequent, up-to-the-minute samples of your student's writing.

What Are the Disadvantages of Dialogue Journals?

The most obvious disadvantage of dialogue journals is that they are very time consuming. Some teachers consider responding to dialogue journals as their "nightly homework." Advocates of dialogue journals argue that all student entries should be responded to—a goal that is very time consuming.

From an assessment and evaluation perspective, the disadvantage is that dialogue journals are a kind of letter writing. Too many assessment and evaluation decisions based on dialogue journals would be drawn from only one genre. This disadvantage can be addressed by using formal paragraphs, book reports, research papers, essays and other forms of writing to inform your instruction.

Where Do I Get More Information About Dialogue Journals?

Atwell, N. (1987). *In the middle: Writing, reading and learning with adolescents.* Portsmouth, NH: Boynton/Cook.

Button, K., & Johnson, M. J. (1996). Interactive writing in a primary classroom. *The Reading Teacher, 49,* 6, 446–455.

Hall, N., & Crawford, L. (1997). Writing back: The teacher as respondent in interactive writing. *Language Arts, 74,* 1, 18–26.

Hall, N., & Robinson, A. (Eds.) (1994). *Keeping in touch: Using interactive writing with young children.* Portsmouth, NH: Heinemann.

Hughes, H. W., & Kooy, M. (1997). Dialogic reflection and journaling. *Clearing House, 70,* 4, 187–191.

Peyton, J. K. (1984). Dialogue writing: Bridge from talk to essay writing. *Language Arts, 61,* 141–150.

Staton, J. (1980). Writing and counseling: Using a dialogue journal. *Language Arts, 57,* 514–518.

Holistic Scoring of Writing

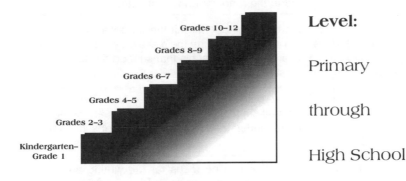

Grades 10–12
Grades 8–9
Grades 6–7
Grades 4–5
Grades 2–3
Kindergarten–
Grade 1

Level:

Primary

through

High School

What Is It?

Holistic scoring of writing is the practice of reading a piece of writing and assigning it a numerical rating based on pre-determined criteria. The ratings usually range from 1 to 4, 1 to 5, or 1 to 6. The piece is evaluated as a whole. Unlike Analytic Trait Assessment of writing, no evaluation is made of individual components or characteristics of the piece.

The procedure usually involves informing the students that they are going to be asked to write a piece that will be evaluated. Typically, they are told that they will be writing in a particular genre, such as a personal experience narrative, an expository piece, a letter, a news article, or a persuasive piece. They are then given a topic or permitted to choose a topic.

Typically, the first day's activity is to create a rough draft. The second day students are encouraged to edit the piece. Frequently the third day is used to copy a final draft as neatly as possible. In some schools the written pieces are holistically scored by the children's teachers. In other situations the scoring is done by raters trained in using rubrics. Rubrics are descriptors of the nature of the writing that would be judged a 1, 2, 3 or 4. Benchmarks or anchor papers, actual samples of students' writings, are used to establish the rubrics and as the comparators that the raters will use.

As with checklists, it works best when teachers at a grade level, within a school, or within a district develop the rubrics for holistic scoring of writing. These rubrics should be designed after careful consideration among teachers, parents, and administrators about what is expected of writers in your school(s). This would include carefully examining state and/or local curriculum guides. Figures 8 and 9 are examples of rubrics for assessing the content of writing (Rickards and Cheek, 1999). They are offered here as examples to spark your thinking about the kinds of rubrics you would like to use.

Figure 8   Rubric for Written Content

4	The writer's ideas are original and suit the purpose of the writing. Ideas are focused on one topic and are clearly developed. Specific details support the topic and add to the reader's understanding.
3	Most of the writer's ideas are original and suit the purpose for writing. Most ideas are focused on one topic, though the piece may include some irrelevant information. There are some details that support the topic and add to the reader's understanding.
2	Few of the writer's ideas are original and the purpose for writing is unclear. The ideas focus on multiple topics, and many details are nonspecific or irrelevant. The reader understands some of the writer's ideas but is confused.
1	Ideas are unoriginal. The writer has no focus for the writing and the purpose is unclear. Ideas are unrelated and/or undeveloped. The reader is confused.
0	The student makes no attempt to write.

Figure 9   Rubric for the Organization of Written Piece

4	The writer uses a strong lead. Ideas are presented in a logical order with a strong beginning, middle, and end. The writer effectively uses transition words to connect ideas.
3	The writer uses an adequate lead. Ideas are presented in a logical order with a beginning, middle, and end. The writer uses some transition words to connect ideas.
2	The writer uses a poor or no lead. The piece lacks a clear idea of a logical order, and/or it lacks a beginning, middle, or end. Few transition words are used to connect ideas.
1	The writer has no main idea, no logical order, and no transition words. There may be insufficient information to evaluate the writer's organization.
0	The student makes no attempt to write.

The examples above are rubrics that are used to assign a single numerical value to a piece of writing. Some teachers find it helpful to use rubrics to assign letter grades to writing. This is simply another application of holistic scoring of writing.

Figure 10, Writing Criteria Checklist, is used in New Jersey by Jodi Brush, a fifth grade teacher, to evaluate the writing of her students. With this rubric she is easily and clearly able to communicate the criteria for each of the grades. The general categories of "strong, developing and limited" are explained in the Grade Five Writing Rubric illustrated in Figure 11.

How Does Holistic Scoring of Writing Inform Instruction?

The scores themselves give a general impression of the overall quality of writing within a class, school or district. The scores, alone, are not particularly helpful in planning instruction. However, because the scores are derived from rubrics, the rubrics may become a highly useful tool for informing instruction.

Refer to Figure 11, Grade Five Writing Rubric, and imagine that you had used this rubric to evaluate your students' writing. Assume you scored a group of them "developing" for "content/organization" because they had attempted transitions but had not written them well. You could pull this group of students together, discuss the rubric, discuss their writing, and use this as a springboard for a lesson or set of lessons on writing transitions. In this way, holistic scoring of writing allows you to focus on skills.

What Are the Advantages of Holistic Scoring of Writing?

The advantage of holistic scoring of writing is the ability it affords to assess and evaluate writing performance, either on a school- or a district-wide basis. Rather than inferring writing ability from scores in punctuation, capitalization, grammar subtests or norm-referenced tests, writing performance may be evaluated with actual writing samples. Trends in scores may be mapped over time and instructional or in-service courses developed.

Teachers have found that sharing the rubrics with students and talking about the differences in the ratings with them helps students understand what constitutes good writing. Jodi Brush engages her students in self-evaluation before they hand in a writing piece. She has them evaluate their writing using the Writing Criteria Checklist (Figure 10) and then has them write an evaluation as illustrated in Figure 12.

What Are the Disadvantages of Holistic Scoring of Writing?

A school or school system may appropriately use the holistic writing scores to evaluate the writing performance of groups of students. However, because the standard error of measurement is so great for any single student, individual scores are not valid (Rhodes and Shanklin, 1993). This means that scores derived from holistic scoring are not particularly helpful to classroom teachers or students.

Figure 10   Writing Criteria Checklist

A+ **Strong** **A**	_____ strong opening and closing _____ single topic _____ understandable with events or information in logical order _____ well developed plot (fiction) _____ sentences and paragraphs are connected/related _____ paragraphed well _____ many supporting details with a lot of explanation _____ descriptive language _____ tried something new or different _____ correct use of tense and pronouns _____ effective and varied word choice _____ complete sentences—no fragments or run-ons _____ variety in sentence structure _____ accurate use of capitalization, end marks, and spelling
B **Developing** **C**	_____ there is an opening and closing _____ single topic _____ understandable with events or information in logical order _____ attempts at plot development (fiction) _____ attempts to connect/relate sentences and paragraphs _____ some paragraphs _____ supporting details _____ some descriptive language _____ generally accurate noun-verb agreement _____ generally accurate use of tense and pronouns _____ generally complete sentences, with some variety in structure _____ accurate use of capitalization and end marks _____ generally standard spelling _____ errors do not detract from meaning
D **Limited** **F**	_____ ineffective, or lack of, opening and closing _____ drifts from topic and may include more than one topic _____ limited or no plot development _____ limited attempts at paragraphing _____ limited attempts at developing ideas _____ limited descriptive language _____ over use of conjunctions (and, then, but, etc.) _____ noun-verb agreement may be inconsistent _____ inaccurate use of tense and/or pro-nouns _____ many run-on, or fragmented sentences _____ lack of sentence variety _____ lack of, or inaccurate use of, commas, semi-colons, end punctuation, and capital letters _____ many spelling errors _____ errors may interfere with meaning

Figure 11 Grade Five Writing Rubric

	Limited	Developing	Strong
Content/ Organization	• May have an opening and/or closing • Drifts from topic • May include more than one topic • Limited attempts at developing ideas • Limited descriptive language	• Opening and closing in evidence • Single focus • Comprehensible with logical sequence • Attempts at transitions • Supporting details • Some descriptive language	• Strong opening and closing • Single focus • Comprehensible with logical sequence • Transitions • Many supporting details with much elaboration • Descriptive language • Some compositional risks
Usage	• Over-use of conjunctions • Noun-verb agreement may be inconsistent • Pronoun reference may be unclear • Errors may interfere with meaning	• Generally accurate noun-verb agreement, verb tense, and pronoun reference • Errors do not detract from meaning	• Correct tense use • Correct pronoun use • Effective and varied word choice
Sentence Structure	• May lack sentence variety • May include run-on sentences and/or sentence fragments	• Generally complete sentences • Some variation in sentence structure	• Complete sentences—no fragments or run-ons • Variety in sentence structure
Mechanics	• Capitalization may be inaccurate • Spelling errors may interfere with meaning • Lack of or inaccurate use of commas, semicolons, and end punctuation	• Accurate use of capitalization • Accurate use of end marks • Generally standard spelling	• Accurate use of capitalization, end marks, and standard spelling

Figure 12   Writing Evaluation

WRITING EVALUATION

Name *Nicle Sanderson*   **Date** *2-4-*

Title *Trick or Treat*

When I grade your writing, I read it through completely. Then I place the Writing Criteria next to your piece and compare them. I look for your strengths (the things you do well) and your weaknesses (the areas you need to improve). Your grade is based on these two things. Before you give your writing to me, I want you to evaluate yourself the same way. Be sure to complete this in a thoughtful manner, so you and I will both benefit from it. Write in cursive and in complete sentences.

MY STRENGTHS *I think that in this piece, I have good paragraph form.*

MY WEAKNESSES *I need to work on run-on sentences, and I have too many descriptive words in one place and not enough in others.*

MY WRITING GOAL(S) *My goals are to work on my weaknesses, and eventually have none.*

WHAT I HAVE DONE TO ACHIEVE MY WRITING GOAL(S) *To achieve my goals I use the writing criteria and evaluation on longer pieces.*

THE GRADE I THINK I DESERVE *A*

EXPLAIN WHY, USING TERMINOLOGY FROM THE WRITING CRITERIA *I did have one or two mistakes in my piece but they were not continuous. There were very few.*

Where Do I Get More Information About Holistic Scoring of Writing?

Cockrum, W. A., & Castillo, M. (1991). Whole language assessment and evaluation strategies. In B. Harp (Ed.), *Assessment and evaluation in whole language programs.* Norwood, MA: Christopher-Gordon.

Goodman, K. S., Bird, L. B., & Goodman, Y. M. (1992). *The whole language catalog: Supplement on authentic assessment.* New York: SRA Macmillan/McGraw-Hill.

Hamp-Lyons, L. (1995). Rating nonnative writing: The trouble with holistic scoring. *TESOL Quarterly, 29,* 4, 759–762.

Hill, B. C., & Ruptic, C. (1994). *Practical aspects of authentic assessment: Putting the pieces together.* Norwood, MA: Christopher-Gordon.

McKendy, T. (1992). Locally developed writing tests and the validity of holistic scoring. *Research in the Teaching of English, 26,* 2, 149–166.

Rhodes, L. K., & Shanklin, N. (1993). *Windows into literacy: Assessing learners K–8.* Portsmouth, NH: Heinemann.

Rickards, D., & Cheek, E. (1999). *Designing rubrics for K–6 classroom assessment.* Norwood, MA: Christopher-Gordon.

Tchudi, S. (Ed.). (1997). *Alternatives to grading student writing.* Urbana, IL: National Council of Teachers of English.

Interest Inventories

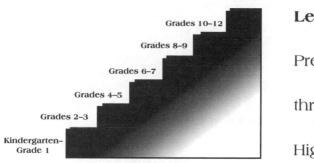

Grades 10–12
Grades 8–9
Grades 6–7
Grades 4–5
Grades 2–3
Kindergarten–Grade 1

Level:

Pre–K

through

High School

What Are They?

We know that learners are more highly motivated when they are working on school activities that tap into their interests. As teachers, we also hope to broaden the interests of our learners. Interest inventories are a tool that can help us reach both of these goals. Interest inventories are questionnaires developed by teachers to tap into children's interests in reading and writing, general interests, school-related interests, or interests in language. You may want to know more about the interests of your students in order to help them select appropriate reading material, to guide them in their selection of writing topics, or in order to make curricular changes. Some teachers appreciate learning the interests of their students simply to "know them better."

The following pages illustrate three kinds of interest inventories: general interests, interests in reading and writing, and interest in school-related topics. The kinds of items we put on interest inventories is, in part, determined by the nature of our student population. Please feel free to use these illustrations as starting points for creating interest inventories that are appropriate for your learners and of greatest use to you.

You may find it helpful to assess students' interests at the beginning of the year and then periodically throughout the year to pick up on changes. Some teachers use interest inventories to begin conversations with students one-on-one or in groups. It is possible to group students by interests for some activities. The inventories will help do this. You will probably see considerable overlap between data from attitude inventories and interest inventories. Used together, they can give you very valuable information about your learners.

Another way to assess interests is to examine the reading logs of your students if they self-select reading materials either for a sustained silent reading period or as part of an individualized reading program. Some schools have sophisticated computer systems in the library that permit printing out lists of the books children have checked out. This is another way

General Interest Inventory

Name_____ Date _____

1. What hobbies do you have?

2. Do you have any collections of things? What Are They?

3. What are your favorite things to do after school? On weekends?

4. When you have free time, who do you like to spend it with?

5. How do you use your computer at home?

6. What are your favorite television programs?

7. What are your favorite movies?

8. If you could travel anywhere, what would be the three places you would go? Why?

Reading and Writing Interest Inventory

Name _____ Date _____

1. What are your favorite books?

2. What kinds of books do you like to read?

3. When you write, what kinds of things do you most like to write about?

4. When do you like to write?

5. When do you like to read?

6. What do you think you should do to become a better reader?

7. What do you think you should do to become a better writer?

School Interest Inventory

Name_____ Date _____

1. Which school subjects do you find most interesting?

2. If you could study anything you wanted in school, what would it be?

3. Of all the school subjects, which is your least favorite? Why?

4. Which subject would you most like to have homework in? Why?

5. Which subject would you least like to have homework in? Why?

6. If you could select themes to study in school (like mystery, adventure, ecology), which ones would you select and why?

7. Which section of the school library is your favorite?

8. Which computer software programs are your favorites? Why?

to assess interests, recognizing however that a book checked out is not necessarily a book read. You could make discussion of these reading records a part of reading conferences. In this way you could either confirm and support the choices the student is making or attempt to broaden the student's range of choices.

How Does an Interest Inventory Inform Instruction?

Teachers often ask learners to complete an interest inventory at the beginning of the year. Once children have responded to the inventory, then the information is used in order to plan activities around topics of interest. For example, several students might have indicated an interest in airplanes, so you can plan a unit on airplanes to meet math, science and social studies objectives and competencies. Students may also indicate social interests and other preferences. When one underachieving student indicated how much she liked pizza, her teacher used that information in planning rewards for her that were personally satisfying.

What Are the Advantages of Interest Inventories?

Interest inventories are a helpful tool in discovering the general interests of your students, as well as their reading- and writing-related interests. Such inventories can assist you in guiding children's choices in reading and writing and in planning instruction. Most teachers assume that if they can tie instruction to interests, the motivation for learning will be greater.

What Are the Disadvantages of Interest Inventories?

The main disadvantage of interest inventories is that they are based on the self-report of children and therefore are subject to amendments based on what children think you want to hear. You can counter this by helping learners understand that you sincerely want to know their interests and that you will use this information as best you can in planning instruction. Therefore, it is necessary that they accurately report their interests.

Some parents are very concerned about "private" information being shared at school. They object to someone asking their children to write personal experience narratives, for example, and would probably object to interest inventories. We need to be sensitive to this issue when developing and using interest inventories, and in some communities it may be necessary to get written parental permission before administering interest inventories.

Where Do I Get More Information About Interest Inventories?

Ceaser, L. (1993). *Reading field experience program.* ERIC ED367658.

Hill, B. C., & Ruptic, C. (1994). *Practical aspects of authentic assessment: Putting the pieces together.* Norwood, MA: Christopher-Gordon.

Manning M., & Manning, G. (1996). Teaching reading and writing. Keeping writing portfolios. *Teaching PreK–8, 27,* 132–134.

Newman, A. (1994). *CONSULT–1 reading. South Avondale elementary school, Cincinnati project. Final report.* Bloomington, IN: Indiana University Reading Practicum Center. EDRS ED371327.

Interviews

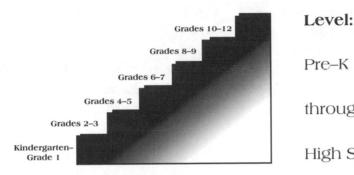

Grades 10–12
Grades 8–9
Grades 6–7
Grades 4–5
Grades 2–3
Kindergarten–Grade 1

Level:

Pre–K

through

High School

What Are They?

Interviews are question-and-answer sessions conducted by the teacher one-on-one with a reader or writer. The purpose of interviews is to learn more about how children view the reading or writing process, how children see themselves as readers and writers, and to gain instructional insight. Interviews are a way for you to listen to your students and, in the process, to learn how to be a more effective teacher.

Interviews are often conducted as part of the "back to school" activities in the fall. You can pull children aside for interviews while the rest of the class is engaged in silent reading. Interviews conducted throughout the year assess children's changing views of their reading and writing processes. You may wish to conduct interviews as part of your regular reading or writing conferences with your students.

Questions that are typically asked about writing include:

- What are you doing well as a writer?
- What is something new you have learned to do as a writer?

- What would you like to be able to do better as a writer?
- When you have trouble with your writing, what do you do?
- If you were going to help someone become a better writer, how would you do it?

When interviewing children about themselves as readers, all of the questions above can be recast for reading. In addition, you might ask:

- What is reading?
- What do you do when you read?
- What parts of this text were difficult for you?
- What made them difficult?
- What parts of this text were easy for you?
- What made them easy?
- When you have difficulty understanding your reading, what do you do?

Interviews conducted during conferences can give you a great deal of insight into your students' thinking. Another powerful opportunity for interviewing occurs as you rove the classroom while children work on reading or writing assignments, or guided reading activities. Stopping by a writer's desk and asking, "How is your writing going?", "Are you having any difficulty with your writing?", and "Do you want to talk about your writing?" can provide you with rich data on the child's immediate work. Likewise, questions asked during guided reading, such as "What parts of this text were challenging for you?" provide opportunities for immediate understanding of the child as reader. (Please refer to the discussion on Assessing Metacomprehension on pp. 17–21.)

Interviews may also give you insight into your students' perceptions of classroom reading tasks. Wixson and associates (1984) developed a fifteen-question interview to assess perceptions of children's use of basal readers, workbooks, and content-area materials. The questions are on page 79.

You could use the work of Wixson and associates as a model for developing your own set of interview questions about reading tasks in your classroom.

A word of caution about conducting interviews: Be careful not to lead your students to give you the answers you want to hear. Don't put words into their mouths. Students will give you honest answers if they believe (through the proof that you give them) that you are sincerely interested in their views. If you lead them, they will understand what that agenda requires and give you exactly what you want to hear.

How Do Interviews Inform Instruction?

Some teachers like to use interviews at the beginning of the school year to get to know their learners and to begin to make personal connections. These early interviews may have three purposes: to learn what your students think reading and writing are, to learn how they feel about reading and writing, and to learn what they are most anxious to study in the school year. Doug Robertson, a fourth grade teacher, asks the following questions:

1. How would you explain what reading is to someone else?
2. What do you like the most about reading?
3. What is your least favorite thing about reading?
4. How would you explain what writing is to someone else?
5. What do you like the most about writing?
6. What is your least favorite thing about writing?
7. What are three things you would really like to study in fourth grade?

The responses you get from the interviews could become the first entries you make in your anecdotal record notebook. Just put the interview sheet into the notebook at each student's section of the three-ring binder. After the interviews are finished, go over them to see what instructional needs you can identify. Make a list, for example, of all those students who don't understand that reading is a meaning-making activity. Notice which of your students think of writing as more a matter of spelling words than creating ideas. Plan to target these students early in the year to build their understanding that reading and writing are about communication.

1. What hobbies or interests do you have that you like to read about?

2. a. How often do you read in school?

   b. How often do you read at home?

3. What school subjects do you like to read about?

   (*Directions:* Display basal reader and content area textbook. Ask each of questions 4 through 10 twice, once for each book.)

4. What is the most important reason for reading this kind of material? Why does your teacher want you to read this book?

5. a. Who's the best reader you know in _____?

   b. What does he/she do that makes him/her such a good reader?

6. a. How good are you at reading this kind of material?

   b. How do you know?

7. What do you have to do to get a good grade in _____ in your class?

8. a. If the teacher told you to remember the information in this story/chapter, what would be the best way to do this?

   b. Have you ever tried _____?

9. a. If your teacher told you to find the answers to the questions in this book, what would be the best way to do this? Why?

   b. Have you ever tried _____?

10. a. What is the hardest part about answering questions like the ones in this book?

    b. Does that make you do anything differently?

    (*Directions:* Present at least two comprehension worksheets to the child and ask questions 11 and 12. Ask the child to complete portions of each worksheet. Then ask questions 13 and 14. Next, show the child a worksheet designed to simulate the work of another child. Then ask question 15.)

11. Why would your teacher want you to do worksheets like these (for what purpose)?

12. What would your teacher say you must do to get a good mark on worksheets like these? (What does your teacher look for?)

13. Did you do this one differently from the way you did that one? How or in what way?

14. Did you have to work harder on one of these worksheets than the other? (Does one make you think more?)

15. a. Look over this worksheet. If you were the teacher, what kind of mark would you give the worksheet? Why?

    b. If you were the teacher, what would you ask this person to do differently next time?

What Are the Advantages of Interviews?

Interviews give you immediate data on children's perceptions of reading and writing processes, as well as other aspects of instruction. You can come to deeper understandings of your students as readers and writers through well-conducted and thoughtfully interpreted interviews.

Interviews permit you to focus on certain aspects of the reading/writing program about which you want to know more. You are also able to probe for more extensive answers. You can sometimes get a child to expand an answer if you simply indicate that you would like to hear more by saying "yes" and looking interested. You can probe by saying, "Tell me more about _____."

What Are the Disadvantages of Interviews?

Interviews are time consuming. You may wish to have students complete a questionnaire in writing and then select students for more extensive one-on-one interviews. Plan to interview first those students about whom you know the least.

Because interviews are a form of self-reporting, they may be invalidated by students giving you the answers they think you want to hear. This can be countered by explaining that you are sincerely interested in what they think, probing for deeper understandings, and being careful not to lead students into certain answers.

Where Do I Get More Information About Interviews?

Church, J. (1994). Record keeping in whole language classrooms. In Harp, B. (Ed.), *Assessment and evaluation for student centered learning.* Norwood, MA: Christopher-Gordon.

Cockrum, W. A., & Castillo, M. (1994). Whole language assessment and evaluation strategies. In Harp, B. (Ed.), *Assessment and evaluation for student centered learning.* Norwood, MA: Christopher-Gordon.

Goodman, Y. M. (1992). Learning through interviews. In Goodman, K. S., Bird, L. S., & Goodman, Y. M. (Eds.), *The whole language catalog supplement on authentic assessment.* New York: SRA, Macmillan/McGraw-Hill.

Wixson, K. K., Bosky, A. B., Yochum, M. N., & Alvermann, D. E. (1984). An interview for assessing students' perceptions of classroom reading tasks. *The Reading Teacher 37*(4), 346–352.

K-W-L Strategy

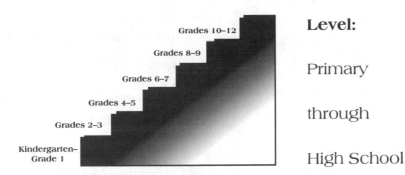

Grades 10–12
Grades 8–9
Grades 6–7
Grades 4–5
Grades 2–3
Kindergarten– Grade 1

Level:

Primary

through

High School

What Is It?

Teachers often find it helpful to discover what learners know about a topic before classroom study of that topic begins. An effective way to learn this is the K-W-L strategy, developed by Donna Ogle. The K-W-L strategy is a technique for organizing children's work as part of a unit, theme, or reading selection. It is primarily an instructional strategy to find out what the children know (K), what they want to know (W), and ultimately what they have learned (L) as a result of their study. Teachers view the strategy as a way to invoke the power of background knowledge and prediction in learning, and as a way to give learners ownership of their learning.

K-W-L is included in this handbook because, as an instructional strategy, it has a great deal of assessment and evaluation potential. Teachers assess and evaluate both through critical examination of the way students answer the questions they (and you) pose, as well as how they record and present what they learn.

K-W-L has found a place in classrooms that are moving from the tradi-

tional transmission of information model to a transactional model, in which there is a focus on construction of meaning and an orientation toward process. The transactional model includes many opportunities for children to experiment, research, and exchange information with one another. Thinking about what I know about a topic and what I want to learn from my reading leads to increased comprehension and self-monitoring.

Questions that guide assessment and evaluation of "K" (What Do We Know?) include:

- Are the children able to identify background knowledge related to the topic?

- Is their background knowledge accurate?

- Do the children see the relevance of their background knowledge in light of the topic?

- Do the children have strategies at their disposal when they discover that background knowledge is limited?

- What are the instructional implications for the ways in which the children handled the "What Do We Know" part of the task? What can I teach them that will improve their ability to do this task in the future?

Questions that guide assessment and evaluation of "W" ("What Do We Want to Know?") include:

- Are the children's questions a valid extension of their background knowledge?

- Are they able to make predictions about what they will find?

- In what ways will I need to support their quest for answers?

- What do their questions reveal about their understandings of how to research information?

- What will I need to do to prepare them to use content area materials or electronic information systems?

Questions that guide assessment and evaluation of "L" ("What Did We Learn?") include:

- How well are the children able to research pertinent information?

- What support do I need to give them to help them deal with content area texts (semantic maps, structured overviews, explanations of technical vocabulary, specific skill instruction)?

- Are the children able to use reading to get answers to their questions?

- Does their reading produce new questions that they are willing to pursue?

- Are they able to organize informa-

tion in ways that answer their questions and stay on topic?

- What assistance do I need to provide them in content area writing (help with text structures, paragraph frames, modeling writing)?

- To what extent are they demonstrating a sensitivity to their audience as they organize and plan to present information?

Jan Bryan (1998) has extended the K-W-L strategy in an interesting way. She has added a fourth column, "Where." Her columns, then, are What I **K**now, What I **W**ant to know, **W**here I can learn this, and I have **L**earned: K-W-W-L. For example, in a study of oceans, children might list under *What I know* "Oceans are salty." Under *I want to learn* they might write "Why are oceans salty?" Then under *Where I can learn this* they might list "encyclopedia, ask a scientist, ask a marine biologist, on the web." Dealing with *Where will I learn this* would cause children to think about resources for learning and lead to independence in learning. Some teachers have added yet another W at the end for "What else do we want to learn?" or "What are my new questions?"

Questions that guide the assessment and evaluation of the second "W" ("Where I can learn this") include:

- Are children using the print resources available in the classroom?

- Are children using electronic resources available in the classroom?

- Are children making good use of the media center?

- Are children aware of and using resources beyond the school?

How Does K-W-L Inform Instruction?

It works well to use the K-W-L strategy as a opener to a unit or theme of study. This helps focus discussion around what the students already know about the topic and what they want to learn. You could create a large wall chart with the three or four columns and give children three or four different colored Post-it Notes. The students write what they already know on one color, what they want to learn on another color and where they will find the information on a third color. These are put on the chart at the beginning of a unit. After completing the topic, students write what they learned on the fourth color note and put them on the chart. You then would help them review the questions they asked to determine if they were answered, all the time asking yourself the assessment and evaluation questions identified above.

Careful observation of children during the initial discussion will help you identify those who have little background knowledge about a topic and those who know more. You may use this information in putting work groups or cooperative learning groups together so that there is a balance within the groups.

The information you obtain by using the K-W-L strategy tells you whether you need to provide instruction/information on a topic. For instance, if students do not have prior knowledge on a topic and are unable to develop questions on what they want to learn, you will know that you need to provide some instruction and information on the topic to build background knowledge, or that the topic is inappropriate for your learners at the present time.

The use of the Post-it Notes will create a colorful display of how much the children are learning as they post notes in the fourth column. In many classrooms this creates an exciting sense of community as they celebrate daily how much they are learning. If you have children put their names on the "want to know" notes, children will be able to share information with classmates as they find it. This further builds a sense of a community as learners read what other students know, want to learn, and have learned.

What Are the Advantages of K-W-L?

Use the K-W-L strategy to assess and evaluate the ways in which learners (1) draw on background information, (2) relate what they know to what they want to know, and (3) use reading and writing abilities to seek, organize, and present information. Anecdotal notes will help you observe the ways learners use the strategies.

What Are the Disadvantages of K-W-L?

From an assessment and evaluation perspective, the disadvantage in K-W-L is the difficulty you may have in identifying individual responses. K-W-L strategies are usually used in group settings, making it more difficult to assess and evaluate an individual's participation. This may be countered by increased care in targeted observations of selected students.

Where Do I Get More Information About K-W-L?

Bryan, J. (1998). K-W-W-L: Questioning the known. *The Reading Teacher, 51,* 618–624.

Glazer, S. M. (1999). Using kwl folders. *Teaching PreK–8, 29,* 4, 106–108.

Ogle, D. M. (1986). KWL: A teaching model. *The Reading Teacher, 39,* 564–571.

Sorrell, A. L. (1996). *Triadic approach to reading comprehension strategy instruction.* Paper presented at the Annual Conference of the Learning Disabilities Association of Texas, Austin, TX. ERIC: ED400670.

Vacca, J. A., Vacca, R. T., & Gove, M. K. (1995). *Reading and learning to read.* New York: HarperCollins College Publishers.

Parent Questionnaires

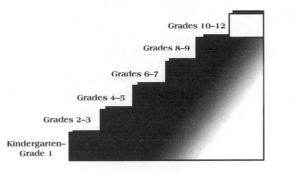

Level:

Pre–K

through

Middle School

What Are They?

The National Research Council report entitled *Preventing Reading Difficulties in Young Children* (1998) is just one example of a growing number of calls nationally for greater cooperation between parents and other caregivers and the schools. Parent questionnaires are one tool schools may use to foster this cooperation. You can give this tool to parents to get their perspectives on their child's literacy development, to involve them in the assessment and evaluation process, and to involve them in goal setting with their child.

Increasingly, teachers understand that good education is a partnership between the home and the school. The parent/teacher conference that is held two or three times a year does not provide enough contact to secure the partnership. Teachers have turned to parent questionnaires as a way of maintaining an on-going dialogue between home and school.

One form of parent questionnaire taps into the parents' perceptions of their child's interest and abilities in literacy, as well as other areas. This beginning of the year parent question-

naire is illustrated on the next pages. Please use this as an example and modify to best suit your needs and the needs of your learners.

The parent questionnaire you use at the beginning of the year will probably not be useful later in the year because your questions will change. The next page illustrates a parent questionnaire you might use periodically throughout the year. Please feel free to modify it as your needs dictate.

Hill and Ruptic (1994) report on the work of Jan Colby. Colby uses a form to evaluate a piece of writing with a child and then shares the writing and the form at the conference, soliciting parental input. The form includes the title of the piece of writing, a section on "what my teacher and I noticed I did well," a section on "my writing goals for next time," and finally a place for the parent(s) to write a response to the writing.

In addition to involving parents in the assessment and evaluation process, teachers have also learned to involve parents in goal setting for/with their child. Church (1994) shares the work of second grade teacher, Tim Moss. Moss uses a form to share his goals, the

Beginning of The Year Parent Questionnaire

Student's Name _____

Parent's Name _____

Welcome to our school! Since parents are the first and best teachers the child has, we can learn much from you. Please help us help your child.

How does your child feel about coming to school?

What things have you done to prepare your child for school this year?

How would you describe your child as a learner?

In what ways does your child show a desire to use written language?

Does your child pretend to write, copy, or trace print?

Does your child respond to signs such as "McDonalds" or "STOP"?

Do you have a set time for reading to your child? If so, when and about how much time?

Comments:

Parent Questionnaire

Student's Name _____

Parent's Name _____

How has your child changed as a writer since our last conference?

How has your child changed as a reader since our last conference?

What do you think your child should learn in order to become a better writer?

What do you think your child should learn in order to become a better reader?

What changes have you seen in your child's use of reading and writing at home?

Are there observations you have made since our last conference that you would like to share with me?

Are there questions or topics that you want us to discuss during our next conference?

child's goals, and to solicit goal statements from parents. The form has three sections: Teacher Goals for This Year, Student Goals for This Year, and Parent Goals for This Year. Church (1994) says that parents tend to respond by listing similar goals across time and grade levels. They are most concerned about their children gaining confidence; working well with others; being responsible, thinking problem solvers; and improving in reading, writing and math.

Susan Mandel Glazer is the director of the Center for Reading and Writing at Rider University in New Jersey. The Center serves a diverse population of students who are multi-aged, multi-ethnic, and have a wide range of interests and accomplishments. The program is designed so that children come to manage their own learning in a curriculum that is divided into composition, comprehension, vocabulary and self-monitoring. The children work on a contract system with the teacher, plus routine activities.

Glazer says that because so much responsibility is placed on the children, it is important to know as much about them before they come to the Center as possible. The Center uses phone interviews as the initial input from parents. The parents are asked to describe the child's reading and writing ability and to give information about the child's personality, work habits and health history. Additionally, parents are asked about the child's previous testing and resulting classifications, any involvement with special education programs, extracurricular activities, siblings, mother's health during pregnancy, complications at birth, age, grade and any retention history. Collecting parent profile data by phone is time consuming, but a quick way to make initial contact with parents.

How Do Parent Questionnaires Inform Instruction?

The information you get from the questionnaires completed early in the year will be valuable to you in setting up your classroom. You may plan some initial instructional grouping based on the reading and writing behaviors described by the parents. You may make tentative plans for children who have had little if any experience with print, for example. You may plan to pull books into the classroom library for those children whom parents report are reading. You may set some individualized goals for your own observations of children in light of information reported by parents.

The questionnaires you use during the year will help you prepare for individual parent-teacher or parent-teacher-student conferences. If you collect the profiles the week before each conference, you may be able to pull work samples and other documentation together for the upcoming conference in response to the parent profile.

What Are the Advantages of Parent Questionnaires?

The greatest advantage of parent questionnaires is that such forms help open a dialogue between teachers and parents about children. When you involve parents in providing you with information at the year's beginning, during conferences, and in evaluation efforts throughout the year, you are clearly signaling your desire for a partnership.

Parents often have valuable information about their children that we cannot learn any other way. This information may be essential in creating instruction best suited to the needs of the learner.

What Are the Disadvantages of Parent Questionnaires?

While most parents are eager to participate in their children's schooling, a few may find parent questionnaires intrusive. They may believe that questions about home-life are beyond the purview of the school. Their reluctance may be countered by telephoning these parents before the form is sent or mailed home to lay the groundwork for completion of the parent questionnaire.

You may find, on hopefully rare occasions, that parents report what they wish to be the case rather than reality. Most parents are quite realistic about their children, but they haven't had the benefit of knowing hundreds of children of a given age, as is the case with many teachers.

Where Do I Get More Information About Parent Questionnaires?

Church, J. (1994). Record keeping in whole language classrooms. In Harp, B. (Ed.), *Assessment and evaluation for student centered learning.* Norwood, MA: Christopher-Gordon.

Egolf, R. H. (1994). Make parents partners in writing assessment. *Learning, 23,* 2, 60–63.

Hill, B. C., & Ruptic, C. (1994). *Practical aspects of authentic assessment: Putting the pieces together.* Norwood, MA: Christopher-Gordon.

Hoyt, L. (1992). Involving students in parent-teacher conferences. In Goodman, K. S., Bird, L. B., & Goodman, Y. M. (Eds.), *The whole language catalog supplement on authentic assessment.* SRA. Macmillan/McGraw Hill.

Morningstar, J. W. (1999). Home response journals: Parents as informed contributors in the understanding of their child's literacy development. *The Reading Teacher, 52,* 7, 690–698.

Paris, S. G., & Ayres, L. R. (1994). *Becoming reflective students and teachers with portfolios and authentic assessment.* Washington, DC: American Psychological Association.

Schwartz, S., & Pollishuke, M. (1991). *Creating the child-centered classroom.* Katonah, NY: Richard C. Owen.

Wolfendale, S. (1998). Involving parents in child assessment in the United Kingdom. *Childhood Education, 74,* 6, 355–359.

Portfolio Assessment

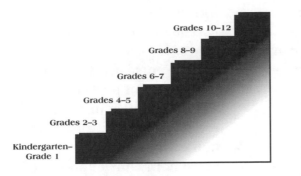

Level:

Pre–K

through

High School

What Is It?

As our profession struggles with the demands for increased testing of students, there are still many of us who believe that we can learn more from examining the on-going, daily work of our learners than we can from test scores alone. The challenge is in how to create an organized system for looking at the work of learners. One answer to this challenge is portfolio assessment. Portfolio assessment involves collecting and evaluating student work samples across time. The samples are housed in a folder—thus the name portfolio. As the artist creates a portfolio of his or her work, so children create portfolios of theirs. In many schools teachers and children are working out the details of how to document learning across the curriculum with portfolio entries. The discussion here will be limited to reading and writing portfolios.

Portfolios in reading and writing seem to be a reasonable way to assess and evaluate growth across time. Many teachers use portfolios because of the benefits they see accruing to their students. Hewitt (1995) has suggested five things portfolios accomplish for students:

1. Asking students to keep portfolios of their work suggests that the work has value, importance.
2. Students who keep portfolios have tangible evidence of their progress.
3. Students who keep portfolios have tangible evidence of their effort.
4. Portfolios suggest that the important comparisons are not to be made with one's peers, but with one's own past accomplishments.
5. Portfolios may provide a means of formal assessment that is based on a system of shared values, such as "clarity of expression," "sentence variety," and so on. When students understand these values, they may attempt to demonstrate them in their day-to-day work, a selection of which will eventually wind up in the portfolio.

I would add one more important accomplishment of a good portfolio system. Students are regularly engaged in evaluating their own work and sharing those evaluations with teachers, parents and peers.

One of the first considerations in launching portfolios is determining the life of the portfolio. Will the portfolio be kept only for the current school year and then sent home, or will it span the child's work across several years of school? Will one portfolio document work in the primary grades and then a new one be started at grade four? How many years a portfolio will be used is an important consideration.

Another important consideration is the distinction between reading and writing folders and portfolios. Reading and writing folders are current collections of on-going work. They house pieces under construction, works in progress. Assessment and evaluation portfolios house completed works that are evaluated by the teacher and student. They are a long-term collection of work samples in reading and writing.

Schools have found it effective to keep two kinds of assessment and evaluation portfolios: one for the current year's work and a second one that moves with the learner from year to year. In all cases, the student and teacher collaborate in deciding which pieces should be placed in each portfolio and in the evaluation of each piece. Pieces are selected from the working reading folder and writing folder for inclusion in the "current year" folder. At the end of the year a few of the best pieces (or most indicative of student growth) are selected for inclusion in the permanent portfolio.

Teachers usually assist children in deciding which pieces should be placed in the portfolio. A discussion about the criteria for selection will be helpful. Students may choose to include a sample of their best work, a set of rough drafts and final product to show how they use the writing process, a reading record to document the num-

ber of books read, or written responses to reading to show critical thinking. One set of criteria for all children may not be appropriate. The portfolio can be individualized to best document each learner's growth as a reader and writer.

Because students have greater ownership of portfolios when they have a hand in choosing the contents, teachers have found it helpful to have students write a "To the Reader" statement that explains the reasons they have made each selection. We often underestimate children's ability to explain why a piece of work is good. A first grade class in New Jersey was given two Post-it Notes and asked to select their two best writing pieces from their writing folder for inclusion in the assessment and evaluation portfolio. They wrote explanations that included "I like the way I used dialogue here," and "I described setting clearly here." And this is only first grade!

In reading and writing we are challenged to select portfolio contents that demonstrate children's use of the processes as well as document quality of their writing products. Following are suggested process and product contents for reading and writing. They are offered here only as *suggestions*. You will need to decide what to include in your portfolios based on district, school, and individual needs.

Writing Process Samples

- Several drafts of a piece and the final version with a narrative written by the student about how the writing process was used.

- Drafts of pieces that were discarded because of decisions to change audience, purpose, or form with accompanying narrative.

- Notes on research done to prepare for writing a piece.
- Editing checklists attached to drafts with an explanation of how the editing improved the piece.
- Summaries of anecdotal notes taken by you that explain your perceptions of how the child used the writing process.

Writing Product Samples

- Essays, reports, projects, letters, poems.
- Finished pieces that illustrate ability to write in various genres.
- Finished pieces that illustrate ability to write across the curriculum.
- Writing pieces that spring from literature.
- Pieces that illustrate particular skill in writing setting, dialogue, characterization, theme, point of view.

Reading Process Samples

- Summaries of your anecdotal notes documenting children's ability to predict, sample, confirm and integrate in reading.
- Summaries of your notes on discussions with a child about what parts of a reading selection proved difficult, why, and what strategies the child used.
- A checklist of the reading strategies the child can use: asking does it look right, does it sound right, does it make sense; rereading; rethinking predictions; skipping a

word and reading on; using picture cues; using rhyming patterns; sounding out; asking for help.

- Running records in which self-corrections are analyzed as a measure of metacomprehension.
- Running records in which sound-throughs are analyzed as evidence of using the graphophonic cueing system; miscues are analyzed to see which of the cueing systems the reader is using.

Reading Product

- Lists of books read.
- Accuracy ratings from running records kept over time.
- Your written evaluations of a child's retellings that document improvement in comprehension over time.
- An audio tape of a child's "best reading" taken over time.

How Does Portfolio Assessment Inform Instruction?

Near the end of a marking period you may want to review with your learners the guidelines, criteria, or rubrics that have been used to define "good writing" as you have been working on it. You would then ask the students to go through their folder/box and make some decisions about what pieces they would like to put in their portfolios. As they are doing this, you will need to be available to give advice where it is needed and generally observe the children making their decisions. (See Student Self-Evaluation on pp. 133–140.)

You will want to encourage students to be very thoughtful about their choices because they are asked to write a reflection on each piece they choose which explains why they chose it, what its strengths are, and what, if any, changes it might need if the child were to continue to work on it. You are likely to see great variety in the choices children make. Examples selected in one classroom of third-graders included a Venn diagram comparing and contrasting two books they have read, a retelling of a story, a journal response to a story, a summary of a book with an illustration, and content-area reading/writing projects, such as a piece of science or social studies writing.

Once the child makes his/her final decisions and has written a reflection for each piece, you might then invite the parent and child to come in together for a conference. In Barbara Sheridan's classroom in New Jersey she has the child sit alone with the parent(s) and explain the portfolio at the beginning of the conference. Then she joins them, sharing her insights into what the child has accomplished and what the next learning steps are. Finally, she meets alone with the parent(s) to discuss strategies on how to work together to continue the progress and/or to discuss any particular problems.

How Does a Portfolio Inform Instruction?

The information you gain from using the portfolio process can guide decisions you make regarding the types of instruction that are needed in the classroom. For example, you may see that most students need some guidance on developing leads for their stories, or you may see that a small group of students is still having trouble with contractions, so you will pull this group aside and give them some specialized instruction.

However, the primary information you will get from a portfolio system is the evidence of growth over time. When you and the children compare reading or writing information from the previous year with this year—or from the fall with the spring—you will see very clearly the proof of your work. This will be affirming and will also give you information for setting goals for the future.

Barbara Sheridan makes an important point. She says that perhaps the most important aspect of using portfolios is that children become better and better at reflecting on their own work. They become more and more thoughtful, more cognitively mature, as they go through their work, choosing pieces and reflecting on each one. In essence, developing a portfolio gives a child more responsibility for his/her own learning.

What Are the Advantages of Portfolio Assessment?

When portfolios are being discussed, terms such as *collaborative, cooperative,* and *student-centered* are frequently heard. These seem to be the greatest advantages of portfolio assessment in reading and writing. The process is collaborative. You and your students are "in it together." This encourages students to take ownership of their learning and communicates the value you place on their work. The process is cooperative. Children often work with other children in developing their "best work." Work samples in writing are the result of editing groups or editing committees, cooperative learning groups, and other cooperative work arrangements. The process is student-centered. Your students play a significant role in selecting pieces to include in their portfolios. They are continually involved in evaluation of their work. In turn, portfolios document the effectiveness of your work as a teacher.

What Are the Disadvantages of Portfolio Assessment?

One of the disadvantages (not inherent in the process) is that some teachers confuse assessment and evaluation portfolios with simple collections of students' work. A portfolio is more than a collection. It is a collection that is carefully, thoughtfully and critically evaluated.

Effectively managed portfolio systems are very time consuming. Many teachers feel this is time well-spent, but nevertheless, a great deal of time goes toward helping students prepare to make selections, making the selections, and evaluating the work.

Where Do I Get More Information About Portfolios?

DeFina, A. A. (1992). *Portfolio assessment: Getting started, teaching strategies.* Jefferson City, MO: Scholastic.

Farr, R., & Tone, B. (1994). *Portfolio and performance assessment: Helping students evaluate their progress as readers and writers.* Orlando, FL: Harcourt Brace and Company.

Glazer, S. M., & Brown, C. S. (1993). *Portfolios and beyond: Collaborative assessment in reading and writing.* Norwood, MA: Christopher-Gordon.

Graves, D. H., & Sunstein, B. S. (Eds.). (1991). *Portfolio portraits.* Portsmouth, NH: Heinemann.

Hewitt, G. (1995). *A portfolio primer: Teaching, collecting, and assessing student writing.* Portsmouth, NH: Heinemann.

Jochum, J., & Curran, C. (1998). Creating individual educational portfolios in written language. *Reading & Writing Quarterly, 14,* 3, 283–307.

Murphy, S., & Smith, M. A. (1991). *Writing portfolios: A bridge from teaching to assessment.* Ontario, Canada: Pippin.

Tierney, R. J., Carter, M. A., & Desai, L. E. (1991). *Portfolio assessment in the reading-writing classroom.* Norwood, MA: Christopher-Gordon.

Yancy, K. B. (1992). *Portfolios in the writing classroom: An introduction.* Urbana, IL: National Council of Teachers of English.

Print Awareness Test

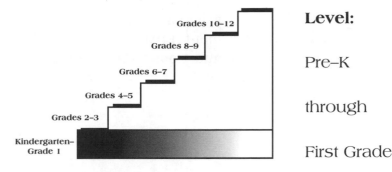

Level:

Pre–K

through

First Grade

Grades 10–12
Grades 8–9
Grades 6–7
Grades 4–5
Grades 2–3
Kindergarten–Grade 1

What Is It?

With increased interest in the development of phonological awareness as a prerequisite to early reading success, teachers of very young children may be interested in how a child has moved from phonological awareness to print awareness. One way to understand a child's knowledge about print and how it functions is print awareness tests. Print awareness tests are teacher-made tests of children's awareness of environmental print.

Environmental print is that print which is easily seen in the child's environment, such as product names, labels, insignias, traffic control signs, and other common forms of print.

The test is usually assembled from product labels, wrappers, and newspaper clippings that are common within the local environment. Each piece of print is glued to card stock or 20-pound bond and placed in a three-ring binder. In this way the binder can be opened, inverted and stood on the edges of the covers, exposing one page at a time. Pages can then be flipped over the binder as each piece of print is exposed.

Pieces of environmental print that are used must be readily evident in the local environment. Examples of print typically used in the test include:

1. The front of a Campbell's soup can label
2. The "Campbell's" piece of the label
3. The round insignia found on the Campbell's soup label
4. The word "Colgate" from a toothpaste box
5. The complete text from one side of a toothpaste box
6. "Coca Cola" from a carton
7. "Dial" from a bar soap wrapper
8. The complete text from a bar soap wrapper
9. "Ragu" from a pasta sauce jar label
10. The complete Ragu Pasta Sauce label
11. The name of a local supermarket from a newspaper ad
12. The name of a local brand of milk from a carton
13. Insignia or design elements from a local milk carton

14. The title from a television programming guide inserted in the local paper

15. "Legos" from a toy carton

16. The Lego insignia from a toy carton

17. A stop sign and the word "STOP" from a stop sign

18. Other well-known examples from your locale

A common set of questions can be asked about each example of environmental print. Figure 13 illustrates the questions that might be asked.

Figure 13   Sample Test Exercises

Ask (pointing to the word, *Colgate*): "Can you tell me what this says?" If the response is correct or "toothpaste" ask, "Does it say 'toothpaste' anywhere else on this page? Can you tell me anything else it says here?" If the first response is incorrect, point to other print and ask, "Can you tell me what any of this says? Can you tell me anything else it says here?"

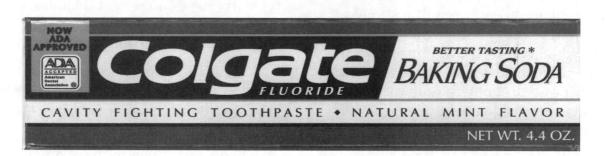

Ask: "Can you tell me what this says?" If the response is "soup," point to *Campbell's* and ask: "Does this say soup?" Point to the Paris exposition seal and ask: "Does this say soup?" Point to "soup" and ask: "Does this say soup? Can you tell me anything else about what it says here?"

With each environmental print example ask questions that respond to what the child says in response to the previous question. Probe for depth of understanding. Probe also to see if the child can distinguish print from picture. With these questions you are trying to understand how attuned the child is to print within the environment, how the child has mastered the language of talking about print, and what the child understands about how print functions in the environment.

How Does the Print Awareness Test Inform Instruction?

Many teachers engage a few children each day in print awareness tasks beginning about the third or fourth day of school. You will probably want to make notes on the things you learn about each child such as whether the child knows where the print occurs in various logos, what the child knows about the print taken out of its usual context, the directionality the child demonstrates when showing where the print says something, whether or not the child knows that it is the words that are being read when one reads, and whether or not the child knows the functions of print.

You can use the information you gain to differentiate instruction. For example, with the children who could recognize almost all the print when it was embedded in its context, knew the names of several letters, knew that the newspaper ads told the price of groceries, and that the print in books was being read, you may choose to read from big books and help them follow along with the print. You will focus on the letters that these children do not know when they appear in stories and encourage them to write as much as possible. On the other hand, with the child who has very little knowledge of environmental print and thinks that the pictures tell the story in books, you may decide to emphasize the print that is found in the room and the school, on the children's clothes, and so on. As these children begin to recognize some print, you might make booklets for them of the print they can read and involve them in listening to the big books with the whole class while drawing attention to the print as you read.

What Are the Advantages of Print Awareness Tests?

The greatest advantage is the ability the test offers you to understand the child's awareness of print in the environment. If the child's responses to your questions are accurate and rich, you may be able to make some appropriate inferences about the degree to which adults have engaged the child in discussion of environmental print. When a child easily recognizes brand names and labels, you can infer that someone has been talking with him or her about that print. This information, combined with data from a parent profile and conferences, will deepen your understanding of the role print has played in the child's life.

Because you create the test with print in your own environment, the child's chances for success are heightened. You may select examples of print that you know are common in your locale. Data from the print awareness test will inform you of the degree to which the child knows that words communicate meaning, that we can give voice to the print on the page, that letters follow each other in a linear sequence, that reading moves from left to right, and that words are distinguished from pictures.

Some print awareness tasks have been found to correlate significantly with spelling, vocabulary, verbal fluency, word knowledge, and general information (Cunningham and Stanovich, 1991).

What Are the Disadvantages of Print Awareness Tests?

The greatest disadvantage of the print awareness test is that you will have to construct it yourself. This is the only way that the print in the test is assured of being significant in your learners' environment. This, of course, is time consuming. The print awareness test must be administered one-on-one, which is also time consuming.

Where Do I Get More Information About Print Awareness Tests?

Clay, M. M. (1991). *Becoming literate: The construction of inner control.* Portsmouth, NH: Heinemann.

Cunningham, A. E., & Stanovich, K. E. (1991). Tracking the unique effects of print exposure in children: Associations with vocabulary, general knowledge and spelling. *Journal of Educational Psychology, 83* (2), 264–274.

McMahon, R. (1996). *The effect of a literacy-rich environment on children's concepts about print.* Paper presented at the Annual International Study Conference of the Association of childhood Educational International, Minneapolis, MN, April 10–13, 1996. EDRS ED399048.

Morrow, L. M. (1997). *Literacy development in the early years: Helping children read and write.* Needham Heights, MA: Allyn and Bacon.

National Research Council. (1998). *Preventing reading difficulties in young children.* Washington, D.C.: National Academy Press.

Notari-Syverson, A. (1996). *Facilitating language and literacy development in preschool children: To each according to their needs.* Paper presented at the Annual Convention of the American Educational Research Association, New York, April 8–12, 1996. EDRS ED 395692.

West, L. S., & Egley, E. H. (1998). Children get more than a hamburger: Using labels and logos to enhance literacy. *Dimensions of Early Childhood, 26,* 43–46.

Reading Conferences

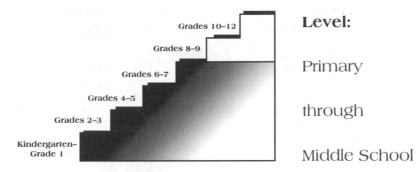

Grades 10–12
Grades 8–9
Grades 6–7
Grades 4–5
Grades 2–3
Kindergarten–Grade 1

Level:

Primary

through

Middle School

What Are They?

Many of us are constantly on the look-out for ways in which we can further individualize our instruction. We want to find ways to know our learners better. One way that is working for many teachers is reading conferences. Reading conferences are typically one-on-one situations where a teacher and learner have an intense discussion about the current work the child is doing in reading. Some teachers hold reading conferences in small groups, but the typical arrangement is one-on-one. The reading conference is a time for the teacher to assess and evaluate the child's progress and to set next learning goals. It is also a time to draw on the assessment and evaluation data you have collected, and to discuss this information with the learner. You may want to give your learners very specific instructions for pre-conference, during-conference, and post-conference activi-ties. The following pages are examples of a checklist you could give older stu-dents to help them prepare for confer-ences and a checklist you could use during conferences.

Key elements in reading confer-ences are the reading folder, the read-ing record, and reading interviews. The reading folder is a portfolio, a working folder, of materials the students will use in reading instruction. Here is kept the important lists of "Things I Am Do-ing Well" and "My Next Goals." These may be kept on sheets of paper stapled into the front cover of the folder. The reading folder also houses all papers related to on-going, current work in reading. These may include writing that is being done in response to read-ing, materials that are being prepared for reading conferences, and lists of books or titles read.

The reading record is an on-going accounting of the reading the child is doing, which may be selections read from the basal as well as trade books read for recreational purposes. If the reading program is literature-based, the list would include all titles read by the child since the last reading confer-ence. The reading record is a form usu-ally prepared with five columns that are headed: Date, author, title, pages read, and conference notes. This form is useful for recording the specific pages

Important Things To Do Before Our Reading Conference

_____ Practice a piece of reading silently that you will read to the me during the conference.

_____ Update your reading folder and reading record.

_____ Select a passage that gave you difficulty and be prepared to discuss how you handled it.

_____ Be prepared to retell what you have read.

_____ Prepare a list of words that you have not been able to figure out yet.

_____ Be prepared to describe a part of the reading you found particularly interesting, exciting, humorous and be ready to tell why.

_____ Be prepared to describe a happening in the book that reminded you of an experience you have had.

_____ Be prepared to discuss why you think the author wrote this piece and to discuss the writing.

_____ Update your list of "Things I Am Doing Well As A Reader" and your list of "My Next Learning Goals As A Reader."

_____ Think of other things about your reading that you want to talk about with me.

Important Things To Do During Our Reading Conference

_____ Report on your progress as a reader. Show me your lists of "Things I Am Doing Well As A Reader" and "My Next Learning Goals As A Reader." Discuss the reasons you have for the recent additions to the list and any evidence you have to support the list. Agree on some next goals.

_____ Read aloud a selection from your reading. I may take a running record. Retell what you have read in as much detail as you can.

_____ Share a list of words that have been difficult for you to read and discuss these with me. Discuss what you did when you had difficulty.

_____ Discuss a part of the reading selection that was interesting, humorous, exciting, or particularly challenging.

_____ Discuss the author's writing.

_____ Talk about the things that are on your mind about your reading.

_____ Here is a list of things you should do after the conference:

- Read on the same topic or selections by the same author
- Complete the goals set during the conference
- Additional follow-up activities that are to be turned in to the teacher.

read each day and for jotting down notes regarding things the reader wants to bring up in the next reading conference with the teacher.

Teachers who conduct reading conferences find them to be important opportunities to learn as much about each child as a reader as possible. One way this is accomplished is to interview the child about his or her views as a reader. These questions may include: What is reading? What do you do when you read? What do you do when you have difficulty as a reader? When you come to a word you do not know, what do you do? The answers to these questions can give you powerful insight into how readers view the reading process and how they see themselves operating as readers. The reading conference may also be a good time to take a running record, to record anecdotal notes, and to assess the need for skill instruction.

How Do Reading Conferences Inform Instruction?

A conference gives you the time to really carefully focus on a child as a reader. This is a wonderful time to hear some oral reading, to perhaps take a running record, to check on goals set at a previous conference, and to set some new goals. Not only is it a time to dialogue with a reader about his or her work, but it is also a time to celebrate accomplishments.

A conference allows a you to determine how a child utilizes reading strategies, not just at the word level, but also at the text level. In other words, is the child predicting, self-correcting, rereading, reading ahead and sounding out? It is a useful source of information for your anecdotal records.

Teachers also use the information gathered from individual conferences to keep in touch with the child about more than just reading. For example, you may discover new interests of the child's or you may seize the opportunity to motivate the child regarding work in school beyond just reading.

What Are the Advantages of Reading Conferences?

Reading conferences are among the richest opportunities you have to assess and evaluate progress in reading. They are intense exchanges between you and your students about their reading performance, their challenges, and their goals. Additionally, they afford the learner the opportunity to engage in self-evaluation and to take responsibility for becoming a better reader. In reading conferences you can diagnose strengths and uncover challenges that then become the next learning goals for that child.

Retellings during conferences give you opportunities to assess and evaluate comprehension. The read aloud piece of the conference is an excellent time for you to evaluate fluency or to take a running record.

What Are the Disadvantages of Reading Conferences?

Reading conferences are time consuming, and you have to practice asking the questions that lead the learner to give you the most information. Tape recording or videotaping conferences will help you analyze the kinds of questions you are asking. Teachers often schedule conferences while the class is working on independent or assigned activities that require little interaction with the teacher. It takes effort on your part to convince children that they are not to interrupt you during conferences except in the case of a real emergency.

Some teachers put a flag or sign on the table to indicate that a conference is in session. Others wear a special hat or a visor to indicate that a conference is not to be needlessly interrupted.

Where Do I Get More Information About Reading Conferences?

Boreen, J. (1995). *The language of reading conferences.* Paper presented at the Annual Meeting of the National Council of Teachers of English (85th, San Diego, CA, November 16–21, 1995) ERIC: ED396263.

Brummett, B., & Maras, L. B. (1995). Liberated by miscues: Students and teachers discovering the reading process. *Primary Voices K–6, 3,* 23–31.

Glassner, S. S. (1995). So little time. *Teaching and Learning Literature with Children and Young Adults, 5,* 2, 67–68.

Manning, M., & Manning, G. (1996). Teaching reading and writing: Tried and true practices. *Teaching PreK–8, 26,* 106–109.

Porterfield, K. (1993). Bringing children to literacy through literature studies. In Harp, B. (Ed.), *Bringing children to literacy: Classrooms at work.* Norwood, MA: Christopher-Gordon Publishers.

Shelor, D. (1993). Bringing children to literacy through literature in primary grades. In *Bringing children to literacy: Classrooms at work.* Harp, B. (Ed.), Norwood, MA: Christopher-Gordon Publishers.

Vacca, J. A. L., Vacca, R. T., & Gove, M. K. (2000). *Reading and learning to read,* (4th ed.). New York: HarperCollins Publishers.

Retellings

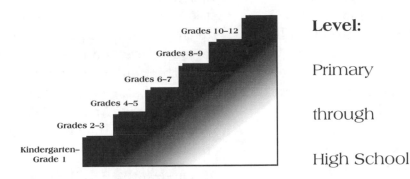

Level:

Primary

through

High School

What Are They?

Literate classrooms are places where readers are excited about what they are reading and are sharing their reactions to their reading with classmates, the teacher, volunteers, visitors and others. Such classrooms are places where discussions of reading are engaged in with enthusiasm. When we listen to these discussions we have no doubt that children have fully comprehended the texts they are reading. How can we take advantage of this enthusiasm to share what learners have read as we evaluate their performance as readers? The answer is retellings.

Retellings are a way of assessing and evaluating students' memories, reactions and understandings of their reading. It is a way of evaluating the quality of their comprehension while honoring the fact that each of us creates our own personal meaning when we read. Since reading is the creation of meaning resulting from interaction between the text and the reader's background knowledge, retellings are a powerful way to measure a student's comprehension. From a reader's retelling, you can assess how he or she created meaning during and after interacting with the text.

Because we believe that reading is an interaction between reader and text, the power of retellings has gained credibility as a measure of comprehension. When we ask questions to measure comprehension, the answers are always evaluated in light of our, or someone else's, interpretation of the text. When we evaluate retellings, we are working to understand this individual reader's construction of meaning. It is important to remember, however, that no retelling can ever represent a reader's complete and total understanding of a text, and that a retelling today may vary from a retelling on the same text at another time. It is also important to remember that fluent readers create meaning that is highly similar to the meaning intended by the author, dependent upon the skill of the reader, the skill of the writer, and the purpose of the reading.

Retellings are thought of as "aided" and "unaided." An unaided retelling is done by asking the reader to retell everything he or she can remember about the text without any assistance from you. During this retelling you should not make any interruptions. Unaided retellings may be prompted by telling the student to assume that you have not read the piece and to tell you everything that he or she can remember. Just as some children are talkative and others are quiet, so some children will offer retellings that are rich in detail and others will tell you little. When you suspect that a child knows more about the piece than the retelling would suggest, you may use the aided retelling approach.

An aided retelling is prompted by asking questions you have thought through in advance. These questions elicit the reader's responses to the text. Examples of such questions are: Have you ever read a similar story? Have you ever been in a similar situation yourself? Why do you think _____ did _____? How did you feel when _____ happened? What more can you tell me about how the story ended? How do you feel about the ending?

In preparing for a retelling, you might wish to briefly outline the important aspects of the selection. If the selection is a narrative piece, you might outline key points regarding setting, characters, plot, and theme. If the piece is expository, you might outline the important facts or concepts you think the reader should remember. As you listen to the unaided retelling, you may want to note points that will guide you in asking questions during the aided retelling.

You will also want to think though what you want to learn about the student's reading before the retelling. For example, are you interested in sim-

ply learning how much can be remembered, or are you interested in discovering what the reader thinks is important to remember? Are you interested in how the reader is able to relate the reading to previous work, or are you interested in the degree to which the reader demonstrates understanding of story structure?

Constance Weaver (1994) offers the following guidelines for using retellings.

1. During the retelling session be friendly and encouraging but do not respond in a way that confirms or disconfirms the accuracy of what the reader is saying.

2. In formulating your questions, be sure to retain any mispronunciations or name changes that the reader used.

3. In asking questions, be careful not to supply any information that the reader has not given you or suggest any insight the reader has not acquired independently.

4. Avoid questions that the reader can answer with a simple yes or no. Instead ask questions that elicit more information such as: What else can you tell me about _____? Who else was in the story? What else happened in _____? What happened after _____? Why do you think _____ happened? How did you feel when _____ happened? Where or when did the story take place? Why was this important to the story?

5. If the reader can tell you almost nothing, it is best to ask that the piece be read silently again. If this fails, try a less difficult or more

motivating selection, or try a different kind of text.

6. Ask questions that elicit the reader's responses to the text and then build on what the reader says in asking more questions.

7. Ask questions to stimulate further thinking about the story and related issues.

8. Ask questions that encourage reflection on the reading itself: How did the reading go for you? Where was it difficult? Where was it easy? What did you do when you came to a difficult word/section?

Retellings can be either oral or written. The advantage of an oral retelling is that you can probe for deeper understandings. The advantage of written retellings is that they can be done by a group of children at one time. You may find that some of your learners prefer one form over the other and that one form is a more valid assessment of comprehension for a given learner than the other. Many teachers prefer oral retellings because they can probe which makes the retelling richer and because your evaluation of reading comprehension is not colored by the child's writing ability.

Following the retelling, you need to evaluate the data to determine what you can learn about the reader. You may wish to employ a rubric to guide this evaluation. The choice here is between a rubric designed to specifically evaluate the retelling of a given text or a generalized rubric to guide evaluation of retellings of any text. Some informal reading inventories use retelling rubrics that are specific to a selection. You could create your own by following the instructions for preparing for a retelling as described above. Rickards and Cheek (1999) offer rubrics for the evaluation of oral story retellings, written story retellings and the retelling of a narrative piece. These are displayed in Figures 14, 15, and 16.

Figure 14   Rubric for Oral Story Retellings

Score Point 4

Without prompting, the student correctly tells the characters and setting, and fully describes the story's problem and solution. Events are described thoroughly and sequenced accurately.

Score Point 3

With a minimum of prompting, the student correctly identifies the characters and setting. He/she explains the story's problem and solution. Events are described and sequenced accurately.

Score Point 2

With prompting, the student identifies the characters, setting, problem, solution, and events, though the information is minimal and may contain slight inaccuracies.

Score Point 1

Even with prompting, the student does not identify the necessary story elements, and/or information contains significant inaccuracies.

Figure 15   Rubric for Written Story Retellings

Score Point 4

The student correctly writes the characters and setting, and fully describes the story's problem and solution. Events are described thoroughly and sequenced accurately.

Score Point 3

The student correctly identifies the characters and setting. He/she explains the story's problem and solution. Events are described and sequenced accurately.

Score Point 2

The student identifies the characters, setting, problem, solution, and events, though the information is minimal and may contain slight inaccuracies.

Score Point 1

The student does not identify the necessary story elements, and/or the information contains significant inaccuracies.

Figure 16   Rubric for Retelling of an Expository Piece

Score Point 4

The reader fully explains the piece's main points and supporting details.

Score Point 3

The reader adequately explains the piece's main points and supporting details.

Score Point 2

The reader explains most of the main points but is unclear about the supporting details. The retelling contains slight inaccuracies and/or minimal information.

Score Point 1

The reader does not correctly identify the main points or supporting details. Information is minimal and inaccurate.

My hope is that you will not simply "adopt" a rubric for use in your classroom or school, but that instead you will "adapt" one so that it is consistent with what you, your colleagues and the parents of your learners value in evaluating reading comprehension. You may find it very useful to develop rubrics for retelling with emergent readers, developing readers and fluent readers.

Another useful tool for evaluating retellings is a checklist (see pp. 112–113). Here you list the elements you wish to see in a retelling and you check them off and write comments as you listen. Retelling checklists for narrative texts and for expository texts follow. The last item on each of these checklists is "comments." Here you might wish to note your observations about the reader's processing of text, evidence of the influence of background knowledge and vocabulary, motivation, challenges in decoding the text, or the appropriateness of this text for the reader in terms of functional reading levels (independent, instructional, frustration).

How Do Retellings Inform Instruction?

There are many important ways in which retellings can inform your instruction. You are able to evaluate students' ability to follow a story line (sequence), remember characters, and understand plot and theme. For example, if you see that there are some students who are not able to remember sequence, you can incorporate that concept into other activities throughout the day. You are also able to gain solid insights into how your learners are interacting with expository texts. For example, if you find children who are unable to retell the details that support a conclusion, you may wish to read several examples of such text, pointing out the structure. You may decide to invite children to write such texts with you using the overhead as a way to display examples.

Retellings not only give you insight into how well students are reading, but they also give you some insight into how they are managing the process. In an aided retelling you can explore the extent to which the reader made predictions, reread for deeper understanding, or used other strategies.

What Are the Advantages of Retellings?

Retellings are truly the reader's creation of meaning, not a response to questions that reflect someone else's creation of meaning on the same text. You are able to focus on how this student responds to a text. Retellings are flexible in that they are both aided and unaided. Aided retellings afford you the opportunity to probe both a student's ability to interact with a text and the meaning that results from that interaction. You can key the items you focus on in an aided retelling to previous reading and classroom events. You can focus on specific aspects of the reading process that are currently instructional goals in your class, or you can focus on aspects of a particular reader's performance that you need to better understand.

Retellings can be scored and used as a statistical measure of comprehension (Goodman, Watson, & Burke, 1987). However, it is important to re-

Narrative Retelling Checklist

Name _____ Date _____

Name of Text _____

Check appropriately: _____ aided   _____ unaided

                             _____ written   _____ oral

_____ Identifies key story characters.

_____ Identifies setting.

_____ Identifies story problem.

_____ Identifies key story episodes.

_____ Identifies problem resolution.

Comments:

Expository Retelling Checklist

Name _____ Date _____

Name of Text _____

Check appropriately: _____ aided   _____ unaided

                            _____ written   _____ oral

Check One:

_____ All important facts are recalled.

_____ Most of the important facts are recalled.

_____ Some of the important facts are recalled.

_____ Supporting ideas are recalled.

_____ Ideas recalled in logical order.

_____ Reader made use of charts, graphs, illustrations.

_____ Reader recalled important conclusions.

_____ Reader stated valid inferences.

_____ Reader read critically.

Comments:

member that this comprehension score is based on only what the reader decides to share and may not be a complete measure of comprehension.

Retellings can be oral or written, and they can be enriched with sketches, diagrams, maps, charts, timelines or other illustrations. Retellings can lend themselves to dramatic presentations. You can take anecdotal records on all of these ways your readers present information.

What Are the Disadvantages of Retellings?

No retelling is ever a complete retelling of all the meaning created by the reader (Goodman, Watson, & Burke, 1987). Therefore, any one retelling, alone, is a source of limited information. We can better understand a reader by examining a series of retellings over time and across a variety of genre and text structures. Retellings can be complex and require very careful analysis. It is helpful to tape-record a retelling for these reasons. Preparation for retellings, scheduling retellings, and the retellings themselves are very time consuming.

Where Do I Get More Information About Retellings?

Brown, S. A. (1996). Immediate retelling's effect on student retention. *Education and Treatment of Children, 19,* 4, 387–407.

Dennis, G., & Walter, E. (1995). The effects of repeated read-alouds on story comprehension as assessed through story retellings. *Reading Improvement, 32,* 3, 140–153.

DeTemple, J. M., & Tabors, P. O. (1996). *Children's story retelling as a predictor of early reading achievement.* Paper presented at the Biennial Meeting of the International Society for the Study of Behavioral Development, Quebec, Canada. ERIC: ED403543.

Gambrell, L. B. (1991). Retelling and the reading comprehension of proficient and less proficient readers. *Journal of Educational Research, 84,* 6, 356–362.

Gambrell, L. B. (1996). *Lively discussions! Fostering engaged reading.* Newark, DE: International Reading Association.

Goodman, Y. M., Watson, D. J., & Burke, C. L. (1987). *Reading miscue inventory: Alternative procedures.* Katonah, NY: Richard C. Owen.

Goodman, Y. M. (1992). Through the miscue window. In *The whole language catalog supplement on authentic assessment.* New York: Science Research Associates.

Glazer, S. M., & Brown, C. S. (1993). *Portfolios and beyond: Collaborative assessment in reading and writing.* Norwood, MA: Christopher-Gordon Publishers, Inc.

Johnston, P. (1983). *Reading comprehension assessment: A cognitive basis.* Newark, DE: International Reading Association.

Kalmbach, J. R. (1986). Evaluating informal methods for the assessment of retellings. *Journal of Reading, 30,* 119–27.

Kalmbach, J. R. (1986). Getting at the point of retellings. *Journal of Reading, 29,* 326–33.

Morrow, L. M. (1985). Retelling stories: A strategy for improving young children's comprehension, concept of story structure, and oral language complexity. *Elementary School Journal, 75,* 647–61.

Morrow, L. M. (1988). Retelling stories as a diagnostic tool. In Glazer, S. M., Searfoss, L. W., & Gentile, L. M. (Eds.), *Reexamining reading diagnosis: New trends and procedures.* Newark, DE: International Reading Association.

Rickards, D., & Cheek, E. (1999). *Designing rubrics for K–6 classroom assessment.* Norwood, MA: Christopher-Gordon Publishers, Inc.

Soundy, C. S. (1993). Let the story begin! *Childhood Education, 69,* 146–150.

Taberski, S. (1997). Three assessment strategies that direct your teaching. *Instructor - Primary, 107,* 83–86.

Weaver, C. (1994). *Reading process and practice: From socio-psycholinguistics to whole language.* (2nd ed.). Portsmouth, NH: Heinemann.

Wood, K. D., & Jones, J. (1998). Tips for teaching. *Preventing School Failure, 43,* 37–39.

Zanowicz, M. (1996). *Story-retelling effects.* Unpublished Masters Thesis, Kean College of New Jersey. ERIC: ED393090.

Retrospective Miscue Analysis

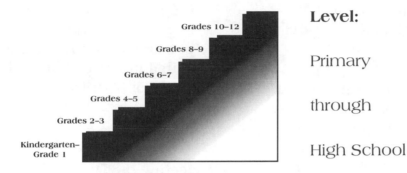

Level:

Primary

through

High School

What Is It?

We understand that good readers know reading is a meaning-making process and that they can monitor their use of the process and take corrective action when it fails. Poor readers do not know these things. But how can we tell if our learners are monitoring their use of the reading process and taking this important corrective action? One very valuable way to do this is to review and analyze their miscues with them. This is called retrospective miscue analysis (RMA). RMA is the process by which you and your student examine the student's oral reading miscues while reflecting upon and evaluating the use of the reading process. It is analyzing the miscues in retrospect—thus the name, retrospective miscue analysis.

Teachers who use RMA find it a powerful way to focus the reader on his or her use of the reading process and reading strategies. When readers examine their own miscues with the guidance of the teacher, they can see how they made use of predicting, sampling, confirming, and integrating—the essential elements of the reading process. They also can see how they used the cueing systems that help readers create meaning—the graphophonic cues, the semantic cues, and the syntactic cues. In RMA, readers can see that good reading is not error-free and that there is a distinction between "good" miscues and "not good" miscues. "Good" miscues deviate from the text without destroying meaning. "Not good" miscues alter meaning too much.

Ann Marek (1987) has done pioneering work in RMA. Her research has shown that one benefit of RMA is that readers' perceptions of reading shift from "text reproduction" to "meaning construction." They become less concerned about getting every word exactly correct and more concerned about creating the richest, most accurate meaning.

Before engaging learners in RMA, you might want to thoroughly study miscue analysis, itself. Understanding miscue analysis and practicing coding miscues and retellings is essential background knowledge for doing retrospective miscue analysis. Goodman, Watson, and Burke's (1987) *Reading*

Miscue Inventory: Alternative Procedures offers an in-depth presentation of miscue analysis. Marek (1991) has offered an outline of RMA procedures, along with her encouragement that you make adaptations to fit your style.

Prior to the RMA

1. Meet with a reader to tape-record the reading of a text. The text may be selected either by you or the reader. The reader should read the entire chapter, short story, or article.

2. During the next week, analyze the reader's miscues.

3. Review the miscues made by the reader and look for patterns that exist in the miscues. Select between 5 and 15 patterned miscues to discuss during the RMA session. Note tape recorder counter numbers for the locations of the miscues you want to play. Select patterns to review based on your perceptions of the reader's needs. If the reader lacks confidence, select miscues that fit the context appropriately. These are miscues that have semantic and syntactic acceptability (good miscues). Focus your discussion on how the reader was working to maintain meaning when he or she made these miscues. If the reader has difficulty sounding out words, select miscues where sounding out has been successfully combined with background knowledge so that you can help the reader see how these are used together. If the reader fails to correct miscues that do not go with the rest of the text, point out some instances where this correction

was made and contrast it to the lack of meaning that was created when the correction wasn't made. If the reader tends to look at initial sounds in words and "bark" any word, select miscues where persistence in sounding out resulted in words that fit the context. Contrast these with substitutions that failed to create meaning.

Conducting the RMA

1. Meet with the reader to conduct the RMA session. Play each of the recorded sections of the previous reading to listen to the miscues you wish to analyze. Marek suggests the following questions as guidelines for the discussion:

   • Does the miscue make sense?

   • Was the miscue corrected? Should it have been?

   • Does the miscue look like what was on the page?

   • Does the miscue sound like what was on the page?

   • Why do you think you made this miscue?

   • Did the miscue affect your understanding of the text?

These questions, and others you create, will lead to discussions of prediction making and sampling from the cueing systems. These questions will also lead to a discussion that is focused on the reader asking important metacomprehension questions of him- or herself, rereading, skipping, and reading on. It is critically important to talk about miscues that were self-corrected. Ask, "What did you think about when you made this correction? How did you know that you needed to make a correction?" Self-corrections are one of the best pieces of evidence we can get that readers are carefully monitoring their use of the reading process.

2. The entire RMA session may be tape-recorded and later transcribed to examine particularly interesting sections, or anecdotal records may be written.

3. Ask the reader to read and retell another selection for later use in RMA.

RMA leads to children being able to carefully and critically analyze their reading. Mary Giard (1993) tells how her first-graders became so comfortable with the language of miscue analysis that it was not uncommon for a child to finish a session with her, walk over to a friend, and say, "Well, today I made four miscues: one was an omission, but the rest were substitutions. I reran and went back to self-correct. Not bad, huh?" (page 80).

Mary's children went on to make note of the strategies they were using to correct miscues. After hearing two reading buddies discuss the running record they had taken on each other, Mary said, "I stood back astonished . . . first-graders understanding strategies, articulating what they needed, and using sophisticated language was one thing . . . taking a running record and understanding its purpose was quite another! I was dumbfounded." (page 80)

How Does Retrospective Miscue Analysis Inform Instruction?

The conversation you have with a child about the miscue made during oral reading can be very enlightening. For example, suppose that the child has correctly decoded initial sounds in words but miscued on the rest of the word. If you ask the child why he or she made that miscue, and the response is something like, "I looked at the first letter" or "I know that first letter," then you will know to help the child focus on the middles and ends of words.

If a child reruns a line of text or a phrase, you might ask why that line was reread. The response of "I just started over" gives you a different instructional signal than a response such as "What I read first didn't make sense." In the first case we have no evidence that the child was monitoring his or her reading. But in the second case such monitoring is very clear.

Another very useful discussion centers around self-corrections. Asking about what a reader was thinking when a self-correction was made is almost always a fruitful discussion. Here we have an opportunity to gain real insight into the way the child views the reading process and whether or not he or she is asking "Does it look right? Does it sound right? Does it make sense?" when they predict and read.

In commenting on student responses to RMA, Yetta Goodman says, "Students who engage in retrospective miscue analysis become articulate about the reading process and their abilities as readers. In order to use language with confidence, students need to feel comfortable to make mistakes, to ask 'silly' questions, to experiment in ways that are not always considered conventional. Readers who are confident, who develop a curiosity about how reading works, and who are willing to take risks in employing 'keep going' strategies are most likely to become avid readers" (Goodman, 1996, p. 608). Could there be a more compelling reason to engage in RMA?

What Are the Advantages of Retrospective Miscue Analysis?

Helping readers understand their use of the reading process and the cueing systems is the greatest advantage of RMA. Some reader's entire perceptions of themselves as readers have changed when they examined how they use the cueing systems and reading strategies. RMA opens a dialogue between you and your students that results in better understandings by all of you. Children learn the language of miscue analysis and are able to correctly use it. RMA leads to greater metacomprehension ability. Insecure readers can begin to see how they may monitor their own creation of meaning and, in turn, get better at doing so. Retrospective miscue analysis gives learners the language they need to discuss their reading with each other in meaningful ways. Another advantage is that readers can take more ownership of their reading and the analysis of it.

What Are the Disadvantages of Retrospective Miscue Analysis?

While not an inherent "disadvantage," RMA requires a teacher who understands miscue analysis and psycholinguistic theory. In fact, this knowledge is essential in light of current understandings about the reading process and how to bring children to literacy. Miscue analysis, itself, takes a good deal of practice in order to become proficient. Likewise, RMA takes a good deal of practice. RMA is very time consuming. You may want to begin using it with the readers in your class about whom you are the most puzzled.

Where Do I Get More Information About Retrospective Miscue Analysis?

Giard, M. (1993). Bringing children to literacy through guided reading. In Harp, B. (Ed.), *Bringing children to literacy: Classrooms at work.* Norwood, MA: Christopher-Gordon Publishers.

Goodman, Y. M., & Burke, C. (1980). *Reading strategies: Focus on comprehension.* Katonah, NY: Richard C. Owen.

Goodman, Y. M., & Wilde, S. (Eds.). (1996). *Notes from a kidwatcher: Selected writing of Yetta M. Goodman.* Portsmouth, NH: Heinemann.

Goodman, Y. M. (1996). Revaluing readers while readers revalue themselves: Retrospective miscue analysis. *The Reading Teacher, 49,* 8, 600–609.

Marek, A. M. (1987). *Retrospective miscue analysis as an instructional strategy with adult readers.* Ph.D. dissertation, University of Arizona, Tucson.

Marek, A. M. (1991). Retrospective miscue analysis: An instructional strategy for revaluing the reading process. In Goodman, K. S., Bird, L. B., & Goodman, Y. M., (Eds.), *The whole language catalog.* Santa Rosa, CA: American School Publishers.

Weaver, C. (1994). *Reading process and practice: From socio-psycholinguistics to whole language.* Portsmouth, NH: Heinemann.

Whitmore, K. F. (1992). Developmental moments: Assessing the strengths of readers. In Goodman, K. S., Bird, L. B., & Goodman, Y. S. (Eds.), *The whole language catalog supplement on authentic assessment.* New York: Science Research Associates.

Running Records

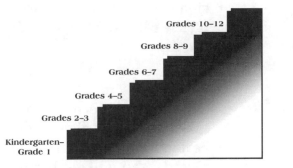

Grades 10–12
Grades 8–9
Grades 6–7
Grades 4–5
Grades 2–3
Kindergarten–
Grade 1

Level:

Kindergarten

through

High School

What Are They?

There was a time, not long ago, when we thought that we could bring children to literacy by teaching them approximately 150 reading skills. Our understandings of the reading process have developed since then. Now we understand that reading is much more than activating and applying skill knowledge. While that is important, it is also important to understand how the reader uses the reading process, how the reader monitors his or her use of the reading process, how the reader applies reading strategies, and how the reader uses the cueing systems.

So now we are challenged with becoming highly skilled observers of how children behave as readers. Running records are one of the most helpful observational/analytical tools we have. Running records are a system for recording (using a set of standard conventions) all that we can observe about a learner's behavior as a reader. Invented by Marie Clay, they are used extensively in New Zealand and are gaining popularity in the United States. More and more U.S. teachers are becoming familiar with running

records as Reading Recovery is more widely introduced into our schools. All reading recovery teachers take running records daily on their learners' reading.

Because running records reflect what really occurs while a reader reads, they assist in our accurate observation and interpretation of the reader's use of the reading process in terms of both strategies and the cueing systems. Running records do not require a typed script. They may be done on any piece of paper. With practice, you can take a running record at any time, anywhere, on any text as the opportunity arises or because what a reader is doing at the moment is critically important.

Clay acknowledges that learning to take a running record can "unsettle teachers" because the process is so simple. All you need to learn before beginning to take running records is the set of marks (conventions) that are used to record reading behavior. Educators in New Zealand argue that all teachers who observe reading behavior through running records should use the same conventions. This way, a teacher in another school or in another school year can look at a past running record and interpret it.

Steps in Taking a Running Record

Step One

Learn the conventions so you can mark easily. (Hint: it will be helpful to you, though not necessary, to tape record the reading in the first running records you do). Accurate reading is coded by making a check mark √ for each word correctly read. The conventions for marking miscues make use of a simple, but effective concept. When the child makes a miscue, you draw an horizontal line. The reading behavior exhibited by the child is coded above the line and what was in the text is coded below the line. Given a line of text that reads "When will the cat leave?", for example, if a reader substituted *what* for *when* while reading "What will the cat leave?", the coding would be:

Substitute $\frac{\text{what}}{\text{when}}$ √ √ √ √

If the reader omitted the word, *the,* reading "When will cat leave?" the coding would be:

Omitted √ √ $\overline{\text{the}}$ √ √

If the reader inserted a word, *fat,* reading "When will the fat cat leave?" the coding would be:

√ √ √ $\underline{\text{fat}}$ √ √ inserted

If the reader, for example, substituted *when* for *what* and then self-corrected, the coding would be:

Self-corrected $\frac{\text{when}}{\text{what}}$ sc √ √ √

Notice that in each example, the reader's behavior was recorded above the line, and the text was represented below the line. For a detailed discussion of the running record conventions, please refer to Clay's *An Observation Survey.*

Step Two

Give yourself permission to make mistakes and move slowly. You can't expect perfection in early attempts at running records. You will get better with practice.

Step Three

Identify a student about whom you would like to know more as a reader. Start with that child. As you get more comfortable, take running records on more children. Set goals for yourself. In kindergarten through grade two, set a goal to do a running record on each student so that no record is older than three weeks old. Establish a schedule by which you can rotate through the class doing running records on this three-week cycle. Beyond second grade, take running records only on children whose behavior as readers is troubling or puzzling to you. SPED also

Step Four

challenge

Select a text for the running record. This text may be one the child has never read before or it may be familiar. Taking a running record on a familiar text will help you determine whether or not the text is of appropriate difficulty and how well the child is using reading strategies that have been taught before. Taking a running record on an unfamiliar text will help you determine how well the child uses the cueing systems and how willing the reader is to take risks.

Whole short stories or expository pieces are best. If not a whole piece, the selection should be between 100 and 200 running words and take about 10 minutes to read (Clay, 1993). Of course, the text has to provide enough challenge to cause the reader to miscue, or the running record will be essentially useless.

Step Five

Fill in the name of the child and the title of the text on the Running Record Sheet. Circle "familiar" or "unfamiliar" depending on whether or not the child has experienced this text before. Ask the student to read the title, or read it yourself. Explain that you are going to make some marks on paper as the student reads aloud to you so that you can know him or her better as a reader. Record all reading behaviors that you can, using the conventions.

There are only three things you should say while taking the running record: the title, "try that again" when you think a rerun over a piece of text would be helpful, and a word when the reader asks you for it. Resist the temptation to *teach* while you are taking the running record. At this point you are simply recording all of the reading behaviors you can for further analysis and teaching later. All that is necessary is that you have visual access to the text the reader is reading. You can sit beside or behind the reader and see the text as you mark the reading behavior. It may be helpful in initial running records to do the marking on a copy of the text. Eventually, you want to be able to do a running record on any piece of paper you have handy.

When we visited primary grade classrooms in New Zealand we saw that almost every teacher had either a table set up with the materials she needed to take running records or a clipboard with running records sheets ready to go.

Figure 17 is an excerpt from a typical running record taken on Lauren's reading of a text in March of first grade. Only a portion of the record is shown here, but the calculations are made on the complete record. At this point in Step Five, we would have listened to Lauren read and used the conventions to record her reading behavior.

Step Six

After the entire text has been read aloud and you have recorded the reading behavior using the conventions, ask the reader to retell everything he or she can remember about what they read. This is call an unaided retelling. Record your impressions of this retelling. If the retelling is not as rich as you would like, assist the reader in thinking of more details. This is called an aided retelling. Circle "aided" or "unaided" accordingly. Questions such as "Remember when _____? What more can you tell me about that _____?" may be helpful in eliciting more details. (Please see Retellings on pp. 107–115.)

Step Seven

Now, without the reader present, you will analyze the running record. We look at each miscue and ask ourselves, "Why do I think the reader made this miscue?" "What was the reader doing when this miscue was made?" Let's ex-

Figure 17   Lauren's Running Record

Name _Lauren_ _____ Date _3/14_ _____ Age _6_

School _Kennedy Elem._   Recorder _Jackson_ _____

Text title: _Brock's farm_ _____

(familiar)/unfamiliar text)

Running Words Errors	Error Rate	Accuracy	Self-correction rate
109/10	1: _11_	_91_ %	1: _6_

Analysis of Errors and Self-Corrections

Lauren draws on all cueing systems in creating meaning. She should be encouraged to pay a bit more attention to visual cues. She used visual cues in making self-corrections. Our next goal is to increase self-correction rate with increased attention to visual cues.

Analysis of Retelling (aided/unaided)

Lauren retold in complete detail without the need for prompting. Her comprehension of the piece was very complete. This selection is at her instructional level.

Figure 17   (continued)

Page		E	SC	Information Used	
				E MSV	SC MSV
4	✓ ✓ ✓ ✓ ✓				
4	✓ ✓ _sister_ /sc / _mother_		1	Ⓜ︎Ⓢ︎V	M S Ⓥ
5	✓ ✓ ✓ _nineteen_ / ninety-seven	1		ⓂⓈV	
	✓ ✓ ✓ _nineteen_ / ninety-seven	1		ⓂⓈⓋ	
6	✓ ✓ ✓ _meatiest_ /sc / _meanest_		1	ⓂⓈⓋ	M S Ⓥ
	✓ ✓ ✓				
	✓ _busted_/_butted_ ✓ — /big _dogs_/_dog_	1 / 1		ⓂⓈV / — / ⓂⓈⓋ	
10	✓ ✓ ✓ ✓				
	✓ ✓ ✓ ✓				
	✓ ✓ _show_/_shovel_ ✓ _manners_/_manure_	1 / 1		ⓂⓈV / ⓂⓈV	
		10	2	MSV /5148	

amine the first miscue in Figure 17. Lauren substituted *sister* for *mother* and then she self-corrected. We do not count self-corrections as errors, so we make no tally in the "E" column, but we do make a tally in the "SC" self-correction column. Then we analyze the miscue twice: once as an error and once as a self-correction, each time asking ourselves which of the cueing systems we think Lauren was drawing on at the time—what knowledge do we think she was using. To do this we write "m s v" in both the "E" and "SC" columns under "Information Used." Do we think Lauren was trying to make meaning when she substituted *sister* for *mother.* The answer is "yes," so we circle the m in the "E" (error) column. We then ask ourselves, "Do we think Lauren was drawing on language cues—her knowledge of the structure of our language—when she substituted *sister* for *mother*?" The answer is "yes" so we circle the s in the "E" column. Then we ask ourselves, "Do we think Lauren was using her knowledge of visual (sound/symbol) cues when she substituted *sister* for *mother*?" The answer is "no." *Sister* and *mother* have very little visual similarity. We do not circle the "v" in the error column.

Because Lauren self-corrected when she miscued on *mother* we now need to analyze this miscue a second time, as a self-correction. We write "m s v" in the "SC" (self-correction) column. In this analysis we are asking ourselves why we think she made the self-correction. We are asking ourselves which of the cueing systems we think Lauren was using when she made the self-correction. Our best prediction is that she reexamined the visual cues, saw that *sister* could not be correct and

made the correction. Because we think she used her knowledge of visual cues, we now circle the "v" in the "SC" column.

We continue our analysis of each miscue in this manner, always asking ourselves why we think Lauren made the miscue—what knowledge she was drawing on in doing so. We then circle the appropriate letter.

After we have analyzed all of the miscues we will tally the number or errors, the number of self-corrections and the number of times we circled "m," "s", and "v." We will then consider the degree to which Lauren is drawing on all of the cueing systems. Here you see that we have observed that she is using them all, but may need to pay a bit closer attention to the visual cues. We then write our analysis of errors and self-corrections, as well as our analysis of Lauren's retelling.

How Do Running Records Inform Instruction?

If you are working with kindergarten, first- or second-grade learners, you will need to set aside some time each day for completing running records. The goal is to complete a number of running records each day in order to maintain an on-going profile for each child. Try to capture a few minutes in which you can be spontaneous in taking a running record on the spot. It works best if you keep plenty of blank forms on hand, so that a running record can be done without having to find a form on which to record it.

The goal, of course, is that all children should be observed carefully by using the running records, but you may find that you take a record more regularly on children who are less fluent. Running records can be useful for more fluent children if you use different genres, such as word problems in math or expository material, or if the purpose for reading is varied from time to time.

You will find that you can use the information from the running records to monitor the growth of individual children, to look at the performance of members of a group to determine whether material under consideration is a good match for them, and to help with long-range planning. You will want to plan instruction on the error patterns that you find are common to the group.

By carefully examining the use of the cueing systems and the self-corrections you can gain insight into which strategies and cues your children are using. You then can make instructional decisions about materials and mini-lessons that will meet the needs of small groups and/or individual children.

In addition to planning appropriate instruction, you will find the running records very helpful in talking to parents and other teachers. It will be especially important for you to share running record information with reading specialists who are working with your learners.

Mary Giard described her use of a running record with a second-grader who was reading an unknown text. This child relied on visual cues throughout the reading. When she had completed the running record, Mary said to her, "I noticed that you tried to use a sounding out strategy for each word that you did not know. Can you also think about what word would make sense given what has been read before?"

Figure 18 is a running record Mary took as Sean was reading a book entitled *The Praying Mantis*. Following the running record, Figure 19 is the transcript of the conversation between Mary and Sean. Pay close attention to Sean's explanations of the strategies he is using and the knowledge Mary has about his reading behavior when this running record and the conference are completed.

As teachers consider beginning running records, I recommend that you use audio or video tapes in the beginning, and that you practice, practice, practice. I believe that having someone to talk to about running records, and having someone to help and support you as you begin running records, will make life so much easier.

What Are the Advantages of Running Records?

The greatest advantages are ease of use (with practice), ease of interpretation, and the important information gained about the reader's use of the reading process and the cueing systems. The percentage of accuracy rating determines one aspect of the degree of challenge presented by texts the child is reading. The running record also provides data for you to use when doing a retrospective miscue analysis with your student. (See Retrospective Miscue Analysis on p. 117–121.)

What Are the Disadvantages of Running Records?

There are two points of controversy about running records often discussed

Figure 18   Sean's Running Record

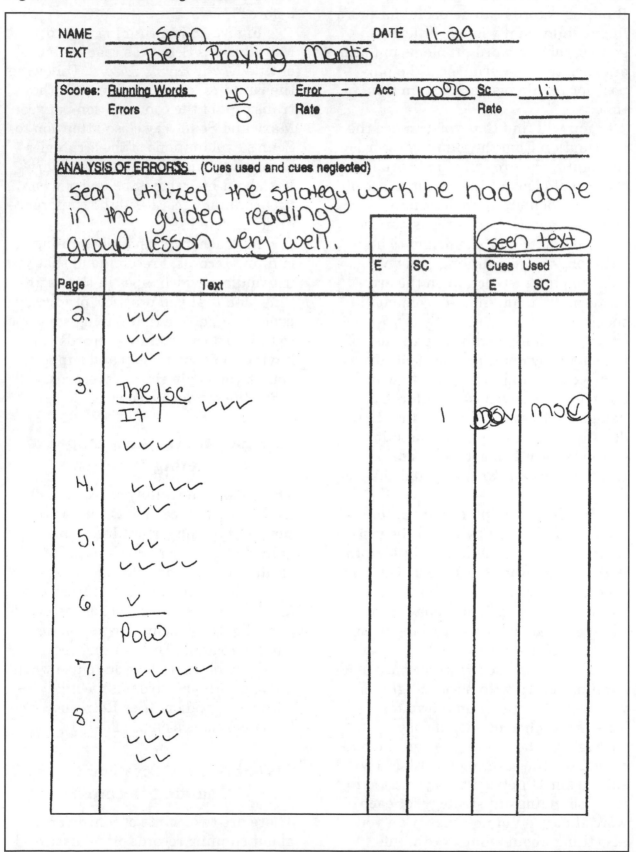

Figure 19 *The Praying Mantis* Running Record Follow-up Transcript

Teacher is Mary Giard
Student is Sean Sevey, first grader

Mary: What did you like about his book?

Sean: I liked the photographs and I liked that the books told us that the praying mantis eats flies everyday.

Mary: So, you learned something new?

Sean: Yes.

Mary: You did a good job reading the book we had a lesson on earlier today. I noticed that you fingerpointed. Why did you do that on this text?

Sean: So I wouldn't get mixed up when I was reading.

Mary: On page 6 I noticed that you hesitated on the word *POW*. What happened there?

Sean: I saw the W. It helped me.

Mary: How?

Sean: pause

Mary: I got ready because I thought you were going to make an error, but you got it.

Sean: I didn't know the O was supposed to be there, but I knew the word was *POW*.

Mary: How did you know that?

Sean: Because I knew that W-O-W name *WOW*. I used that strategy we talked about to change the first letter of the word.

Mary: Good for you. I noticed back here on page 3 . . . initially you said *THE* then you said *IT*. Had you expected the text to say something else?

Sean: I thought it was going to say *THE PRAYING MANTIS* again but then I saw that word *(LOOKS)* and I thought that *THE* wouldn't make sense.

Mary: You're right. *THE LOOKS* wouldn't make sense. I'm glad you caught that. You did a good job integrating all the strategies we have talked about. That was a tough text. I hope you continue to transfer your strategies to new material.

by American educators. The first is that in New Zealand teachers calculate percentages of accuracy when analyzing running records. Some American educators resist this procedure because they believe that mere percentages do not adequately reflect a reader's processing of the text. Percentages of accuracy fail to account for reader purpose and strategy use. The second concern expressed by American educators is the interpretation of meaning. In the New Zealand model, the teacher analyzes the reader's use of meaning by asking, "Does the child use meaning in making the oral reading error?" If what the child says as he or she reads makes sense, even though it is inaccurate, New Zealand teachers believe the child is applying his or her knowledge of the world to reading, so therefore making meaning. For example, if the reader said, "The girl ran to the yellow horse" and the text word was *house,* not *horse,* the New Zealand model would say to credit the reader with making meaning. An American teacher would argue that house and horse do not mean the same thing at all, and therefore the reader should not be credited with making meaning.

American teachers often take a different view of how the meaning issue is to be handled in analyzing a reader's miscues. Many teachers look at the miscue and ask, "Does the miscue mean essentially the same thing as the text word (*home* for *house,* for ex-

ample)?" Only if the meaning of the text has been relatively well maintained would the reader be credited with creating meaning.

I have resolved this for myself by believing that we should take the more liberal view of "meaning" when working with emergent readers and the more conservative view when working with older readers. SPED – high school

Like any form of miscue analysis, running records take time to learn and time to execute, and require that you understand miscue analysis and psycholinguistic theory.

Where Do I Get More Information About Running Records?

Clay, M. M. (1991). *Becoming literate: The construction of inner control.* Portsmouth, NH: Heinemann.

Clay, M. M. (1993). *An observation survey of early literacy achievement.* Portsmouth, NH: Heinemann.

Fountas, I. C., & Pinnell, G. S. (1996). *Guided reading: Good first teaching for all children.* Portsmouth, NH: Heinemann.

Parker, E. L. (1995). Teacher's choices in classroom assessment (reading assessment). *The Reading Teacher, 48,* 7, 622–624.

Weaver, C. (1994). *Reading process and practice: From socio-psycholinguistics to whole language.* Portsmouth, NH: Heinemann.

Student Self-Evaluation

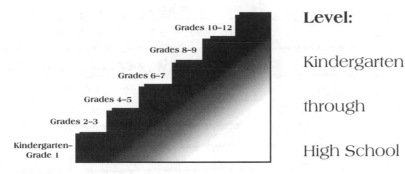

Level:

Kindergarten

through

High School

What Is It?

With increasingly larger classes and over-stuffed curricula, many teachers are looking for ways to help students take more responsibility for their own learning. One way to achieve this is student self-evaluation. Student self-evaluation is the metacognitive process of learners reflecting on their own learning. Through self-evaluation we learn what learners think of their own work. We can gain valuable insight into the learning process by listening to our learners' reflections on their work.

Self-evaluation takes a myriad of forms. It can range from something as simple and unstructured as a brief conversation between you and a student that has been sparked by your asking "How is your writing going?" It can be a ritualized part of daily journal writing, regular letters to parents about a student's self-assessment, or the completion of a self-evaluation form specific to a curriculum area or a learning activity. It can be a part of regular debriefing sessions throughout the day, or a part of the morning meeting.

Mary Giard (1993) shares a marvelous story of self-evaluation that grows out of the work of her first-graders. Mary's students had been engaging in running records and miscue analysis with her for most of the school year. Her learners had learned the language of miscue analysis and could easily discuss their reading using very technical vocabulary. Her children were engaged in buddy reading, and often took running records on each other and debriefed them together. Finally, they had learned so much about the reading process that they came to Mary and asked her to help them create a checklist of the reading strategies they used so that they could more easily remember them and use them as they read and as they discussed their reading with their buddies. The checklist they devised is illustrated in Figure 20. Using the checklist, Mary's children were able to engage in very sophisticated retroactive miscue analysis on their own.

Teachers have created checklists to help readers monitor their use of the reading process. One form of such checklists is based on helping readers learn to ask themselves the three criti-

Figure 20   Reading Strategies Checklist

Reader: _____	Date: _____	
Partner: _____	Title: _____	
Strategies	Yes, it worked	No, it didn't
1. Does it make sense?		
2. Does it sound right?		
3. Does it look right?		
4. Finger Point		
5. Picture Clue		
6. Read something you know		
7. Use your experiences		
8. Reread a book		
9. Rerun, start over		
10. Find word, self correct		
11. Rhyming Pattern		
12. Repeating Pattern		
13. Skip it, Come back		
14. Length of Word		
15. Beginning sound		
16. Give a hint		
17. Ask Someone		
18. Make predictions		
19. Title		
20. Small Word in a Big Word		
21. Insertion		
22. Omission		

Did the reader understand the piece?
How do you know?

Giard

Note: From Giard, M. (1993). Bringing children to literacy through guided reading. In Harp, B. (Ed.), *Bringing children to literacy: Classrooms at work.* Norwood, MA: Christopher-Gordon Publishers. Reprinted with permission.

cal questions that all self-monitoring readers ask: Does it look right? (I made a prediction that the word was _____. Given the graphophonic cues, does my prediction look right?); Does it sound right? (From what I know about how our language works, does my prediction sound like an accurate English sentence?); and Does it make sense? (Does my prediction create reasonable meaning?). A sample self-evaluation checklist for strategic reading follows on the next page.

Students are also encouraged to self-evaluate writing. In a fourth-grade classroom in New Jersey, children were to select the three best pieces of writing in their writing folders and explain why they made each of their selections. Because these children had been discussing writing all year with their teacher and each other in editing groups and editing committees, they wrote comments such as: "I like the hook I used in this story. Readers say it really gets their attention." and "I like the way I built up the suspense in this piece." You might choose to periodically ask students to select a piece of writing and write an evaluation of it. The evaluation may be guided by posting a set of considerations on a chart in the room. The considerations could include:

- This is my current best piece because . . .
- The things I am doing better as a writer that are shown in this piece are . . .
- My most recent writing goals that were met in this piece are . . .
- My next writing goals are . . .

Many teachers are concerned about the lack of real reading that is done during sustained silent reading periods. By creating an evaluation form that children fill out regularly at the beginning of the year, you establish the importance of seriously reading during this time. Questions that could be asked on this form include: How much time did you spend reading during silent reading time today? If you didn't spend all of the time reading, why didn't you? What will help you so that you'll spend all your time reading the next time we have silent reading time? (Rhodes, 1993).

Whole group discussions about how the work of the class is going are another form of student self-evaluation. These discussions may take place at the end of the morning or day, or they may happen as one learning activity is ending. On page 137 is an example of the kinds of questions you might ask for group evaluation titled "Thinking About Our Work." You could copy and distribute them, or make a large wall chart of them. Please use these as a starting point to create your own list.

Some teachers are finding literature logs a valuable tool of self-evaluation. Students are asked to reread the responses to literature pieces written in the logs. Then they write a self-evaluation about the thinking they were doing as they read. If self-evaluation of writing is not happening in other contexts, the writing in the literature log may be subjected to evaluation as discussed above.

Self-evaluation of literature study group activities focuses learners on the importance of the discussions and the quality of work. When you have carefully laid the groundwork for the quality you expect in literature groups, you

Reading Strategy Checklist

Name _____ Date _____

Before I read I:

_____ Think about what I know about the topic.

_____ Make predictions about what the author might say.

_____ When I make predictions I use:
_____ The title
_____ Section or chapter headings
_____ Illustrations
_____ The author's name
_____ What I know about the author's work
_____ Other things I use are:

While I read I:

_____ Check to see if my predictions are proven.

_____ Make new predictions if my predictions were not proven.

_____ Ask myself three important questions about my reading:
_____ When I say a word I'm not sure of do I look at the letters and ask my-self if my prediction look right?
_____ When I read I ask myself if my reading sounds right—does it sound like the way we would say something?
_____ When I read do I ask myself if my reading is making sense?

_____ When my reading does not sound right or look right or make sense, I use a strategy to fix it.

The strategies I use are:

_____ Reread

_____ Read ahead

_____ Rethink

_____ Look at the first letter or the word and think of a word with that letter that would make sense.

_____ Sound out

_____ Put in a word that makes sense

_____ Use picture clues

_____ Ask for help

_____ Other strategies I use are:

Thinking About Our Work

How are we doing?

What worked well in this activity?

What did not work so well?

How can we fix it next time?

How can we tell that we are learning more and getting better at _____?

Were any of us confused?

What can we do to take care of the confusion?

What goals do we have for our next group activity?

How did we do on cleaning up?

can draw on that in having students evaluate their own work. For example, if you had told students that your expectations were that they have read the agreed upon text before the meeting, that they would come to the group prepared to discuss the plot, and that you expected them to offer vocabulary they need to explore, these could become items on a group-evaluation or self-evaluation checklist.

Another form of self-evaluation that is gaining popularity is the student letter to parents. Some teachers have students write a letter every Friday summarizing the highlights of their learning activities for the week and setting goals for next week. In some communities, parents write responses to these letters and return them to school the next week. Other teachers have learners write letters to parents to accompany the report card. "My reading grade is _____ because _____. My goals are _____."

How Does Student Self-Evaluation Inform Instruction?

It can be very useful to have students engage in one or more forms of self-evaluation at the beginning of the year and then revisit that evaluation periodically, or at least at the end of the year.

For example, you might use a student survey for writing at the beginning of the year. The survey asks questions such as "How do you feel about writing?" and "Do you consider yourself a writer?" Then you ask students to produce a piece of writing which you save. At the end of the school year you use the same survey

and ask the students to make comparisons between a current piece of writing and the saved piece looking especially at how they have changed as writers over the year. You might use this same procedure every quarter throughout the school year, to have each student set one or more writing goals for the quarter. The goals could be put in writing along with a plan for how they are going to achieve them. At the end of the quarter, they are asked to assess if they have achieved their goal, and make their goals for the following quarter. If for some reason they have not achieved a goal, they are asked to analyze why and plot out a new strategy that will lead to success. This might best be done as a part of writing conferences.

Another component of student self-evaluation can be the portfolio. If portfolio assessment and evaluation is used in your school, students could choose a piece of their writing for their portfolio at certain points in the school year. They would then be asked to write a reflection piece that deals with questions such as: "Why did you choose this piece?" and "What could you change in the piece to improve it?" Towards the end of the school year, they could be asked to repeat this process and pick the one piece that they would like to go into the portfolio that will go on to the next grade.

Some teachers are finding a powerful way to have students engaged in self-evaluation across the curriculum. This is the student-led conference which takes place at the end of each grading period. In this process, students fill out a form that asks them to write what goals they have had, what they have learned, what goals they have for the next grading period, and how they plan to achieve those goals. As well as dealing with reading and writing, the student-led conferences usually include two or three content areas that the students choose. After the students have written out their plans, a student-led meeting is held with the parents and teacher. The parents and teacher ask clarifying questions and, in general, provide support and guidance throughout the conference.

Parents come away from these conferences understanding what their child is learning and what the goals are for a particular time period. Through these conferences, the student/parent/school connection is strengthened as the parents are built into the goal-setting process.

You will be able to use the information you get from each of these examples of student self-evaluation to guide your teaching. The beginning of school writing surveys will permit you to set goals that are consistent with the students' goals and the curriculum. For example, student's goals may have to do with writing in various genres, creating dialogue, or improving grammar. If you see that some students want to write in a particular genre, you can immerse them in literature of that genre so that they will have good models. If you see there are individual needs in mechanics, you can do focus lessons with small groups.

What Are the Advantages of Student Self-Evaluation?

At the heart of student self-evaluation are two important aspects of learning: responsibility and metacognition. Self-

evaluation is a way for students to take responsibility for their learning. When they have to take a critical look at their behavior as learners, they must see that they are responsible in many ways for their own learning. In this way they are held accountable for their behavior, and out of this accountability comes goal-setting. Metacognition, thinking about their own thinking, is another important aspect of self-evaluation. As you listen to learners reflect on their own learning, you gain insight into your teaching. As you guide them to think about their own learning, you are modeling the kind of thinking that they will ultimately come to do on their own. Self-evaluation is a way to open a dialogue between members of the learning community, and between learners and parents.

What Are the Disadvantages of Student Self-Evaluation?

Self-evaluation relies on the learner to accurately report his or her behavior and evaluations of it. Because of this self-reporting aspect, there is the chance that students will evaluate their work in ways they think you want to hear rather than in ways that truly reflect how they judge their work. It takes time and patience to assist learners to adequately carrying out self-evaluation activities.

Where Do I Get More Information About Self-Evaluation?

Boersma, G. (1995). *Improving student self-evaluation through authentic assessment.* M.A. in Teaching and

Leadership Action Research Project, St. Xavier University, ERIC: ED393885.

Cellini, P. (1997). I wouldn't have missed this meeting for anything! *Primary Voices K–6, 5,* 4, 6–11.

Goodman, Y. M. (1992). A teacher's professional sense. In Goodman, K. S., Bird, L. B., & Goodman, Y. M. (Eds.), *The whole language catalog supplement on authentic assessment.* New York: Science Research Associates.

Haswell, R. H. (1993). Student self-evaluations and developmental change. *New Directions for Teaching and Learning, 56,* 83–99.

Klenowski, V. (1995) *Student self-evaluation processes: Empowering students in learner-centered contexts.* Paper presented at the Annual

Meeting of the American Educational Research Association, San Francisco, CA. ERIC: ED383673.

Lenski, S. D. (1996). Honoring student self-evaluation in the classroom community. *Primary Voices K–6, 4,* 2, 24–32.

Peterson, R., & Eeds, M. (1990). *Grand conversations: Literature groups in action.* New York: Scholastic.

Rhodes, L. K. (1993). *Literacy assessment: A handbook of instruments.* Portsmouth, NH: Heinemann.

Ross, J. A. (1997) *Teaching students how to evaluate their work in cooperative learning: Results of a collaborative action research in-service.* Paper presented at the Annual Meeting of the American Educational Research Association, Chicago, IL. ERIC: ED409353.

Think Alouds

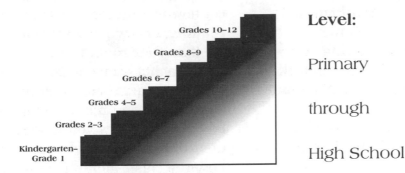

Level:

Primary

through

High School

What Are They?

Have you ever found yourself wishing you could get inside the head of your student? That you could somehow *observe* the thinking a reader is doing *as he or she* reads? Have you wished you could somehow observe metacomprehension happening? There is one small door through which we can begin to make such observations. That door is think alouds. Think alouds are the verbalizations of what a reader is thinking as he or she is reading. Metacomprehension strategies are the reflective thinking readers do as they read. Such thinking involves the conscious application of fix-it strategies when comprehension fails. Think alouds are often thought of as instructional strategies, but they also have power as assessment and evaluation tools.

As instructional strategies, think alouds are a tool for teaching children to engage in the important monitoring of their creation of meaning and their use of corrective strategies. Think alouds require a reader to stop the reading and think aloud about how the reading is progressing, and what the reader is or is not understanding. In

think alouds, the reader makes verbal reports on his or her predicting, confirming and integrating, the understanding of inferences, the asking of "Is this making sense?", and the thinking through of the story. As an instructional strategy, readers are taught to say out loud what is going on in their minds as they read.

As an assessment and evaluation tool, think alouds give you important information about how well the reader is able to engage in metacomprehension activities. By taking anecdotal records on think alouds, you have data on how well the reader is monitoring the creation of meaning and using corrective strategies when meaning fails. Think alouds permit us to "get inside the reader's head" to understand how the reader is using the reading process to construct meaning. We are able to hear the reader use such strategies as predicting, confirming and rejecting predictions, using prior knowledge, rereading and reading ahead, visualizing, and debating where the writer is going with the text.

When using think alouds for assessment and evaluation, ask readers to verbalize their answers to such questions as: Is this making sense? Where do I predict the writer is going with this story? How does the unfolding story match my expectations? What did I do when I came to a difficult part of the text? When do I read on or re-read, and why? By audio taping and transcribing think alouds we can look at what the reader or readers said and try to discern patterns in their responses.

The following page illustrates a Think Aloud Checklist that could be used either by you or your students to evaluate think alouds. The list is not complete enough to cover every eventuality, but it may be useful to you as you and you learners begin to analyze think alouds. Please feel free to modify it in any way that makes it more useful to you.

You could use the checklist simply as a checklist, or you could create a key that learners could use to make the list with the frequency with which they use each of the items. The key might be F = frequently; S = sometimes; R = rarely; N = never. This frequency evaluation could be discussed periodically during reading conferences.

How Do Think Alouds Inform Instruction?

At the beginning of the year, you may need to do a good deal of modeling of think alouds with your students, depending on experiences they have had with them in the past. You can model think alouds while you are reading, and you can also model them as you write. Some teachers pretend that they are a child when they do the modeling. I prefer to model as myself, which I think is more authentic.

Once children understand the process, you can have them do think alouds during guided reading, during reading conferences, during writing conferences, during sustained silent reading, and when you stop by a child's desk as your roam the room.

Teachers have found it easy to integrate think alouds into the everyday curriculum on an informal, but regular basis. Sometimes you might ask a student to play the teacher and explain how the class should think through a problem that comes up in either reading or writing. At other times you might pair students up and ask them to do think alouds with each other. This gives you the freedom to roam the room and listen in on these think alouds.

Dawn Repetti, a second grade teacher, says that she learns a lot about her students by hearing them think aloud. She gains access to the strategies and skills they are using during the reading and writing process. A child doing a think aloud in reading may say something like: "I'm going to start reading this book. I can tell from the picture on the cover that it's about a train. I like trains. I have one at home. We read another book about a train and I sometimes watch a TV show about a train. I always look at the pictures on the cover of the book and on each page before I try to read the words. I'm going to try to sound out this word. I know that it has the 'ch' sound that we learned about last week." From this Dawn can see that the child is applying his prior knowledge, that he remembers the 'ch' lesson done the week before, and is using cues from the pictures to make meaning from the book.

Think Aloud Checklist

Name_____ Date_____

When I think aloud about my reading I sometimes talk about:

_____ How well my reading is going and how I am understanding how it is making sense.

_____ A part that is confusing to me when I am having trouble making sense.

When I am having trouble making sense I sometimes talk about:

_____ The fact that my reading isn't making sense.

_____ Using a part that I just read to help me figure out a word I am not sure of.

_____ Saying what I think the text means in my own words.

_____ Thinking of an experience I've had that I think is like what the text is saying.

_____ What I think the text is saying and what I think is going to happen next.

_____ A synonym that I know for the word that is giving me trouble.

_____ Looking at the first letter of the problem word and thinking if I know a word that begins with that letter that would make sense.

_____ How I am trying to sound out a word.

_____ Questions I have about the reading.

_____ Adding information to the text to see if that makes sense.

_____ Rereading.

_____ Reading ahead.

_____ Other: _____

When we're doing writing, you might ask students to think through the writing process. A student may say something like "I don't know what I'm going to write about. Hmmm, I can't think of anything. I guess I'll draw a picture. Here's an ocean. Look, there's a shark. I think I want to write about a shark. Should I write a make-believe story about a shark, or should I write what I know about tiger sharks? I think I'll write about tiger sharks." Here you can see that the student is capable of generating ideas in a pre-writing activity, knows how to look for a more narrow focus, and is already developing an awareness of the different types of genres. Here the writer is deciding between fiction and expository writing.

You can learn a great deal about your readers and writers using think alouds. It is important, however, to be patient and to provide many, many models.

What Are the Advantages of Think Alouds?

There are many advantages to using think alouds, but probably the most important one is that students gain the very valuable habit of being aware of how they're thinking as readers and writers. This metacognitive skill not only helps you to gain insight into their thinking processes, but it also gives the children a strategy that they can use across the curriculum and in everyday problem-solving.

Because comprehension is such a personal, private activity, think alouds are a way to try to "get inside the head" of a reader. They, along with retrospective miscue analysis, are our best way

of determining to what extent a reader is using metacomprehension strategies.

The information we gain from think alouds permits us to reinforce the self-monitoring behaviors the reader or writer exhibits and to plan instruction to help expand this self-monitoring repertoire.

What Are the Disadvantages of Think Alouds?

Our evaluation of a learner's metacomprehension ability is based on his or her ability to overtly report on what is essentially a covert activity. Our evaluation of a reader's or writer's self-monitoring ability is only as good as that learner's ability to think aloud. Furthermore, our evaluation is based on our own ability to discern patterns in the statements the learner makes during think alouds. Any one statement alone has little or no evaluative power. Only through finding patterns in think alouds can we validly reach conclusions.

Where Do I Get More Information About Think Alouds?

Baumann, J. F., Seifert-Kessell, N., & Jones, L. A. (1992). Effect of think-aloud instruction on elementary students' comprehension monitoring abilities. *Journal of Reading Behavior, 24,* 143–172.

Baumann, J. F., Jones, L. A., & Seifert-Kessell, N. (1993). Using think alouds to enhance children's comprehension monitoring abilities. *The Reading Teacher, 47* (3), 184–193.

Crain-Thoreson, C., & Lippman, M. Z. (1997). Windows on comprehension: Reading comprehension processes as revealed by two think-aloud procedures. *Journal of Educational Psychology, 89,* 579–592.

Garner, R. (1987). *Metacognition and reading comprehension.* Norwood, NJ: Ablex

Glazer, S. M., & Brown, C. S. (1993). *Portfolios and beyond: Collaborative assessment in reading and writing.* Norwood, MA: Christopher-Gordon Publishers, Inc.

Kucan, L., & Bext, I. L. (1997). Thinking aloud and reading comprehension research: Inquiry, instruction, and social interaction. *Review of Educational Research, 67,* 271–300.

Loxterman, J. A., Beck, I. L., & NcKeown, M. G. (1994). The effects of thinking aloud during reading on students' comprehension of more or less coherent text. *Reading Research Quarterly, 29,* 353–369.

Nist, S. L., & Kirby, K. (1986). Teaching comprehension and study strategies through modeling and thinking aloud. *Reading Research and Instruction, 25,* 256–264.

Olshavsky, J. (1977). Reading as problem solving: An investigation of strategies. *Reading Research Quarterly, 12* (4), 654–674.

Wade, S. E., Buxton, W. M., & Kelly, M. (1999). Using think-alouds to examine reader-text interest. *Reading Research Quarterly, 34,* (2) 194–216.

Writing Conferences

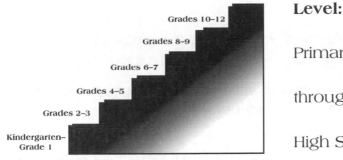

Grades 10–12
Grades 8–9
Grades 6–7
Grades 4–5
Grades 2–3
Kindergarten–Grade 1

Level:

Primary

through

High School

What Are They?

In literate classrooms children change and grow as writers often at amazing rates. We are constantly challenged to keep up with these developing writers. One way to do this is through writing conferences. Writing conferences are typically one-on-one situations where a teacher and learner have an intense, short discussion about the current work the child is doing in writing.

Donald Graves (1994) says, "The purpose of the writing conference is to help children teach you about what they know so that you can help them more effectively with their writing" (p. 59). Typically, the conference is begun by asking the writer what the piece is about, the source of the topic, and what they will write next. Another good conference opener is "How is your writing going?" Graves (1991) suggests that about 80 percent of our conferences enable children to explain what they are doing as writers, and about 10 percent of the conferences present us with a teachable moment in which we can do a quick demonstration. The writing conference is a time for you to assess and evaluate the child's progress and to set next learning goals.

As in reading conferences, you may want to give your learners very specific instructions for pre-conference, during-conference, and post-conference activities. The following examples are of a checklist you could give students to help them prepare for writing conferences and a checklist you could use during conferences.

Post-conference activities may include continuing work on the piece, follow-up to suggestions discussed in the conference, and work on new goals.

Writing folders are a key element in writing conferences. The writing folder is a portfolio, a working folder, in which current writing pieces are kept. Some teachers also have children keep selected finished pieces in the writing folder. Here is kept the important lists of "Things I Am Doing Well" and "My Next Goals." These may be kept on sheets of paper stapled to the front cover of the folder.

Important Things To Do Before Our Writing Conference

_____   Select a piece of writing you want to take to the conference.

_____   Be prepared to explain why you selected this piece.

_____   If you have taken this piece of writing to an editing group or committee, be prepared to explain what happened there.

_____   Collect drafts of the piece and think about why you made changes. Be ready to talk about these decisions.

_____   Update your list of "Things I Am Doing Well As A Writer" and your list of "My Next Learning Goals As A Writer."

_____   Prepare to talk about what you plan to do with this piece next and why.

_____   Think about other things about your writing that you want to talk about with me.

Important Things To Do During Our Writing Conference

_____   Report on your progress as a writer. Show me your lists of "Things I Am Doing Well As A Writer" and "My Next Learning Goals As A Writer." Discuss the reasons you have for the recent additions to the lists and any evidence you have to support the additions. Agree on some next goals.

_____   Share a selected piece of writing with me.

_____   Explain where the writing came from—why you are writing it, and how your writing has progressed.

_____   Explain where your writing is now with this piece.

_____   Explain where you are going next with this piece of writing.

_____   Talk about difficulties you are having with the writing.

_____   Anything you want to talk with me about your writing?

Teachers who conduct writing conferences find them to be important opportunities to learn as much about each child as a writer as possible. The writer finds the conference format predictable and focused on the child's needs.

How Do Writing Conferences Inform Instruction?

A writing conference gives you the time to really carefully focus on a child as a writer. This is a wonderful time to enjoy a writing sample, to talk about goals, challenges and accomplishments. Here is an opportunity to reflect on recent instructional activities in which you have engaged your learners as writers and to talk with a child about how he or she has incorporated these lessons into written work.

What Are the Advantages of Writing Conferences?

Writing conferences are among the richest opportunities you have to assess and evaluate progress in writing. They are intense exchanges between you and your students about their writing performance, their challenges, and their goals. Additionally, they afford the learner the opportunity to engage in self-evaluation and to take responsibility for becoming a better writer. In writing conferences, you can diagnose strengths and uncover challenges that then become the next learning goals for that child.

What Are the Disadvantages of Writing Conferences?

Writing conferences are time consuming, and you have to practice at getting good at asking the questions that lead you to the most information from the learner. Tape recording or videotaping conferences will help you analyze the kinds of questions you are asking. Teachers often schedule conferences while the class is working on independent or assigned activities that require little interaction with the teacher.

Where Do I Get More Information About Writing Conferences?

Flynn, T., & King, M. (Eds.). (1993). *Dynamics of the writing conference: Social and cognitive interaction.* Urbana, IL: National Council of Teachers of English.

Garcia, G. E. (1992). *The literacy assessment of second-language learners.* ERIC, ED348665.

Graves, D. H. (1983). *Writing: Teachers and children at work.* Portsmouth, NH: Heinemann.

Graves, D. H. (1991). *The reading/writing teacher's companion: Build a literate classroom.* Portsmouth, NH: Heinemann.

Graves, D. H. (1994). *A fresh look at writing.* Portsmouth, NH: Heinemann.

Hatch, J. A. (1991). Developing writers in the intermediate grades. *Childhood Education, 68* (2), 76–80.

McIntyre, E. (1993). *Teaching and learning writing skills in a low-SES, urban primary classroom.* ERIC, ED366987.

Section 2

Published Assessment and Evaluation Tools

American Literacy Profile Scales

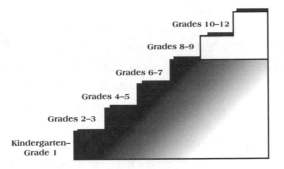

Grades 10–12
Grades 8–9
Grades 6–7
Grades 4–5
Grades 2–3
Kindergarten–Grade 1

Level:

Kindergarten

through

Upper Elementary or Middle School

Year Published: 1995

What Is It?

Have you wished you could take a more developmental perspective with your assessment and evaluation, but haven't been sure how to do that? The *American Literacy Profile Scales* may be the answer you are looking for. It is a set of five profile scales in literacy that cover reading, writing, spoken language, listening and viewing. Each scale covers nine levels—called *bands*—of development labeled from A (lowest) to I (highest).

Each band is defined by a "nutshell statement" which gives a concise description of the behaviors marking that band. On the profile record sheet the band is then further described in detail. The manual contains clearly articulated statements of the contexts in which your observations of behaviors characteristic of that band may be made. Let's consider the following example.

The Nutshell Statement for Band A of the Reading Profile is: *Knows how a book works. Likes to look at books and listen to stories. Likes to talk about stories.*

The detailed descriptors in Band A of the reading profile are:

Concepts about print: Holds book the right way up. Turns pages from front to back. On request, indicates the beginnings and ends of sentences. Distinguishes between upper- and lower-case letters. Indicates the start and end of a book.

Reading strategies: Locates words, lines, spaces, letter. Refers to letter by name. Locates own name and other familiar words in a short text. Identifies known, familiar words in other contexts.

Responses: Responds to literature (smiles, claps, listens intently). Joins in familiar stories.

Interest and attitudes: Shows preference for particular books. Chooses books as a free-time activity.

All of the rest of the reading bands include descriptors under the headings of "reading strategies" and "responses." Some of the other bands include descriptors under "interests and attitudes."

The suggested context for observation of the behaviors described in Reading Band A include reading conferences, shared reading, quiet reading time, discussion with parents, writing sessions and more.

The manual described the properties of profiles in great detail. Some of the characteristics include:

- Profiles are holistic.

- The focus is to demonstrate competence.

- What is to be achieved is described explicitly.

- Profiles allow for a wide range of both formal and informal assessment devices and strategies.

- Profiles provide a way to interpret the vast array of assessment and evaluation data available in classrooms.

- Profiles tend to be more qualitative than quantitative, but can be both.

- Profiles are motivating to students because they can so clearly see their growth.

You are encouraged to engage in profile building with your learners on an on-going basis. It is a matter of constantly collecting data on learners in a variety of ways and then considering what that data says in terms of a child's movement on the profile. You will be able to collect data on a daily, weekly and year-long basis.

The manual contains black-line masters for the forms you will need. These include individual student profile sheets and class record sheets for each profile. Appendices include con-cise presentations of the nutshell statements and the band level descriptions. You might find it helpful to make copies of these documents to share with parents.

The profiles were begun in Victoria, Australia in 1986. The work has been presented at conferences in the United States and other countries. After several workshops with American teachers, the authors of the profiles decided to adapt them for use in American classrooms. The current profiles are the result of input from hundreds of American teachers.

How Do the *American Literacy Profile Scales* Inform Instruction?

The scales are a systematic way for you to make the most out of the assessment and evaluation data you collect. Each band describes attitudes, understandings and behaviors that are developmentally advanced over the descriptors in the previous band(s). By tracking your assessment and evaluation data using these descriptors, you will be able to mark a child's progress through the bands.

By using the class record profile you will be able to quickly see which children are in the same band. You can then look at their individual profile sheets and determine which of the children in a given band need the same kinds of instruction. This will facilitate instructional grouping.

The detailed discussion of the contexts for observation will provide regular reminders for you of the range of observations and other data collection you can do to inform your placement of children within the scales. By using these contexts for observation, you will be completely integrating instruction and assessment.

Student progress is rated with a "0 to 3" scale that is applied to each of the bands. A "0" rating is assigned to a band if the student shows none of the behavior patterns for that band. A "1" is assigned if the student is beginning to show some of the behaviors characteristic of that band; a "2" if some, but not all, of the behaviors are exhibited; and a "3" if the student has established the behavior and consistently exhibits all or most of the behaviors in that band. This rating system can be used to report progress to parents, other teachers and administrators. Further, the rating system will alert you to the areas of greatest instructional focus.

What Are the Advantages of the *American Literacy Profile Scales?*

The scales offer a concise, well-defined way for you to organize and interpret the assessment and evaluation data you collect on your learners as readers, writers, listeners, speakers and viewers. While complete, they are not so detailed as to become "too much to handle."

The manual offers many kinds of support for your efforts in creating and using the profiles. A section on building profiles consists of chapters on getting started, the profile records for each of the areas, and the contexts in which you can use assessment as a part of teaching and learning.

A final section of the manual offers excellent chapters on recording and reporting with the profiles; profiling the literacy skills of students with special needs; the reading classroom; and establishing consistency in rating systems using teacher judgment.

What Are the Disadvantages of the *American Literacy Profile Scales?*

I see "challenges" rather than disadvantages in using this tool. It will take a period of learning on your part to become adequately familiar with the bands and behaviors. This learning will be necessary if you are to become familiar enough with the scales to use them effortlessly and efficiently.

If you are going to the effort to incorporate the scales into your teaching, it would be far better if the other teachers at your grade level—in fact, all of the teachers in your building, were committed to using the scales as well. The scales are comprehensive enough to track the learning of children well throughout the elementary school years and possibly beyond. They will be best-used over a period of years of growth.

Where Do I Get More Information About the *American Literacy Profile Scales?*

Griffin, P., Smith, P. G., & Burrill, L. E. (1995). *The American literacy profile scales.* Portsmouth, NH: Heinemann.

Analytical Reading Inventory

Sixth Edition

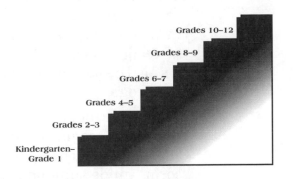

Grades 10–12
Grades 8–9
Grades 6–7
Grades 4–5
Grades 2–3
Kindergarten–Grade 1

Level:

Kindergarten

through

High School

Year Published: 1999

What Is It?

The Analytical Reading Inventory (ARI) is an informal reading inventory offering graded word lists and graded reading passages (from primer through ninth grade) that may, when appropriate, be used with readers from kindergarten through high school. The sixth edition of the ARI has three forms—A, B, and C—of narrative text. It also includes one form of science passages (from grade one through nine) and one form of social studies passages (from grade one through nine).

The authors, Woods and Moe, state that the *Inventory* assists the teacher in gaining specific information about a student's ability to cope with text material at various levels of instruction, the strategies the reader uses to recognize words, and the strategies used to understand the meaning of the text.

When you use the ARI you can determine the following information about a reader:

- Use of prediction/prior knowledge
- Use of word identification strategies
- Oral and silent reading strategies

- Fluency
- Comprehension strategies including retellings and comprehension questions
- Use of the cueing systems—graphophonic, syntactic, and semantic
- Four functional levels—independent, instructional, frustration, and listening levels
- Emotional status
- Interest, attitudes, habits, and ability perceptions (from a reading survey)

The sixth edition of the *Analytical Reading Inventory* has been expanded considerably over the fifth edition. New to this edition are a reading interview, assessment of prior knowledge and predictions, improved qualitative analysis of miscues, and an analysis of fluency.

Further, the sixth edition offers unusually thorough support for you in learning how to use the inventory. Accompanied by an audio tape, a very complete chapter walks you through a case study so that you can learn about all of the components and how to use them.

The procedures for using the ARI are clearly spelled out in careful detail in the manual. The process involves the following:

1. Conducting the interviews. The information from the *Seven Questions about Reading* helps you learn how a reader feels about himself or herself as a reader. The *Reading Interview* helps you understand a student's awareness of the reading strategies he or she is using before, during and after reading.

2. Use graded word lists to determine the point to begin the narrative passages. You begin the passages at the highest level at which the reader correctly read all of the words on the graded word list and correctly used some of the words in context.

3. You explore prior knowledge with the reader about the topic of the selection and have the reader make predictions.

4. As the student reads a passage aloud, you record miscues.

5. After the oral reading, you record information about the reader's fluency. The manual encourages you as you continue your analysis to think about how the oral reading miscues and comprehension interact with the reader's fluency.

6. Following the oral reading, you ask the student to do a retelling. You use either the narrative or expository elements retelling rubric to evaluate the retelling. If the retelling is very thorough, you may not ask any of the comprehension questions. You may decide to ask selected ones. Comprehension questions are designed to both require the reader to respond from the text as well as to respond from the reader's head to the text, interpreting the content by accessing knowledge.

7. Continue through increasingly difficult passages until the frustration level is reached. Use the scoring guide summary to determine scores for word recognition and comprehension and to note the reader's emotional status while reading.

8. Have the reader silently read passages from a different form of the inventory. The purpose here is to find out if the reader is more or less successful when reading silently than when reading orally.

9. Determine the listening level by reading passages to the student and asking the comprehension questions. Stop when you reach the level at which the student comprehends only 75% of the material.

10. Have the student read the science and social studies passages at grade level. Record the oral reading miscues, the retellings and the answers to comprehension questions.

Following the steps outlined above, you are instructed to use the Student Record Summary Sheet which guides you in analyzing the performance on the word lists and the graded passages to determine the independent, instructional, frustration and listening levels. The estimated levels for both the narrative and expository texts are summarized. There are convenient checklists on the form which are useful in evaluating performance on all aspects of the inventory.

The authors readily recognize that both quantitative and qualitative analysis of miscues is necessary for a complete picture of the reader's behaviors. Each miscue is analyzed in terms of graphophonic similarity, syntactic acceptability, and semantic acceptability.

The graded passages in the ARI were written for the instrument. The authors consulted several professional sources on the reading interests of students at varying grade levels in deciding on passage content. The pieces were written to be motivational for both boys and girls and also nonsexist in nature. The science and social passages were selected from textbooks published by Merrill Publishing Company.

The revised Spache formula was used to calculate readability estimates for passages at primer through Level 3. The Powers formula was used for Levels 4 through 6, and the Flesch was used for Levels 7 through 9. The authors recognize, however, that such words as *America* and *atom,* while increasing gradability, are commonly within the background knowledge of readers. The authors used a Vocabulary Diversity Score to show that passages progressively increase in difficulty and are consistent across forms. These data are clearly presented in the manual.

The sixth edition was field tested using 80 advanced undergraduate students enrolled in a course on reading instruction and approximately 200 students in grades two through eight.

How Does the *Analytical Reading Inventory* Inform Instruction?

Clearly, the most useful information you will get from the inventory is the functional reading levels of your students. This will permit you to place students for instruction in material at their *instructional level.* Instructional level is defined as 95% accuracy in word recognition and at least 75% accuracy in comprehension.

If you use the expository passages at grade level as instructed in the manual, you will know for which of your students social studies and science texts are too difficult. A more valid way to measure this would be to take running records on students' reading of the actual social studies and science books you plan to use.

This inventory offers an unusually complete analysis of miscues. You will be able to determine which of the cueing systems your readers are drawing on when reading. By doing a careful analysis across students, you should be able to define instructional groupings for use of the cueing systems and retellings.

What are the Advantages of the *Analytical Reading Inventory?*

The ARI measures reading performance on both narrative and expository texts. This is helpful in that readers, particularly younger readers, often approach expository material very differently than they do narrative material.

Woods and Moe have recognized the importance of retellings as a measure of reading comprehension. Some reading experts view retellings as the most valid and complete way to assess comprehension. Johnston (1983) views retellings as the most straightforward assessment of the results of the inter-action between reader and text. The authors of the ARI have built retellings into the procedure ahead of asking comprehension questions.

The graded passages have been carefully constructed to increase in dif-ficulty and to speak to the reading in-terests of students across the grade span. Careful field testing resulted in important improvements in the instru-ment, such as improvements in the content of the passages and the com-prehension questions.

The manual contains very helpful forms for analysis of reading behavior. The forms are clear, complete and easy to use. You will find the audio tape and case study very useful, especially if you are unfamiliar with the inventory or are new to this kind of assessment and evaluation tool.

What are the Disadvantages of the *Analytical Reading Inventory?*

Though the authors recognized the dif-ferences in reading behavior on exposi-tory text as opposed to narrative text, they have readers read expository text only on grade level. This practice will surely result in failure to accurately evaluate the level at which a reader can adequately understand expository material. This information will tell you that, for example, a child cannot read fourth grade science material with un-derstanding, but it will not tell you

what level of science material the child can read. The procedures offer no assis-tance to the teacher who wants to know at what level children should be placed in expository material.

There is no technical manual. Six pages of the manual are dedicated to a discussion of the development and vali-dation of the ARI. This makes determi-nations of reliability, the comparability of the forms, and the relationship to other measures very difficult to ascer-tain. Furthermore, there is no informa-tion on the generalizability of the results on the ARI to published in-structional materials used in class-rooms.

While the analysis of miscues is quite thorough, scant attention is paid to self-corrections. You are invited only to check a box beside a statement that the reader "monitors the meaning." It is unfortunate that self-corrections are not more thoroughly analyzed.

The time to administer and inter-pret the ARI will be a concern for many classroom teachers. It could easily take an hour per child to use the instrument completely and well.

Where Do I Get More Information About the *Analytical Reading Inventory?*

Johnston, P. H. (1983). *Reading compre-hension assessment: A cognitive ba-sis.* Newark, DE: International Reading Association.

Woods, M. L., & Moe, A. J. (1999). *Ana-lytical reading inventory.* Sixth Edi-tion. New York: Macmillan Publishing Company.

Bader Reading and Language Inventory

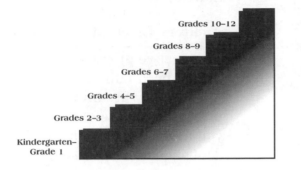

Grades 10–12
Grades 8–9
Grades 6–7
Grades 4–5
Grades 2–3
Kindergarten–Grade 1

Third Edition

Level:

Preprimer

through

Twelfth Grade

Year Published: 1998

What Is It?

The *Bader Reading and Language Inventory* (BRLI) is an informal reading inventory that makes use of graded word lists and graded reading passages to identify students' instructional reading levels. It also contains an extensive set of additional tests useful for diagnosing the nature of reading difficulties and planning remediation. Each of the tests that make up the complete battery are described below.

Student Priorities and Interests

The inventory contains four tools that you may select to use to determine students' reading interests and perceptions of areas in which they need instructional assistance as readers.

English As a Second Language Quick Start

This tool can be used as an initial screening to determine the degree to which the student is able to understand and respond in English.

Word Recognition Lists

These lists include graded lists of ten words ranging from preprimer through

eighth grade, plus a list for high school. While performance on the graded word lists can give some indication of word recognition and decoding ability, their primary use is to help you decide which of the graded reading passages to use. In addition to the graded word lists there are two other fifteen-word lists: Instructional Directions List and Experience Lists. The Instructional Directions list is to be used to determine whether or not the student can recognize words frequently used in instructional materials and tests. The Experience Lists, one for children and one for adults, are used to determine whether or not the student has been able to learn any words that are a routine part of daily life. Finally, a Functional Literacy List covers words that may be encountered in completing forms and managing personal affairs in daily life.

Graded Reading Passages

There are three sets of graded reading passages ranging from preprimer level through twelfth grade. One set is for children, one set is for either children or adults, and one set is for adults.

Scoring criteria differ depending on whether the student is orally reading a passage not previously read silently. A coding system is outlined for you to use in marking oral reading miscues. Miscues are evaluated both quantitatively and qualitatively. Consideration is made in scoring miscues as to whether or not the miscue disrupted meaning.

The qualitative analysis of miscues involves comparing the miscue with the text to determine graphic similarity, phonetic similarity, whether the miscue happened at the beginning, middle or end of the word, syntactic acceptability and semantic acceptability. Other questions are offered in the manual for further analyzing miscues such as "Does the reader have difficulty with particular grammatical functions (verb, adverb, noun)?" and "Does the reader correct the miscue and make the sentence semantically acceptable?"

The author suggests that a combination of retelling and direct questioning is probably best for assessing comprehension. You are encouraged to begin comprehension assessment by asking the student to retell the passage (a retelling key is provided), and to then proceed with general probing questions ending with direct questioning.

Spelling Tests

Seven lists of ten words each are provided in the Diagnostic Spelling Tests. While these tests are intended to give you diagnostic information related to the student's spelling ability, the manual urges that you combine these data with additional evidence gathered from actual writing samples.

Visual Discrimination

Two tests of visual discrimination are provided which require students to match letters and words.

Auditory Discrimination Test

This test requires students to listen to pronounced pairs of words and determine if they are alike or different. The primary purpose of this test is to assist you in deciding whether or not the student should be referred for a hearing test.

Preliteracy Assessment

This is a battery of tests designed to evaluate strengths and weaknesses of students who are unable to read the graded word lists or passages. It contains two interviews that assess book handling and literacy concepts, a test of blending and segmentation, a test of letter knowledge, a test of the ability to hear letter names in words such as /z/ in "zebra," and a test of the ability to recognize words as separate speech entities that can be recorded in print.

Phonics and Structural Analysis Test

The phonics test assesses ability to decode initial consonants, consonant blends, consonant digraphs, short and long vowel sounds, vowel digraphs and reversals. The structural analysis test assesses ability to decode inflectional suffixes, derivational suffixes, prefixes and compound words. These tests are designed to determine if students know phoneme/grapheme correspondences in nonsense words that are phonetically regular.

Cloze Tests

A set of cloze tests is designed to measure beginning readers' ability to make semantically acceptable predictions based on context as a aid to comprehension. A more difficult test requiring prediction of missing words that are both semantically and syntactically acceptable is available for use with students reading at, or above, second-grade level.

Oral Language Expression and Reception

The manual recommends eliciting oral language from a student by showing a picture and asking for description, reading a passage to the student and asking for a retelling, or by asking the student to dictate a story to you. An Oral Language Expression Checklist is provided for your use in evaluating the oral language production. The manual encourages using some of these same activities to evaluate oral language reception.

Writing

Several ways of evaluating written production are offered. They include the ability to write letters, the ability to write words in sentences, near- and far-point copying, writing from dictation, and expressing ideas in writing. A Written Language Expression Checklist is provided for your use in evaluating the written production in terms of handwriting, syntactic development, mechanics, level of abstraction, and organization and presentation of ideas.

Arithmetic Test

The author explains that the arithmetic test is included as a supplement to the battery for two reasons. First, the ability to perform basic arithmetic is not dependent on reading. Good performance on the arithmetic test, in con-

trast to reading, is evidence of potential. Second, the author believes that remedial specialists and teachers should give assistance in all areas of need. Raw scores on the arithmetic test are converted to grade equivalent scores, but no explanation is offered for the creation of those grade equivalents.

Open Book Reading Assessments

These are informal silent reading assessments that include questions to answer or tasks to complete while reading. Instructions are included in the manual for the creation of these assessments. The purposes of the open book tests are to obtain specific information on students' abilities to understand and use content area, vocational, or daily-life reading materials, to plan instruction, and to confirm or supplement other diagnostic data.

How Does the *Bader Reading and Language Inventory* Inform Instruction?

As a classroom teacher you might find the graded word lists and graded reading passages most helpful in placing children instructionally in texts. You might also use selected tests from the battery to diagnose strengths and weaknesses of students whose reading performance is puzzling. It is unlikely that you would have the time to use the complete battery. As a reading specialist, you will find that data from the inventory will be useful in planning instruction whether for the struggling emergent reader or the non-reading adult. The inventory clearly reflects the author's belief that "a thorough assessment includes: personal interviews and reflections, observations, informal and formal tests, and diagnostic teaching. The inventory provides several tools and guides for this model."

What Are the Advantages of the *Bader Reading and Language Inventory?*

Collected within one battery are a variety of assessment and evaluation tools that the reading specialist will find very helpful in diagnosing strengths and weaknesses. The manual is well-written and offers very complete, useful documents such as a referral information form, home information form, an adult intake information form and a variety of checklists and guides for evaluating data. The provisions for assessing and activating background knowledge prior to reading the graded passages and the use of qualitative miscue analysis and retellings are excellent. There is a rather extensive section at the end of the manual on using portfolio assessment. The manual has very detailed suggestions for a variety

of testing sequences, depending on the age of the student and the goals of diagnosis. Reference sections are offered throughout the manual.

What Are the Disadvantages of the *Bader Reading and Language Inventory?*

The graded word lists are decontextualized. There is no provision within the inventory to assess decoding of target words in context. While there may be merit in using an arithmetic test with some struggling readers, the lack of explanation of how grade scores were derived renders this test questionable.

Where Do I Get More Information About the *Bader Reading and Language Inventory?*

Bader, L. A. (1998). *Bader Reading and Language Inventory.* (3rd ed.). Upper Saddle River, NJ: Merrill, an imprint of Prentice Hall.

Basic Inventory of Natural Language

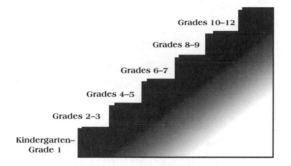

Level:

Kindergarten

through

High School

Year Published: 1991

What Is It?

The *Basic Inventory of Natural Language* (BINL) is a criterion-referenced system designed to assess and evaluate the oral language production of learners in grades K through 12. The BINL has been used in school language development programs such as bilingual, English as a Second Language, natural language, immersion, and in regular classroom programs.

The BINL kits come in two forms: the elementary kit is designed for use in grades K–6, and the secondary kit is for use in grades 7–12. Following one to five days of practice sessions in regular classroom activities, oral language samples are obtained from subjects by asking students to respond to large, colorful photographs. Examiners are instructed to allow students to select their own pictures, and not to ask direct questions of subjects. Instead, examiners ask students to "tell me" about the picture and follow up leading ideas given by the student with "tell me about the . . ." prompts. In giving the test you are asked not to make any corrections of any sort, but rather to

keep the student in the "information-giving" mode.

The Examiner's Manual offers several suggestions for creating and maintaining an atmosphere that will support getting natural language from students. Among them are suggestions to engage the student in a brief, informal conversation before you turn on the tape recorder; to use natural, reinforcing responses to whatever the student says; and to pursue any comment of interest that the student makes.

A minimum of ten utterances are then transcribed and analyzed. The analysis of oral language samples occurs at three levels: word class (determiner, noun, verb, adjective, adverb, preposition, etc.), type of phrase (noun phrase, verb phrase, prepositional phrase), and sentence type (simple sentence, compound sentence, compound/complex sentence). The language profile yielded by the BINL includes a fluency score (the total number of words used in the sample), an average sentence length score (total number of utterances divided into the total number of words used), and a level of complexity score (derived from scoring the lan-

167

guage sample for certain grammatical structures). The BINL system classifies a student as a non-limited, functional, or fluent speaker in each language assessed, and yields a series of proficiency scores in fluency, level of complexity, and average sentence length.

BINL tests are scored in Arabic, Armenian, Cambodian, Cantonese, Chinese, Creole, Dutch, English, Farsi, French, German, Greek, Hindi, Hmong, Ilocano, Inupiaq, Italian, Japanese, Korean, Laotian, Navajo, Philipino, Polish, Portuguese, Russian, Spanish, Taiwanese, Tagalog, Toishanese, Ukrainian, Vietnamese, and Yugoslavian. The BINL may be hand or computer scored.

The Examiner's Manual establishes content validity by reviewing research in support of free-sampling testing as a valid measure of natural language. Cut-off scores for the levels of proficiency were based on grade means and standard deviations obtained by a sample of bilingual students. Cut-off score reliability was established using the chi square test with significance beyond the .001 level. Reliability was established through split-half correlations, with a correlation coefficient of .925 on a randomly selected sample of 7,500 English dominant students in grades K through 12.

How Does the BINL Inform Instruction?

The BINL is typically used as a general screening test. Often kindergarten or first graders are tested either in their first language or in English. Students who perform well in English are enrolled in a regular classroom. Children who perform much better in their first language than in English are enrolled in bilingual classrooms.

What Are the Advantages of the BINL?

The advantages of the BINL are the assessment of oral language proficiency in a free-response, natural language situation, and the number of languages assessed by the system. The variety of scoring possibilities is another advantage. Computer scoring is available in eleven languages and microcomputer scoring is available in English and Spanish. The BINL may be computer-scored at the publisher's facility, microcomputer-scored at the school using keyboard entry of the utterances, microcomputer-scored at the school using written copy transcribed from the tape recording and coded for numeric entry, or hand-scored from written transcriptions of the tape recording. Computer scoring is particularly advantageous when persons trained in grammatical analysis are not available at your school.

What Are the Disadvantages of the BINL?

The BINL is time-intensive. It will take a good deal of time to use the inventory with all of the children in your program. You may find that you will have to select students for assessment rather than test everyone. Guyette (1985) has been critical of the size of the oral language sample required for analysis. A minimum of only ten utterances is acceptable. Guyette asserts that an adequate sample size should be between 50 and 100 utterances per sample.

There is confusion around the scoring of statements of implied meaning. For example, if the child responds to "Where are the toys?" with "on the table" he or she is given credit for a complete sentence answer. The manual does not give explicit instructions on how to reconstruct these implied meanings (Guyette, 1985).

Where Do I Get More Information About the BINL?

CHECpoint Systems, *Basic inventory of natural language authentic language testing technical report.* San Bernardino, CA: CHECpoint Systems, Inc.

Guyette, T. W. (1985). Review of basic inventory of natural language. In Mitchell, J. V. (Ed.), *The ninth mental measurement yearbook.* Lincoln, NE: University of Nebraska Press.

Burns/Roe Informal Reading Inventory

Fifth Edition

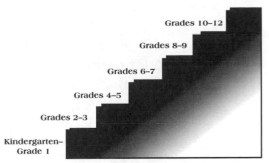

Grades 10–12
Grades 8–9
Grades 6–7
Grades 4–5
Grades 2–3
Kindergarten–Grade 1

Level:

Primary

through

High School

Year Published: 1999

What Is It?

The *Burns/Roe Informal Reading Inventory* (B/RIRI) is designed for use by preservice college students who are learning about inventories, special reading teachers and in-service classroom teachers. It consists of a set of sequentially graded word lists and reading selections designed for analysis of both quantitative and qualitative information. Quantitative analysis is used to determine a reader's independent, instructional, and frustration reading levels, as well as the listening comprehension level. Qualitative analysis is used to examine miscues, the kinds of comprehension questions the reader can or cannot answer, and the quality of retellings. You must use the B/RIRI with one student at a time.

Independent reading level is defined in the manual as the level at which a person can read with understanding and ease, without assistance (p. 3). Quantitatively, this is determined by a word recognition score of 99% or higher and a comprehension score of 90% or higher.

Instructional reading level is defined in the manual as the level at which a person can read with understanding *with* the teacher's assistance. Quantitatively, this is determined by a word recognition score of 85% or higher for a first- or second-grader and 95% or higher for a third-grader or above, and a comprehension score of 75% or higher.

Frustration reading level is defined in the manual as the level at which a person is unable to function adequately because the reading material is too difficult. Quantitatively, this is determined by a word recognition score of below 85% in grades one and two and below 90% in grades 3 through 12, and a comprehension score of below 50%.

Listening comprehension level is defined in the manual as the level at which a person adequately comprehends material that is read by the teacher. The student has 75% or higher comprehension of this material. This is thought to be the level at which the student could probably read if there were no limiting factors present.

The kinds of comprehension questions analyzed in the B/RIRI are: main idea, details, inference, sequence, cause-and-effect, and vocabulary (meaning of a word or phrase). The author claims that the kinds of comprehension questions asked in the *Inventory* correspond to the areas of comprehension addressed in instructional materials used in schools. Therefore, an analysis of the kinds of questions missed will help you decide which instructional tools to use with a given reader.

Roe suggests that oral reading miscues should be analyzed in terms of whether or not they change meaning. She recognizes that even very fluent readers make miscues as their minds are moving beyond the material being spoken. Fluent readers often translate the text into different words with similar meanings. She recommends that you not worry about planning skill lessons for miscues that do not change the meaning of the passages. In the case of readers who make nonsensical miscues, Roe suggests instruction in the use of context clues.

Roe offers a Free Recall Processing Checklist (Irwin, 1991) in the manual. The checklist asks ten questions about the nature of the retelling which are to be rated on a five-point scale from "poorly" to "very well." The checklist also asks for an evaluation of the comprehension processes used by the reader, and offers an eight-item list of factors that might affect comprehension performance.

The basic procedures for administering the *Inventory* are:

1. Set the stage for testing by choosing the appropriate location, establishing rapport, and informing the student about procedures.

2. Administer Graded Word Lists to determine where to start the student in the passages. Use successively easier lists until you reach a list where the student makes no mistakes. Then move up list by list until you find a list where the reader makes one or more mistakes. Begin testing with the graded passages at the level equivalent to the highest level on the word lists where there were no mistakes.

3. Administer Graded Passages, alternating oral and silent passages. Ask the comprehension questions with each passage to determine independent, instructional and frustration levels. A system is offered for marking word recognition miscues. An alternative suggested here is to have the student reread orally the passages that were first read silently. These scores can then be compared with earlier oral reading scores to see if oral reading with the benefit of prior silent reading is dramatically better than oral reading on sight.

4. Administer listening passages to determine listening comprehension level.

5. Analyze the findings.

6. Qualitatively and quantitatively interpret the results (p. 11).

Quantitative analysis includes identification of functional reading levels and listening comprehension level. Performance on both oral and silent reading passages is analyzed as well as the graded word lists. Miscues are counted in total, in miscues resulting in a meaning change, and in self-corrections. The percentage of errors is calculated for each of the kinds of comprehension questions: main idea, detail, sequence, cause and effect, inference and vocabulary.

The qualitative analysis consists of a summary of strengths and weaknesses in word recognition, strengths and weaknesses in comprehension, and a checklist of reading behaviors such as "reads in phrases" and "attends to punctuation."

The fifth edition revisions include explanations of more flexible ways to use an informal reading inventory, the use of retelling, assessment of context clue use, and partial assessments. Case studies to assist teachers new to informal reading inventories have been expanded and a section on frequently asked questions has been added.

Word lists used in the B/RIRI were randomly drawn from the vocabulary lists of two basal reading series. The lists were then administered to students at the level for which the list was intended, the level below and the level above. A word was assigned to a given level if 80% or more of the students from that level, less than 80% from the level below, and more than 80% from the level above successfully pronounced the word.

The Graded Passages of between 60 and 220 words were chosen from three different basal or literature series. Reading levels were checked using the Spache Readability Formula for preprimer through grade three materials and the Fry Readability Graph for material for grades 4 through 12. Only selections that fit the formula exactly were used. Both fiction and nonfiction texts are included.

Comprehension questions were evaluated by "several classes of graduate students in reading education who had experience in constructing informal reading inventories" (p. 222).

How Does the *Burns/Roe Informal Reading Inventory* Inform Instruction?

One of the most helpful aspects of this tool is the procedure of having a student read the first selection silently and then rereading it orally. Then having the student read another selection at the same level only orally. Many students benefit from silent reading before oral reading.

In addition to determining the functional reading levels for accurate instructional placement, you will have some information about miscues that may assist you in instructional planning. This information includes both the frequency with which miscues alter meaning and the place in the word where the miscue was made. These include, for example, single consonants, consonant blends, vowel digraphs, and so on.

What Are the Advantages of the *Burns/Roe Informal Reading Inventory?*

The B/RIRI manual encourages both quantitative and qualitative analysis of your student's reading behavior. While the six categories of comprehension questions cover a significant range of thought, you are encouraged to engage students in retellings as well. The retelling checklist is thorough and helpful.

The use of graded word lists to determine placement in the graded passages is quick and convenient. The passages are varied in content, and the introductory statements give some background information that may be helpful in creating meaning.

The miscue analysis is consistent with current thinking. Each miscue is analyzed in terms of graphic similarity, syntactic acceptability, and semantic acceptability. Explanations of the various reading levels are clear. Included with the *Inventory* are a number of very helpful tables and charts, and clear examples of the administration, scoring and interpretation of the tool.

What Are the Disadvantages of the *Burns/Roe Informal Reading Inventory?*

While there are four forms of the *Inventory,* there is no technical manual. This makes determinations of reliability, the comparability of the four forms, and the relationship to other measures very difficult. Furthermore, there is no explanation offered for the determination of the reading levels—for example, why the independent reading level is set at 99% or higher for word recognition and 90% or higher for comprehension. Since not all informal reading inventories use the same criteria, it would be helpful to know how these particular criteria were determined.

Shapiro (1989) has questioned the generalizability of test results beyond the particular basal series from which the *Inventory* was developed. He suggests that results on a particular measure may be different if a different reading series were employed, and while the results may be generalizable to students placed in the basal used for development, the manual fails to offer adequate detail on those basals.

Where Do I Get More Information About the *Burns/Roe Informal Reading Inventory?*

Roe, B. D. (1999). *Burns/Roe informal reading inventory: Preprimer to twelfth grade.* Fourth Edition. Boston: Houghton Mifflin Company.

Classroom Reading Inventory

Eighth Edition

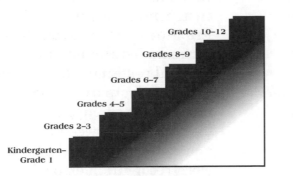

Grades 10–12
Grades 8–9
Grades 6–7
Grades 4–5
Grades 2–3
Kindergarten–Grade 1

Level:

Primary

through

Adult

Year Published: 1997

What Is It?

The *Classroom Reading Inventory* (CRI) is an informal reading inventory designed to evaluate reading behavior traditionally in Form A and in a more process-oriented manner in Form B. The eighth edition of the CRI is a streamlined version of the seventh edition.

The author, Nicholas Silvaroli, explains that traditional informal reading inventories have used what he calls a "subskill" format. This format diagnosed the reader's ability to decode words (word recognition) and answer comprehension questions (fact, inference, vocabulary). Functional reading levels (independent, instructional, frustration) are determined in this format.

Silvaroli calls the more process-oriented format a "reader response format." In this format the oral reading selections are not followed by the traditional comprehension questions. Instead, the reader is asked to use the picture and title to make predictions and to retell the selections to the examiner. The author explains that in the Subskills Format you are able to evalu-ate the student's ability to decode words in and out of context and to evaluate the student's ability to answer factual/literal, vocabulary, and inference questions. In the Reader Response Format the reader is asked to predict what the story will be about and to retell the story or text.

In the Subskills Format comprehension is evaluated by a count of comprehension questions correctly answered. In the Reader Response Format a number is assigned to the quality of the responses given by the students. Both formats establish instructional reading levels, though in Form B the instructional level is called the "Comfortable Reading Level." Comfortable Reading Level is defined as the level at which the student is able to read without difficulty where oral reading is fluent and expressive with few, if any, significant word recognition errors and no difficulty in retelling.

The criteria for determining the functional reading levels (independent, instructional, frustration) are defined as percentages in the manual only for the instructional level. Silvaroli defines the instructional level as at least 95%

accuracy in word recognition and at least 75% comprehension. The other levels are explained but no numerical values are attached. For example, the independent level is defined as "material from which they can extract content without hazards of unfamiliar words and concepts" (p. 8).

There is a Form C of the inventory described as "diagnostic subskills material for high school and adult education students . . . available in a customized format through Brown & Benchmark" (p. v). Form C is not included in the manual.

Silvaroli points out that teachers should analyze decoding errors both quantitatively and qualitatively. He defines qualitative analysis of word recognition errors as "thinking about what the student is actually doing as he or she makes the error" (p. 9). In analyzing word recognition errors, you are instructed to think of them as *significant* (high weighted) or *insignificant* (low weighted). Significant errors are defined as those that impact or interfere with the student's fluency or thought process. Insignificant errors are defined as minor alterations that do not interfere with student fluency or cognition.

Silvaroli handles the scoring of word recognition and comprehension errors quite differently than most informal reading inventories. The typical practice is to set percentage limits for the functional reading levels in word recognition and comprehension. Instead, Silvaroli has set error limits for significant word recognition errors and comprehension errors. For example, with the fifth grade level, 104-word selection in Form A (p. 94), the scoring guide for significant word recognition

errors is 2 errors for Independent, 5 errors for Instructional, and 10 errors for Frustration. In comprehension, the Independent level error limit is 0–1, Instructional error limit is 1.5—2, and Frustration level is 2.5⁺. The manual offers no instruction for how to classify the oral reading if, for example, 4 significant errors are made. It recommends that when there is a discrepancy between word recognition and comprehension—for example, the word recognition error limit is Instructional and the comprehension error limit is Independent—that you rely most heavily on the comprehension score to determine the functional reading level for the selection. The scoring guide provides estimated levels, and you are to make the final diagnosis.

The author recognizes the importance of background knowledge in the reading comprehension process. He recommends that you assess background knowledge before you have a student read a selection. This is done by asking a question. For example, the second grade selection in Form A is titled "A Simple Telephone." The background knowledge assessment consists of you saying, "This story tells how to make a simple telephone. How often do you use the telephone?" (p. 28). You are then asked to rate the background knowledge for the selection as adequate or inadequate.

The testing procedure for Form A consists of having students read the graded word lists and entering the graded passages at the highest level at which all of the words on the list were correctly read. For Form B, where no graded word lists are used, you are instructed to enter the passages at the student's current grade level unless you know the student is reading above or below level. If so, adjust the starting level.

In Form A, you have the student read the graded passages until the frustration level is reached. Then you read the passages to the student to determine listening capacity.

In Form B, you are asked first to model the retelling and prediction process for the reader. Then you move to the entry point passage. You ask the student to look at the picture and title and predict what the selection will be about. Then ask the student to read the selection orally. Following this, you check whether the selection is above, at, or below the reader's comfort level. Following a retelling, you rate the prediction and retelling in terms of the degree of prompting from you that was required by the reader. The retelling is then evaluated on four elements with a rating of from 1 (low) to 3 (high) for predicting, character(s), problems, and outcome. Questions are provided to aid in the retelling, if necessary. A numerical total is calculated across these for the passage. You are then encouraged to write a summary of specific instructional needs and the comfort level.

How Does the *Classroom Reading Inventory* Inform Instruction?

With both Form A and Form B you are able to define instructional reading level. This will be useful especially if you are placing learners in literature for instructional purposes. In Form A the comprehension questions are so limited in type that you may not have much instructional information from them. However, in Form B the retelling

guide may give you information that will be useful in designing instruction. Performance on the Graded Word Lists may yield some information on decoding ability that will inform instruction.

What Are the Advantages of the *Classroom Reading Inventory?*

The CRI is specifically designed for use by teachers and prospective teachers who have not had prior experience with informal reading inventories. As a result, the forms and analyses are highly simplified. The scoring guides eliminate the need for calculating percentages in determining functional reading levels. The system for coding word recognition errors is simple, and consistent with that taught in many beginning reading methods courses.

The eighth edition offers a form for doing a qualitative analysis of word recognition, prediction, and retelling. Consistent with the latest thinking in miscue analysis, decoding errors are judged to be significant or insignificant depending on the interruption to fluency and the reader's thinking.

What Are the Disadvantages of the *Classroom Reading Inventory?*

The manual is lacking in technical information about the development or field testing of the instrument. The graded passages are said to be like basal reader selections, but no information is offered about their source or design other than to identify the readability formulas that were used.

Each graded passage has only five comprehension questions covering recall of facts, drawing inferences, and understanding vocabulary. Five questions does not seem to be an adequate sampling of thinking to permit you to make valid judgments about your student's comprehension of these three areas. Furthermore, comprehension is much more complex that just recalling facts, making inferences, and recalling word meanings. No attempt is made to measure critical thinking or study skills. No attempt is made to analyze metacomprehension strategies. The directions tell you to take the passages away from the student before the comprehension questions are asked. In essence, this becomes a test of recall.

The criteria for the functional reading levels are not numerically defined except for the instructional level. The scoring guides leave you wondering what percentages were used to determine functional reading levels at various grade levels. For example, at the seventh grade level the word recognition score for independent level is 3 significant errors. This is a percentage of 98%. But the manual does not offer this information. Nor is there an explanation of how these percentages were determined.

While background knowledge is assessed by asking a question, for example, in asking "What do you know about elephants?", there are no suggestions in Form A for what to do if a student does not have adequate background information to understand the text.

The lack of technical information makes determinations of reliability, the comparability of the four forms, and the relationship to other measures very difficult.

Where Do I Get More Information About *Classroom Reading Inventory*?

Roe, B. D., Stoodt, B. D., & Burns, P.C. (1995). *Secondary school reading instruction: The content areas.* Boston: Houghton Mifflin Company.

Ruddell, R. B., & Ruddell, M. P. (1995). *Teaching children to read and write: Becoming an influential teacher.* Needham Heights, MA: Allyn and Bacon.

Silvaroli, N. J. (1997). *Classroom reading inventory.* (8th ed.). Boston: McGraw Hill.

Developmental Reading Assessment

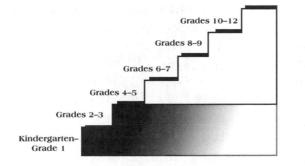

Level:

Kindergarten

through

Third Grade

What Is It?

The *Developmental Reading Assessment* (DRA) is a set of materials and strategies for assessing children's reading development in a literature-based program over time. The materials are designed to help you track the knowledge and behaviors that are characteristic of good readers. The authors have based the materials around the following understandings about good readers (Beaver, 1997, pp. 8–10).

√ Good readers select appropriately leveled reading materials and continue to improve as readers each time they read.

√ Good readers read and sustain their reading for longer periods of time.

√ Good readers preview a book or story before reading it and can predict what might happen.

√ Good readers read aloud quickly and smoothly.

√ Good readers use a variety of strategies.

√ Good readers read for meaning.

√ Good readers read and function within a literacy community.

A set of leveled texts is provided for use in conducting the assessment. You identify the text that you think is best suited to the child you are testing, or you collaborate with the child in selecting a text from an array of texts. You then use the accompanying Observation Guide to introduce the text with previewing and predicting. At lower text levels you have the child read the text aloud as you take a running record. With higher level texts you have the child read the first few paragraphs aloud, make predictions about what will happen next, and read the rest of the story silently. At most levels you ask for a retelling, and take a running record on a section of oral reading.

In short, the DRA is an organized set of materials designed to help you track children's progress as readers over time using literature, taking and analyzing running records, evaluating retellings, and plotting progress on a developmental continuum. The continuum ranges from "early readers" through "transitional readers" to "extending readers." It is intended that the continuum will follow each child from kindergarten through third grade. Across each of the developmental stages in the continuum, you analyze growth criteria in the areas of book selection and sustained reading; previewing and predicting; oral reading and use of strategies; and comprehension. Extensive checklists are provided for each of the sections of growth criteria. You may use the checklists in planning instruction in response to the assessment.

The DRA was developed, field-tested, and revised by primary teachers in the Upper Arlington City School District in Ohio between 1988 and 1996. In May 1996, seventy-eight primary classroom and Reading Recovery teachers from across the United States, and twenty-two teachers in Canada, field-tested the DRA. The current forms reflect the suggestions made by these teachers.

How Does the *Developmental Reading Assessment* Inform Instruction?

The central feature of the DRA is the one-on-one conference. Here you observe and interact with each of your students about a text, recording their responses and behaviors as they read and respond to the texts. The information you collect will enable you to:

- Determine a reader's independent assessment reading level.
- Confirm or redirect ongoing instruction.
- Group students effectively for reading experiences and instruction.

- Document changes over time in reading performance.
- Identify students who may be working below proficiency and need further assessments (Beaver, 1997, p. 16).

A careful analysis of the running records will permit you to discern not only the child's level of accuracy in oral reading, but you will be able to analyze the child's use of knowledge about language and graphophonic knowledge in reading. Further, you will be able to determine the extent to which the child is reading for meaning and strategically using the reading process. These understandings will be valuable to your planning for guided reading activities, skill and strategy instruction, and reading conferences.

You could develop a schedule that would have you assess the reading performance of each of your students at the beginning and again at the end of the school year. However, the DRA will prove a more helpful planning tool the more frequently you use it. You may find that creating a schedule by which you assess each child each quarter of the school year will be most useful to you in planning instruction.

Some schools have developed plans to use the DRA in October/November and again in May/June. They have established levels of proficiency for each grade level at those times. For example, you may decide in your school/district that second-graders, in the spring, will be reading levels 24–28 with 94% accuracy or above with adequate understanding. By establishing these proficiency levels, you will be able to easily identify children who need increased specialized instruction.

What Are the Advantages of the *Developmental Reading Assessment?*

The DRA contains the leveled books and record keeping materials you need to engage in literature-based assessment and evaluation of your students' development as readers. The resources have been collected in one place for you to do a series of assessments across time.

The developmental continuum represents statements describing important developmental characteristics, yet is not too detailed or too time-consuming to use. If your school plans to use the DRA over the years from kindergarten through third grade, you can use a different color ink or highlighter to mark the continuum each year. This will provide a longitudinal record of growth.

What Are the Disadvantages of the *Developmental Reading Assessment?*

Using the DRA requires solid knowledge of the reading process on the part of the teacher. While this is not a criticism of the tool, and in fact is a desirable situation, schools who plan to adopt the DRA will need to plan for adequate in-service training and follow-up. The *Resource Guide* offers some excellent suggestions for implementing the program and learning to use it effectively.

The texts that accompany the DRA have been leveled. The *Resource Guide* makes reference to Irene Fountas and Gay Su Pinnell's *Guided Reading: Good First Teaching for All Children* as a reference for leveled books. However, the leveling system used by Fountas and Pinnell is different than the system used in the DRA. It may be time-consuming to establish uniformity between the leveling system in the DRA and the leveling system used in your school. Fountas and Pinnell describe eighteen levels (A–R). Barbara Peterson [In DeFord, Lyons & Pinnell (Eds.) (1991). *Bridges to Literacy: Learning from Reading Recovery*. Portsmouth, NH: Heinemann] describes twenty levels. The *DRA Resource Guide* refers to forty levels, but offers titles at only selected levels.

Where Do I Get More Information About the *Developmental Reading Assessment?*

Beaver, J. (1997). *Developmental reading assessment resource guide*. Parsippany, NJ: Celebration Press.

Ekwall/Shanker Reading Inventory

Third Edition

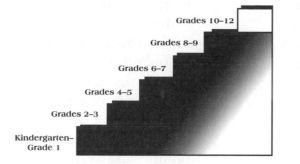

Grades 10–12
Grades 8–9
Grades 6–7
Grades 4–5
Grades 2–3
Kindergarten–Grade 1

Level:

Grade 1

through

Grade 9

Year Published: 1997

What Is It?

The *Ekwall/Shanker Reading Inventory* (ESRI) is an informal reading inventory consisting of eleven subtests. These include graded word lists, oral and silent reading passages, a test of basic sight words and phrases, plus tests of letter knowledge, phonics, structural analysis, contractions, the El Paso Phonics Survey, the Quick Survey Word List and an interest inventory.

The authors suggest that the battery may be used selectively. It may be used as a quick screening device for instructional placement, as a brief individual diagnosis, or as a comprehensive individual diagnosis depending on the subtests you select.

Each of the tests that make up the ESRI is briefly described below.

1. *San Diego Quick Assessment or Graded Word List:* Lists of words in isolation graded from preprimer through ninth grade. The authors suggest that this test may be used to "obtain a quick estimate of the student's independent, instructional and frustration reading levels" (p. 17). It may also be used for both an estimate of where to enter the graded passages and to obtain an initial diagnosis of basic sight vocabulary, phonics and structural analysis skills.

2. *Oral and Silent Reading Passages:* To get an accurate assessment of functional reading levels on both silent and oral reading. The passages were written by Ekwall and contain ten sentences except at the preprimer level. There is usually one comprehension question per sentence. Questions are designed to ask students to recall facts, make inferences, and understand vocabulary. The grade levels of the preprimer through eighth grade were determined using the Harris-Jacobson Readability Formula. At ninth grade, the Powers, Sumner, Kearl formula was used. Performance on the silent reading passages is evaluated in terms of reading speed (time to read the passage) as slow, medium, fast, or median. These values were determined by administering the passages to 170 students at each grade level.

Oral reading errors are coded and counted. Omissions, insertions, substitutions, mispronunciations, words pronounced by you, and repetitions are all counted as errors at each occurrence. Self corrections and disregard of punctuation are not counted as errors. Consecutively repeated words are counted as one error. The authors recognize that you may exercise some judgment in counting minor errors that do not change the meaning.

3. *Listening Comprehension:* In this test you read passages to the student and ask the comprehension questions. The purpose of the test is to obtain the level at which a student can understand material read to him or her. The theory behind this is that a child would be capable of reading material at his or her listening capacity level if decoding and comprehension skills were improved.

4. *The Basic Sight Words and Phrases Test:* To determine which of the 220 basic sight words and 143 basic sight word phrases can be recognized and pronounced instantly by the student.

(Note: Tests five through seven may be thought of as decoding tests.)

5. *Letter Knowledge:* Determines if the student can associate letter symbols with letter names. In one subtest you say the letter names and the student points to the printed letter. In the other subtest you point to the letter and the student says the name.

6. *Phonics:* A test of letter-sound associations. In subtests one through five the student points to a printed letter that corresponds to a sound you indicate in a word. The remaining subtests require the student to actually decode sound/symbol relationships. Across the nine subtests, decoding ability is tested on initial consonant sounds, blends, digraphs, ending sounds, vowels, phonograms, blending ability, phonic substitution, vowel digraphs, and the application of phonics skills in context.

7. *Structural Analysis:* A test of the ability to use structural analysis skills to aid in decoding unknown words. Tests include the ability to hear separate syllables in words, to decode inflectional endings, prefixes, suffices compound words, affixes and syllabication, and the application of structural analysis skills in context.

8. *Knowledge of Contractions Test:* A test requiring students to decode 48 common contractions and tell the two words the contraction stands for.

9. *El Paso Phonics Survey:* Tests decoding and blending 90 phonic elements using nonsense words.

10. *Quick Survey Word List:* Consists of fourteen multi-syllabic nonsense words. Intended to be a quick test of the mastery of phonics and structural analysis skills. May be used as a pretest to determine the necessity of administering Tests four through nine. May be used with students in fourth grade and above who do not have difficulty applying phonics skills.

11. *Reading Interest Survey:* Explores student's general interests, read-

ing interests, and reading experiences.

The manual includes an ESRI Analysis Sheet. You transfer data from the scoring sheets for the individual tests and/or the test summary sheet to this Analysis Sheet. You then examine the student's performance in each area using the guidelines for evaluation provided on the Analysis Sheet.

How Does the *Ekwall/Shanker Reading Inventory* Inform Instruction?

In addition to determining the student's functional reading levels, you will be able to gain a great deal of information about a student's strengths and weaknesses across an array of reading skills. The manual includes a Diagnostic Report Form which will help you organize test data, summarize data, and make recommendations for instruction. Each of the subtests provides adequate coverage of the skill tested to permit confidence in the data. You will be able to specify which skills you should focus your instruction on after analyzing the test data.

What Are the Advantages of the *Ekwall/Shanker Reading Inventory?*

The first word that comes to mind here is *complete*. The complete battery offers a very thorough set of tests for evaluating performance on the application of subskill knowledge. The subtests that ask for application of phonic and structural analysis in context are especially helpful. These tests bring the assessment of this knowledge into much

more realistic formats than the "skills in isolation" tests.

The scoring sheets, analysis sheets, and diagnostic report forms are excellent and should be very helpful to you in making maximum use of the inventory. The section of the manual on how to write a diagnostic report will be very helpful to the novice report writer.

The manual contains a Prescriptive Analysis of Phonics Skills chart. The chart is a grid that you can use to evaluate the student's ability on 96 specific phonics elements. This grid will be especially useful in identifying a student's phonics strengths and weaknesses.

What Are the Disadvantages of the *Ekwall/Shanker Reading Inventory?*

The most serious disadvantage of the ESRI is in the El Paso *Phonics Survey* and the *Quick Survey Word List*. These tests use nonsense words. This is problematic in that it is not at all like the reading act. Where no meaning exists, the student's ability to "read" is seriously compromised. This is an especially difficult act for some students. The author's recognize these difficulties, but have included the tests anyway.

Analysis of reading behavior in this inventory represents exclusively a subskills orientation to reading. No attention is paid to reading strategies, the use of the reading process or metacomprehension. Miscues are analyzed quantitatively only. No attempt is made to understand the reader's use of the cueing systems. Comprehension is measured only through asking limited comprehension questions (fact, inference, vocabulary). There is no opportunity for retelling, though you are advised to say "can you tell me more" if answers are incomplete.

Where Do I Get More Information About the *Ekwall/Shanker Reading Inventory?*

Ekwall, E. E., & Shanker, J. L. (1993). *Ekwall/Shanker Reading Inventory.* (3rd ed.). Boston: Allyn and Bacon.

First Steps Reading Developmental Continuum

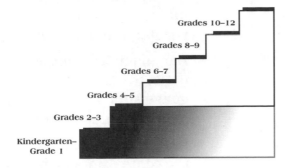

Grades 10–12
Grades 8–9
Grades 6–7
Grades 4–5
Grades 2–3
Kindergarten–Grade 1

Level:

Pre-School

through

Upper Primary

Year Published: 1997

What Is It?

First Steps Reading Developmental Continuum (FSRDC) is one part of a set of resources that provide you a framework for observing children as users of language and planning for their instruction. Developmental continua have been created for reading, writing, spelling and oral language. The complete set of materials consists of the four developmental continua, an accompanying Resource Book for each continuum, and resource materials for working with parents. The *Reading Developmental Continuum* and *Reading Resource Book* are described here.

The continuum was developed by Diana Rees and Bruce Shortland-Jones. The continuum became part of the *First Steps* resource material developed by the Education Department of Western Australia. The *Reading Developmental Continuum* consists of six phases. Each phase has a list of behavioral indicators. The phases are listed below.

Phase 1: Role Play Reading

Indicators are organized under the categories: making meaning at text level, making meaning using context, making meaning at word level, and attitude.

Phase 2: Experimental Reading

Indicators are organized under the categories: making meaning at text level, making meaning using context, making meaning at word level, and attitudes.

Phase 3: Early Reading

Indicators are organized under the categories: making meaning at text level, making meaning using context, making meaning at word level, and attitude.

Phase 4: Transitional Reading

Indicators are organized under the categories: making meaning at text level, strategies for making meaning using context, making meaning at word level, and attitude.

Phase 5: Independent Reading

Indicators are organized under the categories: making meaning at text level, making meaning using context, making meaning at word level, and attitude.

Phase 6: Advanced Reading

Indicators are organized under the categories: making meaning at text level and attitude.

The authors explain that you can identify a child's phase of development by observing that the child is exhibiting all of the key indicators of a phase, but that most children will display indicators from other phases as well.

In addition to identifying key indicators for each phase, the continuum includes major teaching emphases that apply to all phases and other teaching emphases specific to each phase. For example, at Phase 3: Early Reading, one of the key indicators is "beginning to read familiar texts confidently and can retell major content from visual and printed texts, e.g. language experience recounts, shared books, simple informational texts and children's television programs." One of the major teaching emphases at this phase is "ask readers about ideas and information they have found in books. Encourage a range of opinions and reactions, discuss stereotypes and generalizations."

It is important to note that the authors of the continuum place heavy emphasis on the notion that the indicators are not designed to provide evaluative criteria *through which every child is expected to progress in lock-step order*. They reflect a developmental view of teaching in which great consideration is given to individual differences.

The indicators described in the continuum have been developed from a set of theoretical assumptions. The authors emphasize that the indicators and learning activities be interpreted from the perspective of these underlying assumptions about language learning. The assumptions are:

- Language learning takes place through interactions in meaningful events, rather than through isolated language activities.

- Language learning is seen as holistic; that is, each mode of language supports and enhances overall language development.

- Language develops in relation to the context in which it is used; that is, it develops according to the situation, the topic under discussion, and the relationship between the participants.

- Language develops through interaction and the joint construction of meaning in a range of contexts.

- Language learning can be enhanced by learners monitoring their own progress.

- The way in which children begin to make sense of the world is constructed through the language they use and reflects cultural understandings and values.

Using the *Reading Developmental Continuum* involves a five-step process. The first step is to predict where each of your students is on the continuum by looking at the key indicators. The second step is to collect data through observation and work samples to confirm your predictions. The third phase is to involve parents and children. The fourth step is to link assessment with teaching by making use of the major teaching emphases. The final step, monitoring progress, is done through ongoing collection of data, consultation with parents and linking children's current phase of development with teaching.

A companion volume, *First Steps Reading Resource Book*, is a rich source of information for both classroom organization and curriculum. It contains case studies that help you see how children move through the continuum, and how you can use the curriculum resources to facilitate that movement.

How Does *First Steps Reading Developmental Continuum* Inform Instruction?

The continuum provides a well-articulated, developmental perspective on learning to read. As you study the key indicators and look carefully at each of your children as readers, you will begin to look at children and the reading process through "new eyes." You will begin to think developmentally about the reading process, and you will see how each of the major teaching emphases facilitates learning that process and monitoring use of that process.

By looking at the children in your class who exhibit the same key indicators, you will be able to put groups of children together for instruction that either reinforces their learning or moves them to new ground. By visiting the continuum of each of your learners frequently you will notice which children have stalled, and be able to intervene quickly.

What Are the Advantages of *First Steps Reading Developmental Continuum?*

The continuum provides you with a framework for monitoring progress and planning instruction on a very individual basis. The *Reading Resource Book* is an excellent planning and teaching resource. It contains valuable information about organizing to use the continuum, working with children as readers, and meeting the needs of children who are struggling.

The same could be said for the other three continua and resource books in the *First Steps* materials.

What Are the Disadvantages of *First Steps Reading Developmental Continuum?*

Frankly, I don't see any disadvantages. I do see some challenges, however. The continuum is complex. It will require a serious effort on your part to learn it thoroughly and use it well. But this will only help you know your learners better.

The *First Steps* materials can be ordered from Heinemann. In-service training is controlled through the publisher. Training is delivered at the school or district level. Maximum use would be made of the continua if a majority (if not all) of the teachers within a school (or district) agreed to use the materials.

Where Do I Get More Information About *First Steps Reading Developmental Continuum?*

First Steps Training, Heinemann, 800-541-2086, ext 164. Workshops@heinemann.com
First Steps Reading Developmental Continuum. (1997). Westport, CT: Heinemann.

First Steps Reading Resource Book.
   (1997). Westport, CT: Heinemann.

Gates-MacGinitie Reading Tests

Fourth Edition

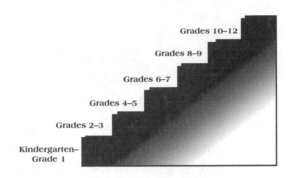

Grades 10–12
Grades 8–9
Grades 6–7
Grades 4–5
Grades 2–3
Kindergarten–
Grade 1

Level:

Pre–K

through

High School

Year Published: 1998

What Are They?

The *Gates-MacGinitie Reading Tests* (GMRT) are norm-referenced tests for measuring reading achievement ranging from pre-reading abilities through adult reading. The Pre-Reading Level was designed to assess the child's knowledge of important background concepts upon which beginning reading skills are built. The pre-reading evaluation (Level PR) contains subtests that measure literacy concepts, oral language concepts (phonemic awareness), letters and letter-sound correspondences, and story listening comprehension. Children are not required to read at this level, as they choose answers from pictures or symbols. Pictures are always named by the teacher.

Level BR can be useful in measuring reading skills of children who make less-than-average progress in reading by the end of grade one. Level R (beginning reading skills) contains subtests that measure use of initial consonants and consonant clusters, use of final consonants and consonant clusters, use of vowels, and the recognition of story words. At this level children are asked to choose pictures with names that begin or end with certain letters, to read words, and to read simple sentences. The teacher reads most of the questions to the children, who then choose answers from pictures or words.

Levels 1 through 12 of the GMRT were designed to provide a general assessment of reading achievement. At levels 1 and 2 (first and second grade) the subtests are word decoding, word knowledge, and comprehension. At these levels, the vocabulary subtests are primarily a test of decoding skills. Children need to either recognize or sound out words that correspond to pictures. Comprehension of passages ranging from one sentence to five sentences is measured by asking children to choose the picture that illustrates the passage or answers a question about the passage.

At levels 3 through 12, the vocabulary subtest is a test of word knowledge. The student's task is to select the word or phrase that means most nearly the same as the test word. The comprehension test measures the student's ability to read and understand prose passages and verse. Students respond to questions in a multiple-choice format.

Level AR is designed for post-high school, colleges, community colleges, adult education programs, GED programs, vocational and training schools. Norms are available on community college students.

The *Gates-MacGinitie* may be scored by machine through the Riverside Scoring Service or locally by hand. Self-scorable answer sheets are available for levels 4 through AR.

Raw scores may be converted to a variety of derived scores. These derived scores are national percentile ranks (NPR), normal curve equivalents (NCE), national stanines, extended scale scores (ESS), and grade equivalents (GE). The NPR for a particular raw score tells you the percentage of students in that same grade whose raw scores were lower. The NCEs are percentile ranks that have been statistically transformed into a scale of equal units of reading achievement. These scores, ranging from 1 through 99, are suitable for computing averages. Stanines describe a student's level of achievement in relationship to the achievement of other students at the same grade level. Stanines divide the range of reading achievement into nine unequal bands. The ESSs permit you to follow a student's progress in reading over a period of years on a single, continuous scale. In this way, a student's achievement can be ranked within a group that includes all of the students in all the grades. Like NCEs, ESSs can be averaged.

Reliability and validity measures are documented in the *Technical Report*. Test, retest reliability coefficients range well into the .80s, and correla-

tions between the *Gates-MacGinitie* and the *Iowa Tests of Basic Skills* range between .67 and .84 for vocabulary, and .53 and .83 for comprehension.

How Does the *Gates-MacGinitie* Inform Instruction?

The *Gates-MacGinitie* is often used to get the Normal Curve Equivalent scores that are used in Title One reports to show year-to-year gains. The test tends to highlight students' deficits rather than their strengths, so reading specialists often use it in conjunction with other measures such as an informal reading inventory, anecdotal records, writing samples, running records, and students' written reflections on their work.

Sarah Ramsey, a K–6 Language Arts specialist from Illinois for grades K–6, uses the *Gates-MacGinitie*. Because of her work as a Title I teacher, she is required to report Normal Curve Equivalent (NCE) scores. In her annual reports, she needs to document the gains the students have made during the school year. Because the *Gates-MacGinitie* measures both vocabulary and reading comprehension skills she uses it as a pre- and post-test.

Sarah says that she finds that the test is useful in that it is one measure that the classroom teacher hasn't made on an informal basis. You can see very concrete results that have taken place during the school year. She finds that the results of this test help her in talking to parents about student performance, and it is also a very specific way to show students that they are progressing in their reading.

What Are the Advantages of the *Gates-MacGinitie Reading Tests?*

One strong advantage of the GMRT is that test data can help you in making individual and program evaluation decisions. The early levels, for example, can give you information on which children may have difficulty in reading unless they receive modified instruction. At the older levels, for example, you can learn which children are not progressing at the rate you would expect or who needs additional instruction in comprehension skills.

The manuals for scoring and interpretation offer very complete discussions for using the scores in instruction. One section of the manual entitled "Working with students whose comprehension scores are low," for example, offers specific instructional suggestions for helping students when decoding/word recognition is inaccurate, when vocabulary is limited, or when background knowledge is limited.

The Manuals for Scoring and Interpretation give very clear and complete instructions for out-of-level testing for students whose reading achievement is far below or above average. Norms are available for out-of-level testing. Additionally, the Manuals offer clear and accurate discussions of appropriate ways of using the derived scores.

Specific norming information was not available at the time of this writing. I suggest you ask Riverside for a copy of the *Preliminary Norms Booklet.* The material I had available at this writing said one copy of this booklet is available at no charge, but it was not yet available when I asked for it.

What Are the Disadvantages of the *Gates-MacGinitie Reading Tests?*

The GMRT views reading very much as a product, not as a process. The emphasis is on how well a student reads and not on how a reader uses the reading process. No way exists for measuring ability in prediction, sampling, confirming, and integrating information read with known information. Because the test is timed, it measures the rate of comprehension rather than power of comprehension. In comprehension, only very narrow aspects are measured. There is no way to distinguish literal from inferential comprehension, and no measure of critical thinking exists. It is not possible to determine the degree to which the reader uses metacomprehension strategies, nor is it possible to assess study skills such as using reference materials, reading charts and graphs, or using illustrations. The reader is asked to deal only with short pieces of text, and comprehension is measured only in the multiple-choice format.

As has been said about other tools in this Handbook, it is unfortunate that grade equivalent scores are used in spite of the 1981 resolution of the International Reading Association (IRA) advocating the discontinuance of such scores. The IRA resolution stated that the misuse of grade equivalents promotes misunderstanding of a student's reading ability, and urged that those who administer standardized reading tests stop using grade equivalents to report performance of either individuals or groups of test-takers. The resolution further asked the president or executive director of the Association to write to test publishers urging them to eliminate grade equivalents from their tests. It is ironic that Walter MacGinitie was once the President of the International Reading Association and yet a reading test bearing his name persists in using grade equivalent scores.

Where Do I Get More Information About the *Gates-MacGinitie Reading Tests?*

International Reading Association. (1981). *Resolution: Misuse of grade equivalents.* Newark, DE: International Reading Association.

MacGinitie, W. H., & MacGinitie, R. K. (1989). *Gates-MacGinitie Reading Tests, Manual for Scoring and Interpretation.* Chicago: The Riverside Publishing Co.

Riverside Publishing. (1999). *Preliminary Norms Booklet.* Itasca, IL: Riverside Publishing. A Houghton Mifflin Company.

Gray Oral Reading Tests

Third Edition

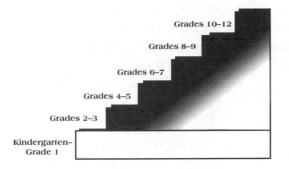

Grades 10–12

Grades 8–9

Grades 6–7

Grades 4–5

Grades 2–3

Kindergarten–
Grade 1

Level: Normed for ages

7 years, 0 months

through

18 years, 11 months

Year Published: 1992

What Is It?

The *Gray Oral Reading Tests–3* (GORT) is a norm-referenced, oral reading test that measures a reader's speed, accuracy and comprehension. In administering either Form A or Form B of the test, you enter the reading passages based on the student's grade level. Each passage has a prompt that you read to the student to introduce the passage. The student then reads the passage orally while you time the reading and mark deviations from the text on a copy of the text. Following the reading, you read the multiple-choice questions to the student as he or she follows along in the Student Book, and you record the responses.

Analysis of performance involves both computation of scores and analysis of miscues. The length of time required to read the passage is converted to a rate score, the number of deviations from the text is converted to an accuracy score, and these scores are then added together to derive the passage score. The comprehension score is determined by the student's performance on the five multiple-choice questions following the reading. The

questions are designed to measure literal, inferential, critical and affective comprehension. A total score, the Oral Reading Quotient (ORQ), is derived by combining the Passage Score and Comprehension Score. The ORQ is described by the authors as an overall index of the student's ability to read orally. Raw scores for rate, accuracy, the passage score, and the comprehension score are converted to grade equivalent, percentile scores, and standard scores. Explaining grade scores, the authors note, "Today, most authorities in assessment discourage the reporting of test results in terms of grade equivalents. We believe that examiners will find standard scores and percentiles more valuable than grade equivalents when reporting scores to others" (Wiederholt & Bryant, 1992, p.23). Miscue analysis is the last step in evaluating the reader's performance.

Miscues are analyzed for meaning similarity, function similarity, graphic/phonemic similarity, multiple sources and self corrections. Analyzing miscues for meaning similarity is a way for you to judge the student's use of comprehension strategies—is the reader attempting to make meaning? The analysis of function similarity allows you to judge the degree to which the reader is drawing on grammatical cues. In analyzing miscues for graphic/phonemic similarity you can draw conclusions about the reader's ability to use specific word attack skills. By counting miscues that demonstrate use of multiple sources of information, such as grammatical cues and phonic cues, you can judge a student's use of multiple reading strategies. The final miscue analysis is of self-corrections which allows you to judge the degree to which the reader is monitoring his or her own use of the reading process and taking corrective action. By calculating the percentages of use for each of the miscue categories, you can determine the degree of balance the reader is bringing to the use of the cueing systems.

The GORT-3 was normed on a stratified sample of 1,485 children residing in 18 states in 1985 and 1986. An additional 226 persons were tested in 1990. The norming sample, while small, appears to be representative of the 1990 census. Reliability has been well established through test-retest with alternate forms. The correlation coefficients generally range from .80 to .92. The standard error of measurement is low on all subtests.

The manual establishes acceptable concurrent validity with other widely used tests as well as acceptable content and construct validity. The reliability and validity of the GORT-3 is well established.

How Do the *Gray Oral Reading Tests-3* Inform Instruction?

The *GORT-3* affords you the opportunity to compare how well a student is reading in terms of rate, accuracy and comprehension with others in a national sample. One of the most useful scores is the Oral Reading Quotient, a composite score. This score is constructed to have a mean of 100 and a standard deviation of 15. A quotient below 70 indicates very poor performance. A quotient above 130 indicates very superior performance. If your purpose in using a norm-referenced measure of oral reading performance is to compare a child's performance against that of others, the Oral Reading Quotient will be very useful.

A very useful analysis is to look at a reader's strengths and weaknesses across subtests. This analysis permits you to determine whether the differences in performance across subtests is significant. For example, when comparing a standard score performance on rate with a standard score performance on accuracy, the minimum difference must be 2.5 in order to have a statistically significant difference at the .05 level. If your student had a standard score of 8 for rate and a standard score of 3 for accuracy, the difference is 5. This means that at the .05 level of confidence, the difference is statistically significant. The student is reading much too fast for his level of accuracy.

Your analysis of the miscues may do more to inform instruction than any of the other analyses. When you calculate the percentage of use for each of the miscue categories (meaning similarity, function similarity, and so on) you can easily see whether or not the student is drawing on all cueing systems in reading. For example, a student who has a very low percentage on meaning similarity and a very high percentage on graphic/phonemic similarity may be relying too heavily on the phonics cueing system and not adequately reading for meaning. This student will benefit from a review of his or her miscues and guided reading activities focusing on meaning. Of critical importance is the percentage of self-corrections. Self-corrections are clear evidence that the reader is reading for meaning, understands that reading is a process, and is monitoring his or her use of the process. Students with a low self-correction percentage will need help in learning to ask themselves of their reading—"Does it look right? Does it sound right? Does it make sense?"

What Are the Advantages of the *Gray Oral Reading Tests-3?*

The greatest advantage of the *GORT-3* is that you can get normative data on oral reading performance using a test that is significantly updated from the first edition in 1967. The Examiner's Manual is excellent. It is clearly written, easy to use, and offers many resources. The rationale and overview of the test are clear. The construction of the test and norming of the scores are clearly explained. There is an excellent section offering suggestions for instruction regarding adjusting rate, reading for meaning, using function clues, graphic/phonemic skills, and self-corrections. A bibliography of resources for use in designing instruction is included in the manual.

The analysis of miscues is a strong advantage in using this test. The in-structions for conducting the miscue analysis are clearly articulated in the manual.

What Are the Disadvantages of the *Gray Oral Reading Tests-3?*

The oral reading passages are very short in comparison to the kinds of texts children read daily in school. The lack of congruence between school reading tasks and the test passages limits your ability to infer performance in school from this test. Further, comprehension is measured by only five questions on each passage. This is a very traditional, and perhaps limited, view of comprehension.

The administration of the test is complicated. Basal and ceiling levels must be determined, a marking system for recording deviations from text must be learned, and the analysis of miscues is demanding. However, none of these administrative tasks should discourage you from using the test. You will need practice before you are likely to feel comfortable with administering the test. Tape recording the oral reading of test passages is strongly recommended.

Where Do I Get More Information About the *Gray Oral Reading Tests-3?*

Wiederholt, J. L., & Bryant, B. R. (1992). *Gray Oral Reading Tests, Third Edition, Examiner's Manual.* Austin, TX: Pro-ed.

Gray Oral Reading Tests–Diagnostic

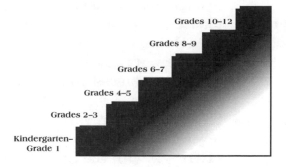

Grades 10–12

Grades 8–9

Grades 6–7

Grades 4–5

Grades 2–3

Kindergarten–
Grade 1

Levels:

Ages 5 years 6 months

through

12 years 11 months

Year Published: 1991

What Is It?

The *Gray Oral Reading Tests-Diagnostic* (GORT-D) is an expanded version of the GORT-3. The authors recognize that the GORT-3 is limited to paragraph reading and that some students have not developed the ability to handle passage reading or they experience significant difficulties in doing so. The GORT-D is an expansion of the first test to include a diagnostic instrument for students who exhibit difficulty reading paragraphs.

The seven subtests of the GORT-D are designed to measure a reader's ability to use what the authors have called "meaning cues" (within the reader), "function cues" (within the flow of language), and "graphi/phonemic cues" (within the words). The subtests are described below.

Meaning Cues

Two subtests assess the reader's ability to create meaning with print. The first, Paragraph Reading, is a modified version of the GORT-3's passage and comprehension scores. The student reads the graded passages aloud, and you

record the length of time in seconds to read the passage and the number of words read incorrectly. This data is converted to a Rate and Accuracy Score. You then ask comprehension questions which yield a Comprehension Score. The three scores, Rate, Accuracy, and Comprehension generate a total score for each paragraph. The total scores for all paragraphs are summed and create the Paragraph Reading Score.

The Word Identification subtest is the second subtest designed to measure the ability to make meaning with print. This subtest measures word recognition and vocabulary by having the reader pronounce four words that appear in a group and pick the two of the four words that go together in some way.

Function Cues

Three subtests assess the reader's ability to use function or grammar cues. Morphemic Analysis measures ability to use inflectional endings, contractions, and compound words. Contextual Analysis assesses the reader's use of the function cues as they appear in context. In this test readers produce a word missing in a sentence when they have only the beginning letter of the word. The Word Ordering subtest presents a series of words in random order. The words need to be reordered to make a sentence.

Graphic/Phonemic Cues

Two subtests assess the ability to use graphic/phonemic cues: decoding and word attack. In decoding the student is tested in onset recognition, rime recognition and blending using nonsense words. For example, the student is shown "C al Cal" and asked to pronounce it. In the word attack test the student is shown a word, such as *potato* and asked to find and say some small words that are in the bigger word. For *potato,* that would be *pot, at, to, tat.*

The authors state that one of the major purposes of the GORT-D is to locate students who are having difficulties and to quantify their reading ability by comparing their specific oral reading performance with that of their agemates.

On each of the subtests, raw scores may be converted to percentile scores, standard scores and grade equivalent scores. Composite Quotients are obtained by comparing performance across the subtests for Meaning Cues, Function Cues and Graphic/Phonemic Cues. Differences of more than nine points are statistically significant at the .05 level.

The test was normed on 831 examinees residing in 13 states. The authors claim that the norming sample is representative of the national population in terms of sex, residence, race, ethnicity and geographic area.

Reliability of the test is established by measures of internal consistency, and test-retest with alternate forms. Internal consistency coefficients range from .96 on decoding to .72 on morphemic analysis. Alternate form reliabilities tended to be lower. Only the Paragraph Reading and Decoding subtests showed adequate reliability coefficients.

Concurrent validity was assessed by correlating performance on the GORT-D with the GORT-3 and two other tests. Coefficients were described by the authors as "moderate." With a median coefficient of .53 I think one would have to consider this "low." Concurrent validity of the GORT-D is not well established.

How Do the *Gray Oral Reading Tests-Diagnostic* Inform Instruction?

The way in which the authors have designed this test is consistent with the way in which many of us think about teaching and evaluating reading. This is in terms of the cueing systems: making meaning, using language knowledge, and using the graphophonic cues. To this extent you will be able to analyze performance and determine areas of strength and instructional need. If you wanted normative data on your student's ability to use these cueing systems, the GORT-D provides that. However, if the normative data is not important to you, you can probably learn much more about your student's use of the cueing systems by carefully analyzing running records.

You may find the Composite Quotients the most helpful information if you want to know how your student compares nationally. This score is available for the Total Reading Score, the Meaning Cues Score, and the Function Cues Score. This will permit useful comparisons of performance across the subtests and will illustrate areas of weakness in the use of all but the graphophonic cueing systems.

What Are the Advantages of the *Gray Oral Reading Tests–Diagnostic?*

The GORT-D affords the opportunity to gain considerably more diagnostic information than you can get from the GORT-3 alone. The most compelling reason to use this test is the normative data available.

What Are the Disadvantages of the *Gray Oral Reading Tests–Diagnostic?*

The greatest disadvantages of this test are the low levels of validity and reliability. Further, limited analysis is made of the use of the cueing systems. You would know much more about your student's use of the cueing systems from a running record than you will from this test.

This is clearly a philosophical issue, but I take exception to the use of nonsense words on the decoding test. The use of nonsense words moves this subtest far away from the reading act. I do not believe that the practice of finding little words in bigger words, as is done in the word attack test, is reflective of the way in which most readers attach words.

The work of Vacca, Vacca & Gove (2000) has demonstrated that children typically learn graphemic bases — groups of letters whose pronunciation is consistent from one word to the next. These bases constitute the rime of the word. Children attack words by decoding the onset (part of the syllable before the vowel) and then blending it with the rime. This process is very different than finding little words in bigger words.

Where Do I Get More Information About the *Gray Oral Reading Tests–Diagnostic?*

Bryant, B. R., & Wiederholt, J. L. (1991). *Gray Oral Reading Tests-Diagnostic*. Austin, TX: pro-ed.

Vacca, J. A., Vacca, R. T., & Gove, M. K. (2000). *Reading and learning to read*. (4th ed.). New York: Addison Wesley Longman.

Language Assessment Scales Reading/Writing

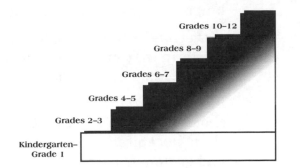

Grades 10–12
Grades 8–9
Grades 6–7
Grades 4–5
Grades 2–3
Kindergarten–Grade 1

Level:

Grade 2

through

High School

Year Published: 1988

What Is It?

The *Language Assessment Scales Reading/Writing* (LAS R/W) measures English language skills in reading and writing that are thought necessary for functioning in mainstream academic environments. LAS R/W is not an achievement test. It is designed for use as a screening device for placement and reclassification for language-minority learners who are minimally proficient in English—defined by the examiner's manual as "those who are at least able to produce a simple sentence orally" (p. 2).

The authors, Duncan and DeAvila, state that reviews were conducted of state guidelines, district curriculum guides, expected learning outcomes, and ESL instructional materials in designing the test. The LAS R/W is a successor to the LAS Oral. Reading competency is assessed through the combined results of tests of vocabulary, fluency, mechanics and usage, and comprehension sections. Writing competency is assessed through sentence completion and sentence-writing activities. The test is available in three sets of forms.

Grades 2–3   Forms 1A and 1B
Grades 4–6   Forms 2A and 2B
Grades 7–9+ Forms 3A and 3B

The authors recommend that new or entering students be tested with a form one level lower than the grade level as suggested by age. Then testing can be adjusted higher or lower depending on level of competence.

Test content varies considerably across form levels. The content of each level (1–3) is described below as it is described in the manuals.

LAS R/W Form 1A & 1B

Vocabulary: Ten multiple choice items per form that measure ability to match pictures to words.

Fluency: Ten multiple-choice items per form that measure overall language fluency and the ability to infer a missing word based on a knowledge of language usage and semantics.

Reading for Information: One story and ten true/false questions per form which measure the ability to identify information.

Mechanics and Usage: 15 multiple-choice items per form that measure skills in capitalization, punctuation, and grammar usage.

Finishing Sentence: Five open-ended items per form that measure the ability to complete a sentence correctly.

What's Happening?:   Five graphic prompts per form, each designed to elicit one sentence.

LAS W/R Form 2A & 2B

Vocabulary: Ten multiple-choice items per form that measure ability to match pictures to words.

Mechanics and Usage: 15 multiple-choice items per form that measure skills in capitalization, punctuation, and grammar usage.

Fluency: Ten multiple-choice items per form that measure overall language fluency and the ability to infer a missing word based on a knowledge of language usage and semantics.

Reading for Information: One story and ten multiple-choice questions per form which measure the ability to identify information.

Finishing Sentences: Five open-ended items per form that measure the ability to complete a sentence correctly.

What's Happening?:   Five graphic prompts per form, each designed to elicit one sentence.

Let's Write: Graphic prompts to elicit a story-writing sample.

LAS R/W Form 3A & 3B

Synonyms: Ten multiple-choice items per form that measure recognition of same-meaning words.

Fluency: Ten multiple-choice items per form that measure overall language fluency and the ability to infer a missing word based on a knowledge of language usage and semantics.

Antonyms: Ten multiple-choice items per form that measure identification of opposite-meaning words.

Mechanics and Usage: 15 multiple-choice items per form that measure skills in capitalization, punctuation, and grammar usage.

Reading for Information: One story and ten multiple-choice questions per form which measure the ability to identify information.

What's Happening?:   Five graphic prompts per form, each designed to elicit one sentence.

Let's Write!:   Graphic prompts to elicit a story-writing sample.

Forms A and B at each level have been designed to be equivalent and so may be used as pre- and post-tests for program entry and exit information or in a test/retest situation. Duncan and DeAvila suggest combining LAS R/W with LAS Oral for a complete assessment of listening, speaking, reading and writing skills. They caution that combining the LAS R/W with any other test of oral language proficiency may invalidate program placement decisions.

The manuals offer some important testing cautions. General instructions for the test and subtests may be given in whatever language, mixture of languages, or dialects is necessary for students to understand what they are to do. However, actual test items must not be translated. You may assist students with mechanical tasks, but not in a way that would give away any answers. You are advised to encourage students to "make your most careful choice" rather than telling them to "guess."

The LAS W/R may be given either timed or untimed. The authors, reluctant to set time limits, advise that students at the lowest levels of proficiency will be better assessed if the test is untimed.

Reading raw scores are determined by adding the scores on the first four subtests in Forms 1 and 2, and the first five subtests in Form 2. The writing raw scores are determined by adding the scores on the last two subtests in Form 1 and the last three subtests in Forms 2 and 3. Raw scores are converted for both reading and writing to standardized scores that have a maximum of 100. The standardized scores are then used to determine competency levels in reading and writing. Standardized scores of 0–59 equate to a competency level of 1, meaning non-reader or non-writer; standardized scores of 60–79 equate to a competency level of 2, meaning limited reader or limited writer; standardized scores of 80–100 equate to a competency level of 3, meaning competent reader or competent writer. The authors state that "competent" on the LAS R/W means that the student's reading and writing skills are equivalent to those of "mainstream students achieving at or above the 40th percentile on a nationally-normed test."

An overall reading/writing competency is determined by converting the standardized scores to scaled scores, and then comparing scaled scores to the three competency levels. The standard error of measurement (SEM) for the scaled scores is 4.0.

The manual states that the bandwidths between Levels 1 & 2 and Levels 2 & 3 are created by plus or minus one SEM. These gray areas are approximately eight Scaled Score points wide. It is in these areas that student classification errors are most probable. The authors suggest that when students fall into these classification bands that additional data be collected. They recommend retesting, teacher and parent judgment, and use of the LAS Oral.

The norming sample for the LAS-R/W was made up of 1,129 language majority students and 2,840 language minority students for a total of 3,969. Data were collected on students in the Southwest, the Northeast, the Midwest, and the Pacific. Concurrent validity is established with the California Test of Basic Skills (CTBS) with correlation coefficients between LAS Writing and CTBS Language of .80, and CTBS Reading of .75. Correlation coefficients between LAS Reading and CTBS Language and Reading were .91 and .88, respectively. Item analysis correlations range from .78 to .86. The validity and reliability of the LAS-R/W are adequately established.

How Does the *Language Assessment Scale* Inform Instruction?

This tool should be thought of as a screening device rather than a diagnostic instrument. The LAS/RW provides information on the child's ability to use the conventions of English writing and how much mastery the child has of the rules for using the syntax of English.

The number of test items is small. This suggests that the results have greater utility as a screening measure for admission or exit from a program than as a diagnostic test.

The purpose is to assess competence to function in a mainstream class and to help you in making entry and exit decision for students in ESL programs. The LAS/RW should be used in conjunction with the *Language Assessment Scales, Oral.*

What Are the Advantages of the *Language Assessment Scales Reading/Writing?*

The LAS R/W are easy to administer and interpret. The reading subtests appear to have adequate face and construct validity. The writing subtest actually elicits written responses that are holistically scored. The manuals offer rubrics and benchmarks for the scoring of writing. Explanations of the scores and rationales for assigning scores to samples are very clear and helpful. The instructions for determining inter-rater reliability are clear.

The fact that the test can be untimed makes it truly a power test rather than a rate test. This increases the likelihood that you will be able to make more accurate placement decisions.

The manuals offer clear guidelines for scoring the tests. Tables are easy to use.

What Are the Disadvantages of the *Language Assessment Scales Reading/Writing?*

The fluency subtest in each of the three levels is probably misnamed. The test is described as measuring overall language fluency and the ability to infer a missing word based on knowledge of language usage and semantics. This subtest no doubt does measure the ability to infer a missing word, and that ability does depend on language usage and semantics. However, this subtest is not a measure of reading fluency, particularly when it is administered in an untimed mode.

The black line illustrations, particularly those in the "What's Happening?" subtests are sometimes very difficult to understand. Students are told to write only one sentence telling who or what is in the picture and what is happening. This would be very difficult to accomplish with some of the pictures, especially if the subtest were timed within the recommended range of 5 to 12 minutes, depending on the form.

No rationale is offered in the manual for the cut-off scores for the levels of competence. It is very difficult to judge the accuracy of these cut-off scores under these circumstances. Furthermore, the manual refers the examiner to a Technical Report for data on reliability and validity studies. None of this information is available in the manuals.

The manuals list 72 elementary, middle, and high schools, mostly in Texas, California, and Arizona, where pilot studies and the "national tryout" of the *LAS R/W* were conducted. No information is given about the nature or results of these studies.

Where Do I Get More Information About *Language Assessment Scales Reading/Writing?*

Duncan, S. E., & DeAvila, E. A. (1988). *Language assessment scales: Reading/writing forms 1A and 1B.* Monterey, CA: CTB/McGraw-Hill.

Duncan, S. E., & DeAvila, E. A. (1988). *Language assessment scales: Reading/writing forms 2A and 2B.* Monterey, CA: CTB/McGraw-Hill.

Duncan, S. E., & DeAvila, E. A. (1988) *Language Assessment Scales: Reading/writing forms 3A and 3B.* Monterey, CA: CTB/McGraw-Hill.

Learning Record Assessment System

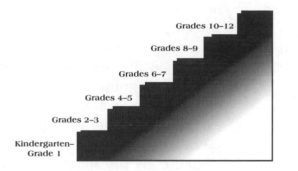

Level:

Kindergarten

through

Twelfth Grade

What Is It?

The first edition of this handbook reviewed the *Primary Language Record.* The *Primary Language Record* was developed in England, and influenced by work in the United States, Australia and New Zealand. It gained considerable attention in the United States. Ultimately, teachers at the Centre for Language in Primary Education in London entered into a productive partnership with teachers in California which resulted in the creation of the *California Learning Record.* This assessment tool has become known in the United States as the *Learning Record Assessment System* (LRAS). In the United States, the system has been expanded to include middle and secondary schools.

The LRAS provides a structure of portfolio assessment across subject areas and enables teachers to be more accountable to parents and the public. Teachers, parents, and learners are all involved in using the LRAS. The record accounts for the student's work both in English and other languages. The LRAS is based on the belief that the

teacher's professional knowledge and effectiveness are enhanced by careful observation and careful, accurate record keeping.

The principles that guided the development of the record are:

- Thoughtfulness over rote learning
- Performance over assumptions of deficit
- Individual development meshed with grade-level expectations
- The strengths of being bilingual and of understanding cultures beyond one's own (Barr et al, 1999, p. 2).

The LRAS is explained in two well-written handbooks: one for grades K–6 and one for grades 6–12. The K–6 Handbook is explained here. The 6–12 handbook is highly similar, offering some changes appropriate to the age level. The focus is on students in the process of learning and on the work they complete as learners. The LRAS consists of three parts: A, B, and C. Part A is completed in the fall, or whenever the child enters school. This part includes a record of the discussion between the parent(s) and teacher. The purpose of this discussion is to let the parents share their knowledge about the child at home and at school, and to share hopes, expectations, and concerns. The manual suggests topics to be discussed, such as the child's enjoyment of story and storytelling, favorite stories, kinds of reading the child does at home, what the parents have observed about the child's language, and the goals the parents would like to set for the year.

The second section of Part A is the record of a language/literacy conference between you and the child. The child is asked to bring books recently read (in any language) and writing samples to the conference. The child is asked to talk about him or herself as a reader, writer, and a language user both in and out of school. Encouragement is offered to the child to discuss what he or she thinks about achievements, concerns, and areas for improvement in language and literacy.

Part B guides you in observing students as they work and in looking for evidence of student progress and documenting that progress. Part B, to be used during the second and third quarters of the school year, is divided into three parts: B1, Talking and Listening; B2, Reading; and B3, Writing. Each of these sections is described below.

Components of LRAS Part B

B1, Talking and Listening, asks you to comment on the child's use of spoken language, use of talk for learning and thinking, use of talk for particular purposes, and talking and listening with different people in different settings. You are also asked to comment on the teaching that has helped, or would help, in this area.

B2, Reading, asks you to comment on the child as a reader in English or other community languages, where the child is operating in terms of reading scales that describe stages of development in terms of becoming a reader and reading across the curriculum, indications of the child's pleasure in reading, the child's ability to reflect on his or her reading, and the strategies the child has used. This section also offers a place to comment on experiences and teaching that have been helpful. The reading scales are very helpful descriptions of the criteria by which you can developmentally classify students, both as beginning readers and as readers across the curriculum.

B3, Writing, asks you to comment on the writer's confidence and development, the types of writing done across the curriculum, the child's affective responses to writing alone and with others across a variety of genres, the influence of reading on writing, and the writer's understanding and use of written language, spelling, and conventions. A final section on writing is where you can record the results of experiences and instruction in writing.

In addition to the main body of the Learning Record, there are optional observation and sample sheets that offer you a framework for observing your students' development in language and literacy. The Talking and Listening Observation/Sample Sheets present a grid on which you can record both learning and social contexts, and then observations and anecdotal records. The Reading and Writing Observation Sheets are designed for you to record anecdotal records about your observations of the child's development as a reader, how the child responds to books, the kinds of books the child uses, and specific information about reading behavior. Similarly, a writing observation section includes your comments on the child's pleasure and confidence as a writer, the degree of the child's involvement in writing, the extent to which the child draws on background experiences in writing, and specific information about writing behavior. The optional observation sheets and the reading and writing samples you are encouraged to collect are to be used in completing the formal parts of the Learning Record.

Part C, completed during the fourth quarter of the school year, organizes comments written by you and the parents, as well as records of conferences with the child. These are reflections on the child's learning across the school year. Part C allows for reporting on fourth-quarter accomplishments, as well as recognizing and evaluating the year's work. This reflective stance underscores the notion that learning is ongoing and cumulative.

How Does the *Learning Record Assessment System* Inform Instruction?

Teachers who have valued anecdotal records and other forms of careful observation of student learning see the Learning Record as a way to give structure and organization to these observations. Teachers who use the record report that it helps to keep them focused on curriculum goals, and that it is an excellent tool for communicating with parents.

Some teachers have found it helpful, after the very initial observations of learners, to identify one or two children a day for in-depth observation. This observation schedule will permit you to begin individualizing instruction very early in the year, in part, because you will have come to understand individual strengths and what each child wants to learn and his/her personal goals in learning to read and write.

You will find it helpful while you are completing these conferences with individual children, to have the other children engaged in choice activities that do not require much teacher intervention. If you schedule an hour-long period of choice activities each morning you will be able to observe several children and hold three conferences.

You will find the Learning Record is a basic assessment tool in terms of planning for whole group, small group, and individual instruction. For example, you may discover that only two children know how to use a comma for punctuating items in a series. You will then plan a mini-lesson on using commas for the whole class. If you discover that three or four children are not comfortable with the strategy of using what they know about sentence structure to make predictions about unfamiliar words, then you can teach those three or four how to use the knowledge that they have in oral language in their reading. You may find that only one child is interested in writing that involves dialogue or in writing a scientific report. If so, then you can make plans to teach those children individually.

What Are the Advantages of the *Learning Record Assessment System?*

The LRAS offers a well-organized system for managing information on your students as readers, writers, listeners, and speakers. The forms presented with the LRAS are thoughtfully designed and will be a valuable tool to help you organize important information drawn from the child, the parents', and your own understandings.

One of the greatest advantages in using the LRAS are the outstanding manuals that accompany it. The manuals offer detailed and up-to-date information to guide your observations. They are rich in illustrations of complete forms, so that you have clear and easily used models. In a sense, the LRAS manuals are a kind of "in-service training" in some of the latest thinking about the reading and writing processes and the careful, thoughtful, professional observation of learners and their work.

Appendices include excellent developmental scales in reading and writing, a set of stages in English language learning, a school performance scale, and The Learning Record itself.

What Are the Disadvantages of the *Learning Record Assessment System?*

One disadvantage inherent in the LRAS is also true of any well-designed anecdotal records/portfolio-type system. The physical management of the forms and materials is challenging. However, the LRAS manuals offer very good suggestions that should alleviate much of this concern.

Where Do I Get More Information About the *Learning Record Assessment System?*

Barr, M., Ellis, S., Hester, H., & Thomas, A. (1988). *The primary language record: Handbook for teachers.* Portsmouth, NH: Heinemann.

Barr, M. A., Craig, D. A., Fisette, D., & Syverson, M. A. (1999). *Assessing literacy with the learning record. A handbook for teachers, grades k-6.* Portsmouth, NH: Heinemann.

Barr, M. A., & Syverson, M. A. (1999). *Assessing literacy with the learning record. A handbook for teachers, grades 6–12.* Portsmouth, NH: Heinemann.

Metacomprehension Strategy Index

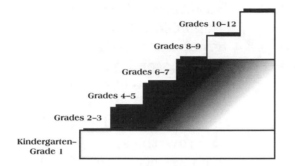

Grades 10–12
Grades 8–9
Grades 6–7
Grades 4–5
Grades 2–3
Kindergarten–
Grade 1

Level:

Middle

through

Upper Elementary

Year Published: 1990

What Is It?

The *Metacomprehension Strategy Index* (MSI) is a 25-item, multiple-choice questionnaire designed to assess students' awareness of reading strategies they use before, during, and after reading a narrative text selection. We know that good readers are actively involved in the reading process. They are aware that reading is a process involving the reader in thinking about his or her own comprehension. This ability to monitor one's own use of the reading process and to take strategic action when the process fails is what is known as metacomprehension ability.

The MSI measures students' awareness of a variety of metacomprehension behaviors within six broad categories. *Predicting and verifying* (Item nos. 1, 4, 13, 15, 16, 18, 23) involves assessing the ability to predict story content, to use predictions as a purpose for reading, evaluating predictions, and generating new ones. *Previewing* (Item nos. 2, 3) involves assessing students' awareness of previewing text, activating background knowledge, and providing information

for making predictions. *Purpose setting* (Items nos. 5, 7,21) assesses students' understanding of the importance of reading with a purpose. *Self questioning* (Item nos. 6, 14, 17) assesses students' understanding of the importance of generating questions to be answered as a reader. *Drawing from background knowledge* (Item nos. 8, 9, 10, 19, 24, 25) involves assessing students' understandings of the importance of activating background knowledge to draw inferences and make predictions. *Summarizing and applying fix-up strategies* (Item nos. 11, 12, 20, 22) measures students' awareness of the importance of strategies such as summarizing, re-reading, suspending judgment, and reading on when comprehension breaks down. It is recommended that you read the questions and possible answers to students so that students' limited decoding ability or slow reading rate will not interfere with the ability to perform on the questionnaire.

The strategies assessed by the MSI were determined by an assessment of the strategies taught in several metacomprehension instructional studies. (Please refer to the "more in-

213

formation" section at the end of this review). This lends construct validity to the instrument. Validity has been further established by correlating performance on the MSI with performance of students receiving metacomprehension strategy training. Students who received training in metacomprehension strategies scored significantly higher on the MSI than students in a control group. Reliability has been established through internal consistency measures yielding a coefficient of .87.

How Does the *Metacomprehension Strategy Index* Inform Instruction?

Your analysis of children's performance on the MSI can be very useful in planning instruction in strategic reading. You could examine performance on each of the six strategy areas tested. For example, if a student marked very few of the answers that confirm the ability to predict and verify, you would want to either plan a focus lesson on this for this child or you may wish to draw together a group of children who scored poorly on that strategy for instruction.

It would be useful to compare the total score on the MSI with the performance of your children on either a norm-referenced achievement test, or state or district performance assessments. For example, you may notice that a child who scored 22 or 23 total correct responses also scored at the 92nd percentile on a norm-referenced test. This, along with your own observations, would confirm that this child is comprehending well and reading strategically. Conversely, if you had a

child who scored poorly on a state or district assessment and also had a low score on the MSI, you would see that one way to help this child improve in reading would be to focus on strategies in guided reading instruction, small group instruction, shared reading, and reading conferences.

The use of guided reading, running records, and retrospective miscue analysis would be excellent ways to improve the strategy use of children who perform at low levels on the MSI.

What Are the Advantages of the *Metacomprehension Strategy Index?*

The MSI is built on sound theory and research in that it examines before reading strategies, during reading strategies, and after reading strategies. It is a convenient way for you to get a quick assessment of the ways in which children in your class perceive their use of reading strategies. Examination of the data at the strategy level, as well as the overall score, will be useful in planning instruction.

The authors offer very helpful illustrations of ways in which the index may be used in planning instruction.

What Are the Disadvantages of the *Metacomprehension Strategy Index?*

The number of items allocated to each of the six areas of strategy use is very uneven. For example, seven items deal with predicting and verifying while only two items deal with previewing. This makes comparison across strategy areas less valid than it would be if the items were more evenly distributed. However, the authors point out this issue in discussion and caution about interpreting the MSI.

It is difficult to determine that any of the during reading items are devoted to asking whether or not decoding predictions are correct, make sense, or sound right. The correct response to one "during reading" item is "check to see if my guesses are right or wrong." This could relate to decoding predictions, but that is not at all clear. Another correct response is "try to see if my guesses are going to be right or wrong." It is, again, unclear as to what these guesses are about.

The MSI is reprinted in Figure 21 on the following pages with the permission of the author and the International Reading Association.

Where Do I Get More Information About the *Metacomprehension Strategy Index?*

Baumann, J. F., Seifert-Kessell, N., & Jones, L. (1987, December). *Effects of think-aloud instruction on elementary students' ability to monitor their comprehension.* Paper presented at the National Reading Conference, St. Petersburg, FL.

Paris, S. G., Cross, D. R., & Lipson, M. Y. (1984). Informed strategies for learning: A program to improve children's reading awareness and comprehension. *Journal of Educational Psychology, 76,* 1239–1252.

Schmitt, M. C. (1990). A questionnaire to measure children's awareness of strategic reading processes. *The Reading Teacher,* March, 1990, 454–461.

Figure 21   Metacomprehension Strategy Index

Metacomprehension Strategy Index

Directions: Think about what kinds of things you can do to help you understand a story better before, during, and after you read it. Read each of the lists of four statements and decide which one of them would help you the most. *There are no right answers.* It is just what *you* think would help the most. Circle the letter of the statement you choose.

I. **In each set of four, choose the one statement which tells a good thing to do to help you understand a story better *before* you read it.**

1. Before I begin reading, it's a good idea to:
   A. See how many pages are in the story.
   B. Look up all of the big words in the dictionary.
   C. Make some guesses about what I think will happen in the story.
   D. Think about what has happened so far in the story.

2. Before I begin reading, it's a good idea to:
   A. Look at the pictures to see what the story is about.
   B. Decide how long it will take me to read the story.
   C. Sound out the words, I don't know.
   D. Check to see if the story is making sense.

3. Before I begin reading, it's a good idea to:
   A. Ask someone to read the story to me.
   B. Read the title to see what the story is about.
   C. Check to see if most of the words have long or short vowels in them.
   D. Check to see if the pictures are in order and make sense.

4. Before I begin reading, it's a good idea to:
   A. Check to see that no pages are missing.
   B. Make a list of the words I'm not sure about.

C. Use the title and pictures to help me make guesses about what will happen in the story.
D. Read the last sentence so I will know how the story ends.

5. Before I begin reading, it's a good idea to:
   A. Decide on why I am going to read the story.
   B. Use the difficult words to help me make guesses about what will happen in the story.
   C. Reread some parts to see if I can figure out what is happening if things aren't making sense.
   D. Ask for help with the difficult words.

6. Before I begin reading, it's a good idea to:
   A. Retell all of the main points that have happened so far.
   B. Use the difficult words to help me make guesses about what will happen in the story.
   C. Reread some parts to see if I can figure out what is happening if things aren't making sense.
   D. Ask for help with the difficult words.

7. Before I begin reading, it's a good idea to:
   A. Check to see if I have read this story before.
   B. Use my questions and guesses as a reason for reading the story.
   C. Make sure I can pronounce all of the words before I start.
   D. Think of a better title for the story.

Underlined responses indicate metacomprehension strategy awareness.

8. Before I begin reading, it's a good idea to:

   A. Think of what I already know about the things I see in the pictures.

   B. See how many pages are in the story.

   C. Choose the best part of the story to read again.

   D. Read the story aloud to someone.

9. Before I begin reading, it's a good idea to:

   A. Practice reading the story aloud.

   B. Retell all of the main points to make sure I can remember the story.

   C. Think of what the people in the story might be like.

   D. Decide if I have enough time to read the story.

10. Before I begin reading, it's a good idea to:

    A. Check to see if I am understanding the story so far.

    B. Check to see if the words have more than one meaning.

    C. Think about where the story might be taking place.

    D. List all of the important details.

II. In each set of four, choose the one statement which tells a good thing to do to help you understand a story better *while* you are reading it.

11. While I'm reading, it's a good idea to:

    A. Read the story very slowly so that I will not miss any important parts.

    B. Read the title to see what the story is about.

    C. Check to see if the pictures have anything missing.

    D. Check to see if the story is making sense by seeing if I can tell what's happened so far.

12. While I'm reading, it's a good idea to:

    A. Stop to retell the main points to see if I am understanding what has happened so far.

    B. Read the story quickly so that I can find out what happened.

    C. Read only the beginning and the end of the story to find out what it is about.

    D. Skip the parts that are too difficult for me.

13. While I'm reading, it's a good idea to:

    A. Look all of the big words up in the dictionary.

    B. Put the book away and find another one if things aren't making sense.

    C. Keep thinking about the title and the pictures to help me decide what is going to happen next.

    D. Keep track of how many pages I have left to read.

14. While I'm reading, it's a good idea to:

    A. Keep track of how long it is taking me to read the story.

    B. Check to see if I can answer any of the questions I asked before I started reading.

    C. Read the title to see what the story is going to be about.

    D. Add the missing details to the pictures.

15. While I'm reading, it's a good idea to:

    A. Have someone read the story aloud to me.

    B. Keep tack of how many pages I have read.

    C. List the story's main character.

    D. Check to see if my guesses are right or wrong.

16. While I'm reading, it's a good idea to:

    A. Check to see that the characters are real.

    B. Make a lot of guesses about what is going to happen next.

    C. Not look at the pictures because they might confuse me.

    D. Read the story aloud to someone

Underlined responses indicate metacomprehension strategy awareness.

17. While I'm reading, it's a good idea to:
    <u>A.</u> Try to answer the questions I asked myself.
    B. Try not to confuse what I already know with what I'm reading about.
    C. Read the story silently.
    D. Check to see if I am saying the new vocabulary words correctly.

18. While I'm reading, it's a good idea to:
    <u>A.</u> Try to see if my guesses are going to be right or wrong.
    B. Reread to be sure I haven't missed any of the words.
    C. Decide on why I am reading the story.
    D. List what happened first, second, third, and so on.

19. While I'm reading, it's a good idea to:
    A. See if I can recognize the new vocabulary words.
    B. Be careful not to skip any parts of the story.
    C. Check to see how any of the words I already know.
    <u>D.</u> Keep thinking of what I already know about the things and ideas in the story to help me decide what is going to happen.

20. While I'm reading, it's a good idea to:
    <u>A.</u> Reread some parts or read ahead to see if I can figure out what is happening if things aren't making sense.
    B. Take my time reading so that I can be sure I understand what is happening.
    C. Change the ending so that it makes sense.
    D. Check to see if there are enough pictures to help make the story ideas clear.

III. In each set of four, choose the one statement which tells a good thing to do to help you understand a story better *after* you have read it.

21. After I've read a story it's a good idea to:
    A. Count how many pages I read with no mistakes.

    B. Check to see if there were enough pictures t go with the story to make it interesting.
    <u>C.</u> Check to see if I met my purpose for reading the story.
    D. Underline the causes and effects.

22. After I've read a story it's a good idea to:
    A. Underline the main idea.
    <u>B.</u> Retell the main pints of the whole story so that I can check to see if I understood it.
    C. Read the story again to be sure I said all of the words right.
    D. Practice reading the story aloud.

23. After I've read a story it's a good idea to:
    A. Read the title and look over the story to see what it is about.
    B. Check to see if I skipped any of the vocabulary words.
    <u>C.</u> Think about what made me make good or bad predictions.
    D. Make a guess about what will happen next in the story.

24. After I've read a story it's a good idea to:
    A. Look up all of the big words in the dictionary.
    B. Read the best parts aloud.
    C. Have someone read the story aloud to me.
    <u>D.</u> Think about how the story was like things I already know about before I started reading.

25. After I've read a story it's a good idea to:
    <u>A.</u> Think about how I would have acted if I were the main character in the story.
    B. Practice reading the story silently for practice of good reading.
    C. Look over the story title and pictures to see what will happen.
    D. Make a list of the things I understood the most.

Underlined responses indicate metacomprehension strategy awareness.

Motivation to Read Profile

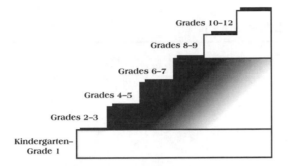

Grades 10–12
Grades 8–9
Grades 6–7
Grades 4–5
Grades 2–3
Kindergarten–
Grade 1

Level:

Second

through

Sixth Grade

Year Published: 1996

What Is It?

The *Motivation to Read Profile* (MTRP) consists of a written survey and a conversational interview designed to assess children's self-concepts as readers and the value they see in reading. The authors have drawn extensively on the research that demonstrates that self-perceived competence and task value are major determiners of both motivation and engagement in tasks. The Reading Survey is a self-report, group-administered tool, and the Conversational Interview is used one-on-one with students.

The Reading Survey assesses self-concept as a reader and value of reading. It consists of 20 items with a 4-point response scale. Ten items each are devoted to self-concept and value. The survey may be group administered and takes 15–20 minutes to complete.

The Conversational Interview consist of three sections. The first section explores motivational factors related to reading narrative texts; the second section asks questions about reading informational texts; and the third section focuses on more general factors related to reading motivation such as "your

favorite author" or "who gets you really interested and excited about reading books?"

The Reading Survey was very carefully designed. An initial pool of 100 survey items was developed in accordance with criteria such as grade-appropriateness and adequate reflection of self-concept and value placed on reading. Three reading graduate students reviewed the 100 items and the items that received 100% agreement across all three teachers were retained in the pool. Then four classroom teachers reviewed these items for measurement of self-concept and measurement of value of reading. Items that received 100% agreement across the four teachers were retained in the pool.

The final version of the survey was administered to 330 third and fifth grade students in 27 classrooms in four schools. Factor analyses were done to determine the final survey items.

Reliability coefficients establish moderately high reliability of the instrument. Validity was adequately established by comparing performance on the *Profile* with academic performance in reading.

The *Profile* and administration and scoring instructions follow in Figures 22–27. These materials are re-printed here with the permission of the author and the International Reading Association.

Figure 22   Motivation to Read Profile Reading Survey

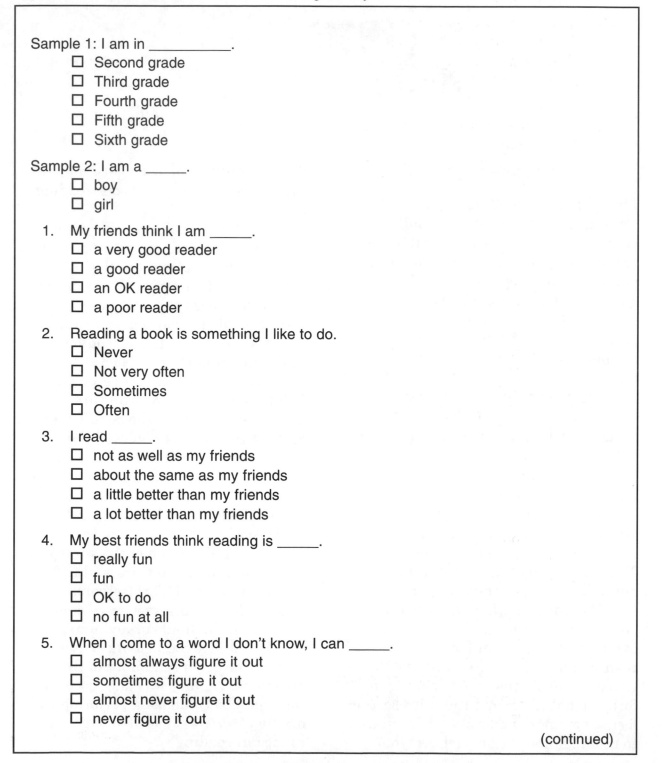

Sample 1: I am in _____.
   ☐ Second grade
   ☐ Third grade
   ☐ Fourth grade
   ☐ Fifth grade
   ☐ Sixth grade

Sample 2: I am a _____.
   ☐ boy
   ☐ girl

1. My friends think I am _____.
   ☐ a very good reader
   ☐ a good reader
   ☐ an OK reader
   ☐ a poor reader

2. Reading a book is something I like to do.
   ☐ Never
   ☐ Not very often
   ☐ Sometimes
   ☐ Often

3. I read _____.
   ☐ not as well as my friends
   ☐ about the same as my friends
   ☐ a little better than my friends
   ☐ a lot better than my friends

4. My best friends think reading is _____.
   ☐ really fun
   ☐ fun
   ☐ OK to do
   ☐ no fun at all

5. When I come to a word I don't know, I can _____.
   ☐ almost always figure it out
   ☐ sometimes figure it out
   ☐ almost never figure it out
   ☐ never figure it out

(continued)

6. I tell my friends about good books I read.
    ☐ I never do this.
    ☐ I almost never do this.
    ☐ I do this some of the time.
    ☐ I do this a lot.

7. When I am reading by myself, I understand _____.
    ☐ almost everything I read
    ☐ some of what I read
    ☐ almost none of what I read
    ☐ none of what I read

8. People who read a lot are _____.
    ☐ very interesting
    ☐ interesting
    ☐ not very interesting
    ☐ boring

9. I am _____.
    ☐ a poor reader
    ☐ an OK reader
    ☐ a good reader
    ☐ a very good reader

10. I think libraries are _____.
    ☐ a great place to spend time
    ☐ an interesting place to spend time
    ☐ an OK place to spend time
    ☐ a boring place to spend time

11. I worry about what other kids think about my reading _____.
    ☐ every day
    ☐ almost every day
    ☐ once in a while
    ☐ never

12. Knowing how to read well is _____.
    ☐ not very important
    ☐ sort of important
    ☐ important
    ☐ very important

13. When my teacher asks me a question about what I have read, I _____.
    ☐ can never think of an answer
    ☐ have trouble thinking of an answer
    ☐ sometimes think of an answer
    ☐ always think of an answer

(continued)

14.   I think reading is _____.
      ☐ a boring way to spend time
      ☐ an OK way to spend time
      ☐ an interesting way to spend time
      ☐ a great way to spend time

15.   Reading is _____.
      ☐ very easy for me
      ☐ kind of easy for me
      ☐ kind of hard for me
      ☐ very hard for me

16.   When I grow up I will spend _____.
      ☐ none of my time reading
      ☐ very little of my time reading
      ☐ some of my time reading
      ☐ a lot of my time reading

17.   When I am in a group talking about stories, I _____.
      ☐ almost never talk about my ideas
      ☐ sometimes talk about my ideas
      ☐ almost always talk about my ideas
      ☐ always talk about my ideas

18.   I would like for my teacher to read books out loud to the class _____.
      ☐ every day
      ☐ almost every day
      ☐ once in a while
      ☐ never

19.   When I read out loud I am _____.
      ☐ a poor reader
      ☐ OK reader
      ☐ good reader
      ☐ very good reader

20.   When someone gives me a book for a present, I feel _____.
      ☐ very happy
      ☐ sort of happy
      ☐ sort of unhappy
      ☐ unhappy

Figure 23   Motivation to Read Profile Conversational Interview

Name _____ Date _____

A.   Emphasis: Narrative text

Suggested prompt (designed to engage student in a natural conversation): I have been reading a good book . . . I was talking with . . . about it last night. I enjoy talking about good stories and books that I've been reading. Today I'd like to hear about what you have been reading.

1.   Tell me about the most interesting story or book you have read this week (or even last week). Take a few minutes to think about it. (Wait time.) Now, tell me about the book or story.

Probes: What else can you tell me? Is there anything else? _____

_____

_____

_____

_____

2.   How did you know or find out about this story? _____

_____

_____

☐ assigned   ☐ in school
☐ chosen   ☐ out of school

3.   Why was this story interesting to you? _____

_____

_____

_____

B.   Emphasis: Informational text

Suggested prompt (designed to engage student in a natural conversation): Often we read to find out about something or to learn about something. We read for information. For example, I remember a student of mine . . . who read a lot of books about . . . to find out as much as he/she could about . . . . Now, I'd like to hear about some of the informational reading you have been doing.

1.   Think about something important that you learned recently, not from your teacher and not from television, but from a book or some other reading material. What did you read about? (Wait time.) Tell me about what you learned.

(continued)

Probes: What else could you tell me? Is there anything else? _____

_____

_____

_____

2.   How did you know or find out about this book/article? _____

_____

_____

☐ assigned   ☐ in school
☐ chosen   ☐ out of school

3.   Why was this book (or article) important to you? _____

_____

_____

_____

C.   Emphasis: General reading

1.   Did you read anything at home yesterday? _____ What? _____

_____

_____

2.   Do you have any books at school (in your desk/storage area/locker/book bag) today
that you are reading? _____ Tell me about them. _____

_____

_____

_____

3.   Tell me about your favorite author. _____

_____

_____

_____

4.   What do you think you have to learn to be a better reader? _____

_____

_____

_____

(continued)

5. Do you know about any books right now that you'd like to read? Tell me about them.

_____

_____

_____

6. How did you find out about these books? _____

_____

_____

7. What are some things that get you really excited about reading books? _____

_____

_____

Tell me about . . .

_____

_____

8. Who gets you really interested and excited about reading books?

_____

Tell me more about what they do.

_____

_____

Figure 24   Teacher Directions: Reading Survey

Distribute copies of the Reading Survey. Ask students to write their names on the space provided.

Say:

     I am going to read some sentences to you. I want to know how you feel about your reading. There are no right or wrong answers. I really want to know how you honestly feel about reading.

     I will read each sentence twice. Do not mark your answer until I tell you to. The first time I read the sentence I want you to think about the best answer for you. The second time I read the sentence I want you to fill in the space beside your best answer. Mark only one answer. Remember: Do not mark your answer until I tell you to. OK, let's begin.

Read the first sample item.

Say:
Sample 1: I am in (pause) first grade, (pause) second grade, (pause) third grade, (pause) fourth grade, (pause) fifth grade, (pause) sixth grade.

Read the first sample again.

Say:
This time as I read the sentence, mark the answer that is right for you. I am in (pause) first grade, (pause) second grade, (pause) third grade, (pause) fourth grade, (pause) fifth grade, (pause) sixth grade.

Read the second sample item.

Say:
Sample 2: I am a (pause) boy, (pause) girl.

Say:
Now, get ready to mark your answer.
I am a (pause) boy, (pause) girl.

Read the remaining items in the same way (e.g., number _____, sentence stem followed by a pause, each option followed by a pause, and then give specific directions for students to mark their answers while you repeat the entire item).

Figure 25   Scoring Directions: Reading Survey

The survey has 20 items based on a 4-point scale. The highest total score possible is 80 points. On some items the response options are ordered least positive to most positive (see item 2 below), with the least positive response option having a value of 1 point and the most positive option having a point value of 4. On other items, however, the response options are reversed (see item 1 below). In those cases it will be necessary to recode the response options. Items where recoding is required are starred on the scoring sheet.

Example: Here is how Maria completed items 1 and 2 on the Reading Survey.

1. My friends think I am _____.
    ☐ a very good reader
    ◼ a good reader
    ☐ an OK reader
    ☐ a poor reader

2. Reading a book is something I like to do.
    ☐ Never
    ☐ Not very often
    ☐ Sometimes
    ◼ Often

To score item 1 it is first necessary to recode the response options so that
    a poor reader equals 1 point,
    an OK reader equals 2 points,
    a good reader equals 3 points, and
    a very good rider equals 4 points.

Since Maria answered that she Is a good *reader* the point value for that item, 3, is entered on the first line of the Self-Concept column on the scoring sheet. See below.
    The response options for item 2 are ordered least positive (1 point) to most positive (4 points), so scoring item 2 is easy. Simply enter the point value associated with Maria's response. Because Maria selected the fourth option, a 4 is entered for item 2 under the Value of Reading column on the scoring sheet. See below.

Scoring sheet

Self-Concept as a Reader   Value of Reading
*recode 1.<u>3</u>   2.<u>4</u>

To calculate the Self-Concept raw score and Value raw score add all student responses in the respective column. The Full Survey raw score is obtained by combining the column raw scores. To convert the raw scores to percentage scores, divide student raw scores by the total possible score (40 for each subscale, 80 for the full survey).

Figure 26 Reading Survey Scoring Sheet

Student name _____

Grade _____ Teacher _____

Administration date _____

Recoding scale
1 = 4
2 = 3
3 = 2
4 = 1

Self-Concept as a Reader

*recode	1. _____	
	3. _____	
*recode	5. _____	
*recode	7. _____	
	9. _____	
*recode	11. _____	
	13. _____	
*recode	15. _____	
	17. _____	
	19. _____	

SC raw score: /40

Value of Reading

	2. _____	
*recode	4. _____	
	6. _____	
*recode	8. _____	
*recode	10. _____	
	12. _____	
	14. _____	
	16. _____	
*recode	18. _____	
*recode	20. _____	

V raw score: /40

Full survey raw score (Self-Concept & Value). /80

Percentage scores   Self-Concept [____]

                           Value   [____]

                           Full Survey   [____]

Comments: _____

_____

_____

_____

Figure 27   Teacher Directions: Conversational Interview

1. Duplicate the Conversational Interview so that you have a form for each child.

2. Choose in advance the sections or specific questions you want to ask from the Conversational Interview. Reviewing the information on students' Reading Surveys may provide information about additional questions that could be added to the interview.

3. Familiarize yourself with the basic questions provided in the interview prior to the interview session in order to establish a more conversational setting.

4. Select a quiet corner of the room and a calm period of the day for the interview.

5. Allow ample time for conducting the Conversational Interview.

6. Follow up on interesting comments and responses to gain a fuller understanding of students' reading experiences.

7. Record students' responses in as much detail as possible. If time and resources permit you may want to audiotape answers to A1 and B1 to be transcribed after the interview for more in-depth analysis.

8. Enjoy this special time with each student!

How Does the *Motivation to Read Profile* Inform Instruction?

By using the Reading Survey, you can very quickly and quite easily determine which of your learners see themselves positively as readers and value reading. Likewise, you can also determine which of your learners view themselves negatively as readers and/or do not value reading. If a student indicated on the Reading Survey that "I read not as well as my friends" and that "reading is boring," you could perhaps pair this child with a "reading buddy" of like-accomplishment and help them locate texts that can be read with ease.

If you have a child who scores low both on self-concept as a reader and value of reading, you will know that you must intervene to help turn the perceptions around. While this will be painfully slow, in most cases, it is extremely important. Having this child take the "author's chair" in a lower-grade classroom to share his or her work and talk about the writing may be a useful strategy here.

A child who scores lower on the value scale than the self-concept scale may benefit from work in a cooperative learning group where other students are seen taking advantage of reading to accomplish tasks. Perhaps readers' theater would be beneficial to this child.

Analysis of single items on the survey across all of your students may be useful. For example, if several of your students indicate that "When I come to a word I don't know, I can never figure it out," you might pull that group together and explore their word attack ability or their use of reading strategies.

The Conversational Interview will help you identify the kinds of reading tasks your students find most interesting. You can then build on this interest. You may discover particular reading topics or reading activities that a majority of your class would enjoy and value.

What Are the Advantages of the *Motivation to Read Profile?*

The MTRP offers you a quick way to gain insight into the self-perceptions of your students as readers and the extent to which they value reading. The Conversational Interview assists you in probing for greater insight than the survey along produces.

The *Reading Teacher* article in which the profile is presented offers an informative review of the research undergirding self-perception and valuing of reading as a function of motivation. The reference list identifies helpful sources for deepening and ex-

tending your understanding of these concepts.

What Are the Disadvantages of the *Motivation to Read Profile?*

Inherent in any self-report instrument is the possibility that students will make answers on the survey, or offer verbal responses in the interview, that reflect what they think you want them to say, rather than their true beliefs.

The interview can substantiate survey responses to some extent, but your careful observation of your learners over time and across a variety of reading activities will provide the best information about motivation.

Where Do I Get More Information About the *Motivation to Read Profile?*

Gambrell, L. B., Palmer, B. M., Codling, R. M., & Mazzoni, S. A. (1996). Assessing motivation to read. *The Reading Teacher, 49,* 518–533.

An Observation Survey of Early Literacy Achievement

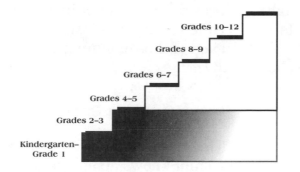

Grades 10–12
Grades 8–9
Grades 6–7
Grades 4–5
Grades 2–3
Kindergarten–Grade 1

Level:

Kindergarten

through

Grade 2

Year Published: 1993

What Is It?

An Observation Survey (AOS) is a set of systematic observation measures that you can use to guide your observations of individual student's work on tasks related to learning to read and write. The Survey, devised by Marie Clay, is widely used in New Zealand and is gaining popularity in the United States. As Reading Recovery programs become more widespread, more and more American teachers are becoming familiar with the tool.

AOS is written for classroom teachers who want to become careful observers of young children as they learn to read and write. The Survey will also be useful to teachers who work one-on-one with children who are having difficulty in learning to read and write. Clay makes it clear that training must accompany any attempts to use the observation tasks. She urges that you and a group of colleagues begin using the tasks together and dialoguing about your experiences and what you are learning.

Clay says that in order to plan effective instruction, we need answers to two basic questions: "What typically occurs for children like those I teach as learning takes place over the school year?" and "How is this individual child changing over time in relation to what typically occurs?" (Clay, 1993, p. 3). AOS is intended to help you make the observations necessary to answer these questions. Through the observation tasks, you will be able to observe children's responses for competencies and confusions, for strengths and weaknesses, for the processes and strategies used, and for evidence of what the child already knows.

AOS consists of six distinct and carefully defined tasks. Each is described below as they are defined in the manual.

Running Records

This is considered the pivotal task among all of the observation tasks in AOS. The running record is your observation and recording of all the child's behaviors as he or she is reading text aloud. Using a standard set of conventions, the oral reading is coded. A check for directional movement is made. Errors (miscues) are analyzed to see what kinds of information sources in the print (cueing systems) are used. The analysis consists of asking: Meaning— Does the child use meaning? Does what he reads make sense even though it might be inaccurate? Structure—Is what he said possible in an English sentence? Visual information—Does he use visual information from the letters and words, or the layout of print?

Next you check to see if you can determine the use of any cross-checking strategies. In cross-checking, two sources of information are used and one is checked against the other. For example, he may predict the reading of a word and then check what he said against the letters in the printed word. Next, an analysis is done of any self-corrections. Here you study the kinds of information the reader was using up to the point at which the error occurred, and then examine what additional information may have been used to make the self-correction. Finally, an error rate, accuracy percentage, and self-correction rate is calculated for the reading of easy texts, instructional texts, and hard texts. Conversion tables are included to assist you in these calculations. (Please refer to Running Records on p. 123 in this Handbook).

Letter Identification

This task permits you to observe what letters the child knows and can identify. Large print alphabets of both upper- and lower-case letters are supplied. The manual offers suggestions for you to use as prompts. Three kinds of responses are scored as correct: an alphabet name; a sound that is acceptable for that letter; and a re-

sponse saying "it begins like . . .", giving an accurate example of a word with that beginning letter. Tables for converting raw scores to stanine scores are provided both for children in Ohio and children in New Zealand, for this and each of the remaining tasks except *Writing*.

Concepts About Print

This task permits you to observe what a child knows about the way we print languages. Most of the items tell you something about what the child is attending to on the printed page. Concepts that are tested here are: the front of the book; that print and not pictures tell the story; that there are letters and clusters of letters called words; that there are first letters and last letters in words; the function of spaces; and the function of punctuation marks. Two booklets are required to do these tasks. They are *Sand* (Clay, 1972) and *Stones* (Clay, 1979).

Word Tests

This task permits you to observe the high frequency words the reader knows that are drawn from the "Ready to Read" series of instructional materials used in New Zealand. The manual offers a second version of the Word Test, The Ohio Word Test. This version was constructed from high frequency words found in the Dolch Word List. Clay suggests that the test may be used to indicate the extent to which a child is accumulating a reading vocabulary during the first year in school. Repeated testings will indicate the extent to which growth in reading vocabulary is occurring.

Writing

This task will help you observe examples of the child's writing behavior. You can make judgments about letter formation, the number of letter forms known, and the number of words known and correctly written. Here we can observe the child's knowledge of letters and of left-to-right sequencing. This task suggests that you take three samples of the child's stories on consecutive days or for three consecutive weeks and rate them for level of linguistic organization (from letters only to multiple sentences and themes); for message quality (from uses and invents letters to successful composition); and for directional principles (from no evidence of directional knowledge to extensive text with good arrangement and spacing). Each of the three dimensions is rated on a scale from 1 to 6. A rating of 1–4 in any category is evaluated as not yet satisfactory. A rating of 5–6 is evaluated as probably satisfactory.

Writing Vocabulary

This task permits you to observe all the words a child can write in a 10-minute period. The child is asked to write his or her name and then "all of the words you know how to write." The manual offers prompts you can use for children who are reluctant to do this. Clay states that this task has high test/retest reliability and a high relationship with reading words in isolation. No data are offered. In scoring this task, each completed word correctly spelled is given one point. Reversed letters are scored as correct when the intended letters are clear. The Writing Vocabulary task is inap-

propriate for older children who can write 50 or more words.

Hearing and Recording Sounds in Words (Dictation Task)

In this task, you can observe the child's recording of a sentence you dictate. The task is scored on the basis of the child's ability to hear the sounds in the words he or she wants to write. Scoring involves counting the child's representation of the sounds (phonemes) by the letters (graphemes). In doing this task, you select one of five alternative sentences. The child is given credit for every correctly written phoneme/grapheme correspondence whether the word is correctly spelled or not.

The manual concludes with a chapter on the summarization of the Survey results. This is particularly helpful in that it guides you in analyzing the strategies the child uses on the text, with words and with letters and sounds. Both useful and problem strategies are identified.

How Does *An Observation Survey* Inform Instruction?

Many of us want to maximize the information we get from observing our children at work as readers and writers. AOS becomes an "on the job training manual" for those of us who want to become better kid watchers. Each of the tests or tasks within the survey, once you have used them, will change the way you look at readers and writers in the future.

The *Survey* will become a rich source of information for you to include in anecdotal records and checklists. It will provide you with the information necessary to planning essential next step instruction and to placing learners in groups for that instruction.

I suggest that as you begin to use this tool that you move into it slowly. Try not to do too much at once. You might set goals such as, "Today I will observe _____, _____, and _____." It works best if you team up with a colleague who agrees to implement the *Survey* at the same time as you. This way you can compare notes, share accomplishments, and work through challenges together.

With some of your learners you will need to use only selected tasks within the survey. It will be useful to use the complete survey with some of your learners. Perhaps you will want to begin with those learners about whom you are most puzzled as readers and writers.

As you become more adept at observing the work of your children, you will need to carefully plan time into each day not only to use aspects of the survey, but to roam the room as they are working so that you can maximize your observations.

What Are the Advantages of *An Observation Survey?*

In the manual, Clay makes the following statement: "In developmental psychology young children were always studied by direct observation. Studies of how children learn to speak have been exciting, and so have the more recent studies of young children learning to read and write. But teachers must go beyond reactions like 'Ooh! Ah!,' or 'I am surprised!' and 'Isn't that cute!' and try to understand what is happening and why it is happening"

(Clay, 1993, p. 3). Herein lies the greatest advantage of the survey. The tasks help you become a better, more informed observer of your students as readers and writers. Clay offers a thoughtful and informative chapter on the reading and writing processes.

The manual is highly readable and very complete. Directions for administration and interpretation of each of the tasks are easy to use. Clear and useful forms for recording data and interpreting it are included for reproduction and use. Stanine scores are offered for all but the Running Record and Writing tasks. These scores may be useful in tracking growth over time. However, the real advantage of AOS is that, unlike most tests that look at achievement, these tasks give you the opportunity to carefully observe children behaving as readers and writers, meeting challenges as they do the real-life work of readers and writers.

What Are the Disadvantages of *An Observation Survey?*

The *Survey* is not an instrument you can just pick up and use. It requires that you have a rather extensive understanding of the reading process—including the cueing systems—and the writing process. It takes careful study and practice.

The manual offers very limited information on the establishment of the validity and reliability of the instruments. While Cronbach Alpha or Pearson coefficients are given as reliability measures on the Ohio data, the information about the subjects in these studies is essentially useless.

While there is a measure of accuracy noted with the Running Record, no measure of comprehension is included. The ability of a reader to retell the passage in a free response mode or with assisting questions may be of greater interest to you than the percentages of accuracy. This seems to be an important disadvantage of the survey.

The usefulness of the Word Test is highly doubtful. Unless American teachers are using the "Ready to Read" material, the original version of the task would be of little use. The Ohio version is drawn from the Dolch list of high frequency words. Teachers using real literature in beginning reading programs may not find the Dolch list words to be indicative of the reading vocabulary their students are developing.

Where Do I Get More Information About *An Observation Survey?*

Clay, M. M. (1972). *Sand—the concepts about print test.* Auckland, NZ: Heinemann Publishers.

Clay, M. M. (1979). *Stones—the concepts about print test.* Auckland, NZ: Heinemann Publishers.

Clay, M. M. (1989). Concepts about print: In English and other languages. *The Reading Teacher, 42,* 268–277.

Clay, M. M. (1991). *Becoming literate: The construction of inner control.* Portsmouth, NH: Heinemann.

Clay, M. M. (1993). *An observation survey of early literacy achievement.* Portsmouth, NH: Heinemann.

Clay, M. M. (1998). *By different paths to common outcomes.* York, ME: Stenhouse Publishers.

Qualitative Reading Inventory–II

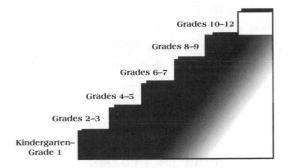

Grades 10–12
Grades 8–9
Grades 6–7
Grades 4–5
Grades 2–3
Kindergarten–
Grade 1

Level:

Kindergarten

through

Junior High School

Year Published: 1995

What Is It?

The *Qualitative Reading Inventory–II* (QRI II) is an individually administered informal reading inventory that provides both qualitative and quantitative analysis of reading performance using word lists, and narrative and expository texts. At each level the authors, Leslie and Caldwell, have provided the means to assess background knowledge for the particular topic and the assessment of comprehension through both retellings and questioning. The QRI II provides the traditional quantitative scores (independent, instructional, frustration), but you are encouraged to evaluate these scores in light of the reader's background knowledge, the type of text read, and the means of assessing comprehension. Therefore, the inventory is called Qualitative. Leslie and Caldwell suggest that the instrument may be used by classroom teachers to estimate reading levels, match students to appropriate texts, as data for reading portfolios, and to verify a suspected problem. They further suggest that the inventory can be used by the reading

assessment specialist to determine reading level and describe specific reading behavior as a guide for instructional intervention (Leslie & Caldwell, 1995, p. 20).

The design of the inventory is research-based. The authors have conducted a thorough review of the research on early reading assessment, factors related to comprehension, and factors related to word identification in designing the QRI–II. They offer rationales for their design decisions based upon research in the reading field, generally within the last fifteen years.

The QRI–II contains graded word lists and graded passages ranging from preprimer level through junior high. The word lists are used to assess accuracy of word identification, to assess speed and automaticity of word identification, and to determine the starting point for reading the graded passages. About the somewhat controversial issue of using the word lists as one measure of automaticity, the authors state: "Some may argue that use of word lists for assessment is not an authentic task. We agree. Readers do not curl up with a good list of words. However, the ability to identify words accurately and quickly out of context is a characteristic of the skilled reader. Therefore, use of the word lists may provide an important piece of assessment information. Readers who take more than one second to accurately identify a word may not have achieved automaticity for that word" (p. 9). The passages are used to determine functional reading levels for word identification in context, for comprehension in context, to assess the reader's ability to read different types of texts, and to comprehend in both silent and oral reading.

Further, the passages are used to assess prior knowledge related to the passage topic, to do oral reading miscue analysis, to measure comprehension through unaided recall, to measure comprehension through questioning, to evaluate automaticity, and to assess strategic reading. The strategic reading assessment includes an examination of which comprehension questions missed initially can be correctly answered when the student is encouraged to look back at the text. The strategic reading assessment can also be used to analyze think-aloud procedures, note-taking ability, the use of context, and listening comprehension.

Unique to the QRI–II is the scoring of background knowledge and prediction making prior to reading the passages. The manual offers a set of exemplar statements for scoring the responses to the background information questions on a scale of 0 to 3. The authors state that their experience suggests that students who score at least 55% of the possible points on the background knowledge task, score above 70% on the comprehension ques-

tions on the same passage. Actual statements made by average readers in the pilot studies are offered as exemplars for scoring the prediction statements. The predictions are rated on a scale of 0 to 3 depending on the number of idea statements the reader predicts that are in the passage. The authors state that prediction-making is a skill that can be modeled and taught, and therefore should be evaluated.

The manual offers two kinds of forms for analysis of the data. The "Student Profile Sheet" is used to record word identification, oral reading, and silent reading data across the lists and passages. The "Comparisons: Describing Specific Reading Behaviors" form is used to compare a student's reading behavior across different contexts. Specific questions are asked to guide your analysis of the student's behavior in both word identification and comprehension.

Pilot research was conducted over a two-year period. A sample of 213 children in Kindergarten through Grade 8 were used. Normative data were used, where available, from both the *California Achievement Test* and the *Iowa Test of Basic Skills*. The manual offers detailed descriptions of these pilot studies and the development of the word identification tasks, the development of the prior knowledge assessment tasks, the development of the measures of comprehension, and the development of the passages. Reliability of the QRI–II was determined through measures of interscorer reliability, internal consistency and alternate-form reliability. Correlation coefficients consistently were in the .98–.99 range for interscorer reliability. The data on internal consistency suggest that, if a student consistently receives scores that differ by as much as 50%, you can reliably conclude that he or she is better at answering one kind of question than another. Alternate-form reliability tests yielded coefficients all above .80, and 75% of them were above .90. In establishing construct validity, the authors demonstrate evidence that the QRI II measures at least two constructs that are generally agreed to be central to the reading process: word recognition and comprehension.

How Does the *Qualitative Reading Inventory–II* Inform Instruction?

You can use the inventory to determine functional reading levels, but you can learn a great deal more about your students. You can determine your student's strengths and needs as you carefully analyze why a student is not reading well. The authors have provided a comprehensive set of questions to guide your analysis. They are:

Can the student identify words accurately?

Can the student identify words automatically?

When reading orally, does the student:

Correct word identification errors that do not make sense?

Make word identification errors that are contextually appropriate?

Make word identification errors that suggest use of graphic or letter clues?

Can the student comprehend successfully in:

Narrative material?

Expository material?

Familiar material?

Unfamiliar material?

Material with pictures?

Material without pictures?

What is the quality of the student's recall?

Does the student organize recall in stories according to elements of the story structure?

Does the student organize recall in exposition according to main idea and details? (p. 18)

As a classroom teacher, you will find the QRI–II useful in estimating a student's reading level, in matching students to text, for information to include in reading portfolios, and to dig deeper into a suspected reading problem. As a reading specialist, you will be able to use the QRI–II as a source of information for intervention instruction.

What Are the Advantages of the *Qualitative Reading Inventory–II*?

The greatest advantage of the QRI–II is that it profiles the strengths and learning needs of a reader using different types of text according to the reader's prior knowledge. The considerations for prior knowledge, predictions, text type, retellings, and miscue analysis place this inventory squarely on the cutting edge of the most recent research and theory on reading and reading instruction.

The authors present a very thorough and scholarly review of the pertinent research literature that informed their design of the instrument. By carefully reading the manual, you can know why each aspect of the instrument is included. The instrument also affords a variety of assessment purposes and options.

The QRI–II yields an analysis of word recognition in which only uncorrected, meaning-changing miscues are counted. This measure is called an Acceptable Accuracy score. It is based on a qualitative analysis of miscues, and gives a much more fair and reasonable measure of word recognition accuracy than the traditional practice of counting every error with equal weight.

The manual is well-written and very complete. The QRI–II is clearly one of the best-documented informal reading inventories available.

What Are the Disadvantages of the *Qualitative Reading Inventory–II?*

While Leslie and Caldwell have certainly succeeded in developing a qualitative instrument, there is one instruction in the "Counting Oral Reading Miscues" section (p. 52) of the manual that flies in the face of the theoretical orientation that drives the instrument. The authors say, "The examiner can determine independent, instructional, and frustration levels by counting all miscues. We call this Total Accuracy. Or the examiner may choose to count only those miscues which change or distort passage meaning. We call this Total Acceptability. It is not necessary to do both. The diagnostic philosophy of the examiner will determine which scoring system

to use."

For much of the forty-year history of informal reading inventories, a total accuracy count was in vogue. We counted every oral reading error with equal weight. No consideration was made of the degree to which the errors (now called miscues) altered meaning. One must wonder for how many children we underestimated what they could read with understanding because of this practice. Our more recent understandings of the reading process lead us to believe that even the most fluent readers make mistakes when they read. Our goal is not "mistakeless" oral reading. Our goal is miscues that do not significantly alter meaning in light of the purpose for reading. It is troublesome that Leslie and Caldwell presented the traditional, "total accuracy" measure as equally acceptable as the "acceptable accuracy" measure.

When using an informal reading inventory to determine instructional reading level for placement, care must be exercised. While the instrument will yield an indication of instructional level, the student's reading performance on actual instructional material should be the final determiner. Nevertheless, the criteria for determining instructional level are important. Leslie and Caldwell suggest that, on oral reading passages where the word recognition score is instructional and the comprehension score is independent, the total passage level should be considered instructional. This may place too much emphasis on the word recognition score and result in instructional placement that is lower than appropriate. You should exercise considerable caution in following this guideline.

Where Do I Get More Information About the *Qualitative Reading Inventory–II?*

Caldwell, J. (1985). A new look at the old informal reading inventory. *The Reading Teacher, 39,* 168–173.

Leslie, L. (1993). A developmental-interactive approach to reading assessment. *Reading and Writing Quarterly, 9,* 5–30.

Leslie, L., & Caldwell, J. (1995). *Qualitative reading inventory–II.* New York: HarperCollins College Publishers.

Reader Self-Perception Scale

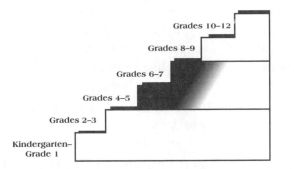

Level:

Grades Four

through

Six

Year Published: 1995

What Is It?

The *Reader Self-Perception Scale* (RSPS) is an instrument to measure how intermediate-grade learners feel about themselves as readers. The scale is based on a theory of self-efficacy which states that a person's judgments of his or her ability to perform an activity affects the way in which the activity is performed. Children who have made positive associations with reading see themselves as better readers and therefore read more often, for greater lengths of time, and with greater efficiency. The authors of the scale state that "self-efficacy judgments are thought to affect achievement by influencing an individual's choice of activities, task avoidance, effort expenditure, and goal persistence" (Henk & Melnick, 1995, p. 471).

The authors identify four sources of information that intermediate grade children use to make reader self-perception judgments. These four overlapping sources of information make up the scale. They are:

- *Progress* (PR)—One's perception of present reading performance compared with past performance.

- *Observational Comparison* (OC)—How a child perceives his or her reading performance to compare with the performance of classmates.

- *Social Feedback* (SF)—Direct or indirect input about reading from teachers, classmates, and family members.

- *Physiological States* (PS)—Internal feelings the child experiences during reading.

The RSPS consists of one general item designed to prompt children to think about their reading ability and 32 additional items covering the four sources of information described above. Students are asked to indicate their degree of agreement on a five-point scale to statements that deal with overall reading ability, aspects of word recognition, word analysis, fluency and comprehension. In Figure 28, the authors suggest that before duplicating the instrument you cover or remove the bracketed source of information codes.

Data on the norming sample are not provided by the authors. However, descriptive statistics by scale and grade level are given. You derive a raw score for each of the four scales, and then compare your student's score with the mean for his or her grade level (see Figure 29). For example, if your fourth-grade student had a raw score of 34 on the Progress (PR) scale you would compare that in Figure 30 with the mean fourth grade score of 39.6. Because your student scored more than one standard deviation (SD) below the mean for his grade level, you may conclude that his perception of his progress as a reader compared to his past performance is in the low range.

Reliability of the instrument has been well established through internal consistency coefficients. The construct validity of the instrument is established through linkage to well re-garded learning theory and research in the affective domain.

The Reader Self-Perception Scale (Figure 28), the *Reader Self-Perception Scale Directions for Administration, Scoring and Interpretation* (Figure 29), and the *Reader Self-Perception Scale Scoring Sheet* (Figure 30) are reprinted here with the permission of the authors and the International Reading Association.

How Does the *Reader Self-Perception Scale* Inform Instruction?

You will interpret each of your learner's scores on each of the four scales as either "high, average or low." In the case described above where a child's perception of current performance is lower than his perception of his past performance, this would be a good time to have a one-on-one conference with the child and try to learn why he feels this way. You may gain insight into some instructional changes you can make on his behalf.

You could administer the scale in the fall and again in the spring to learn how your students' self-percep-tions changed over the school year. If these data became part of a portfolio, you could track such progress from year to year.

Perhaps the most instructionally useful application is in the instance where you establish a goal of improv-ing your learners' self-perceptions as readers. If your goal is, for example, to better match reading interests to texts, to be sure that children are reading at their instructional level, to provide ample time for recreational reading, and to build excitement about books and reading throughout the year, you might administer the scale several times across the year to monitor progress.

What Are the Advantages of the *Reader Self-Perception* Scale?

The scale is well grounded in the theory and research on self-perception and motivation. It can be easily admin-istered to groups of learners.

What Are the Disadvantages of the *Reader Self-Perception Scale?*

The scale yields only a general indica-tion of a child's self-perception of read-ing ability and must be used along with your own observations, work samples, and conversations with your learners. Further, like all self-report assessment tools, students may tell you

Figure 28 Reader Self-Perception Scale

Listed below are statements about reading. Please read each statement carefully. Then circle the letters that show how much you agree or disagree with the statement. Use the following:

    SA = Strongly Agree
    A   = Agree
    U   = Undecided
    D   = Disagree
    SD = Strongly Disagree

Example: **I think pizza with pepperoni is the best.**   SA   A   U   D   SD

If you are *really positive* that pepperoni pizza is best, circle SA (Strongly Agree).
If you *think* that it is good but maybe not great, circle A (Agree).
If you *can't decide* whether or not it is best, circle U (undecided).
If you *think* that pepperoni pizza is not all that good, circle D (Disagree).
If you are *really positive* that pepperoni pizza is not very good, circle SD (Strongly Disagree).

	1.	I think I am a good reader.	SA	A	U	D	SD
[SF]	2.	I can tell that my teacher likes to listen to me read.	SA	A	U	D	SD
[SF]	3.	My teacher thinks that my reading is fine.	SA	A	U	D	SD
[OC]	4.	I read faster than other kids.	SA	A	U	D	SD
[PS]	5.	I like to read aloud.	SA	A	U	D	SD
[OC]	6.	When I read, I can figure out words better than other kids.	SA	A	U	D	SD
[SF]	7.	My classmates like to listen to me read.	SA	A	U	D	SD
[PS]	8.	I feel good inside when I read.	SA	A	U	D	SD
[SF]	9.	My classmates think that I read pretty well.	SA	A	U	D	SD
[PR]	10.	When I read, I don't have to try as hard as I used to.	SA	A	U	D	SD
[OC]	11.	I seem to know more words than other kids when I read.	SA	A	U	D	SD
[SF]	12.	People in my family think I am a good reader.	SA	A	U	D	SD
[PR]	13.	I am getting better at reading.	SA	A	U	D	SD

[OC]	14.	I understand what I read as well as other kids do.	SA A U D SD
[PR]	15.	When I read, I need less help than I used to.	SA A U D SD
[PS]	16.	Reading makes me feel happy inside.	SA A U D SD
[SF]	17.	My teacher thinks I am a good reader.	SA A U D SD
[PR]	18.	Reading is easier for me than it used to be.	SA A U D SD
[PR]	19.	I read faster than I could before.	SA A U D SD
[OC]	20.	I read better than other kids in my class.	SA A U D SD
[PS]	21.	I feel calm when I read.	SA A U D SD
[OC]	22.	I read more than other kids.	SA A U D SD
[PR]	23.	I understand what I read better than I could before.	SA A U D SD
[PR]	24.	I can figure out words better than I could before.	SA A U D SD
[PS]	25.	I feel comfortable when I read.	SA A U D SD
[PS]	26.	I think reading is relaxing.	SA A U D SD
[PR]	27.	I read better now than I could before.	SA A U D SD
[PR]	28.	When I read, I recognize more words than I used to.	SA A U D SD
[PS]	29.	Reading makes me feel good.	SA A U D SD
[SF]	30.	Other kids think I'm a good reader.	SA A U D SD
[SF]	31.	People in my family think I read pretty well.	SA A U D SD
[PS]	32.	I enjoy reading.	SA A U D SD
[SF]	33.	People in my family like to listen to me read.	SA A U D SD

Figure 29   Reader Self-Perception Scale Directions for Administration, Scoring and Interpretation

The Reader Self-Perception Scale (RSPS) is intended to provide an assessment of how children feel about themselves as readers. The scale consists of 33 items that assess self-perceptions along four dimensions of self-efficacy (Progress, Observational Comparison, Social Feedback, and Physiological States). Children are asked to indicate how strongly they agree or disagree with each statement on a 5-point scale (5 = Strongly Agree, 1 = Strongly Disagree). The information gained from this scale can be used to devise ways to enhance children's self-esteem in reading and, ideally, to increase their motivation to read. The following directions explain specifically what you are to do.

Administration

For the results to be of any use, the children must: (a) understand exactly what they are to do, (b) have sufficient time to complete all items, and (c) respond honestly and thoughtfully. Briefly explain to the children that they are being asked to complete a questionnaire about reading. Emphasize that this is not a *test* and that there are no *right* answers. Tell them that they should be as honest as possible because their responses will be confidential. Ask the children to fill in their names, grade levels, and classrooms as appropriate. Read the directions aloud and work through the example with the students as a group. Discuss the response options and make sure that all children understand the rating scale before moving on. It is important that children know that they may raise their hands to ask questions about any words or ideas they do not understand.

The children should then read each item and circle their response for the item. They should work at their own pace. Remind the children that they should be sure to respond to all items. When all items are completed, the children should stop, put their pencils down. and wait for further instructions. Care should be taken that children who work more slowly are not disturbed by children who have already finished.

Scoring

To score the RSPS, enter the following point values for each response on the RSPS scoring sheet (Strongly Agree = 5, Agree = 4, Undecided = 3, Disagree = 2. Strongly Disagree = 1) for each item number under the appropriate scale. Sum each column to obtain a raw score for each of the four specific scales.

Interpretation

Each scale is interpreted in relation to its total possible score. For example, because the RSPS uses a 5-point scale and the Progress scale consists of 9 items, the highest total score for Progress is 45 (9 x 5 = 45). Therefore, a score that would fall approximately in the middle of the range (22-23) would indicate a child's somewhat indifferent perception of her or himself as a reader with respect to Progress. Note that each scale has a different possible total raw score (Progress = 45, Observational Comparison = 30, Social Feedback = 45. and Physiological States = 40) and should be interpreted accordingly.

Figure 30   Reader Self-Perception Scale Scoring Sheet

Student name _____

Teacher _____

Grade _____   Date _____

Scoring key: 5 = Strongly Agree (SA)
4 = Agree (A)
3 = Undecided (U)
2 = Disagree (D)
1 = Strongly Disagree (SD)

Scales

General Perception	Progress	Observational Comparison	Social Feedback	Physiological States
1. _____	10. _____	4. _____	2. _____	5. _____
	13. _____	6. _____	3. _____	8. _____
	15. _____	11. _____	7. _____	16. _____
	18. _____	14. _____	9. _____	21. _____
	19. _____	20. _____	12. _____	25. _____
	23. _____	22. _____	17. _____	26. _____
	24. _____		30. _____	29. _____
	27. _____		31. _____	32. _____
	28. _____		33. _____	
Raw score	_____ of 45	_____ of 30	_____ of 45	_____ of 40

Score interpretation

High	44+	26+	38+	37+
Average	39	21	33	31
Low	34	16	27	25

what they think you want to hear rather than what they truly believe. This further increases the importance of you using observations and other sources of data to support or refute information learned from the scale.

The number of items for each of the scales is sufficiently low as to suggest that you might place more credibility in an overall evaluation rather than individual scale scores.

Data are not presented on the norming sample which makes it impossible for you to judge the validity of the norms for your students.

Where Do I Get More Information About the *Reader Self-Perception Scale?*

Henk, W. A., & Melnick, S. A. (1995). The reader self-perception scale (RSPS): A new tool for measuring how children feel about themselves as readers. *The Reading Teacher, 48,* 470–481.

Reading Miscue Inventory:
Alternative Procedures

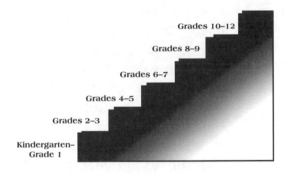

Level:

Primary

through

Adult

Year Published: 1987

What Is It?

The *Reading Miscue Inventory* (RMI) is a set of procedures for recording and analyzing the miscues a reader makes during oral reading. The authors, Goodman, Watson and Burke, assert that teachers are more easily able to make changes in their reading curriculum when they have "a window on the reading process" (Goodman, Watson, & Burke, 1987, p. ix). Miscue analysis gives you this window on the reading process. Through miscue analysis you are able to determine what a reader understands about the reading process, the way the reader uses the cueing systems, and how effectively the reader monitors use of the process. Miscue analysis helps you understand how a reader transacts with a text in order to build meaning. Through miscue analysis, you are able to see how a reader's language, thought, and experiences function in reading. The RMI offers explanations of general procedures for data collection, general procedures for analyzing miscues, and four alternative procedures for analyzing miscues.

The authors identify four purposes for using the RMI that are especially helpful to teachers (p. 8):

- Determine the varying causes of miscues.

- Highlight the strengths of high-quality miscues.

- Pinpoint specific and repetitive problems.

- Distinguish these problems from difficulties caused by the syntactic complexity or conceptual load of the reading material.

Of course, this information is then used to create a reading program tailored to the strengths and needs of the learner.

The RMI is administered one-on-one. The authors suggest that you select a reader who appears to have persistent problems. However, you should probably wait until you have had considerable experience with miscue analysis before you administer the RMI to a seriously troubled reader. Goodman, Watson, and Burke further recommend that you select reading material that the student has not read. The material should contain content with which the reader will be familiar. The material should be an entire text, such as a complete story, a poem, article, or chapter. The authors recommend a text of at least 500 words for use with most students.

familiar content

The student is asked to read directly from the original text from which you have prepared a typescript or a photocopy. While the student reads, you code the miscues on your copy of the text with a set of markings carefully described and illustrated in the RMI Manual. Following the reading, you ask the student to give you an unaided retelling. Following that you can ask open-ended questions that will aid in a further retelling.

The miscues are analyzed by asking a series of questions about each miscue. The questions deal with the syntactic and semantic acceptability of the miscue, whether or not the miscue results in a meaning change, is the miscue attributable to a dialect variation, is it corrected, does it have graphic and sound similarity, and the grammatical function of the miscue.

The RMI presents four alternative procedures to the original Reading Miscue Inventory described above. The essential difference between the original version and Procedure I is that the alternative procedure asks fewer questions about each miscue. A very complete coding form and student profile form accompany Procedure I.

Alternative Procedure II focuses attention on the sentence. The first three questions explore whether or not there is syntactic acceptability, semantic acceptability, and a meaning change

within the *sentence* in which the miscue occurred. The remaining questions explore the graphic and sound similarity of the miscue. The Procedure II Coding Form guides your examination of the language sense of the reader and the degree of graphic and sound similarity in words that were substituted in context. Procedure II also contains a Reader Profile and a Retelling Summary Form.

The RMI Manual describes the differences between Procedure II and III as follows: "Procedure III provides the same kind of information about a reader as does Procedure II. It too is constructed so that its major focus is on the sentence within the story or article. The major difference between Procedures II and III is that in Procedure III, the typescript is used for marking the miscues as well as for coding them. It is therefore less time-consuming because the marking, coding, and analysis are all on the typescript. Neither a Coding Form nor a Reader Profile is necessary" (p. 116).

Procedure IV is the simplest procedure, but requires a great deal of knowledge about miscue analysis on your part. This procedure is probably the most helpful to the classroom teacher because it does not require a typescript. It could be easily done during a reading conference with a student. In this procedure, you keep a tally of the sentences by asking: Does the sentence, as the reader read it, make sense within the context of the selection? Sentences that are fully acceptable, partially acceptable, or corrected are coded "yes." The form accompanying Procedure IV is called an "Individual Conference Form" and it includes a place to record the tallies that are used to calculate a comprehending score (a percentage of sentences that were acceptable), retelling information, and your comments.

The Burke Reading Interview is a part of the RMI. The Interview is based on the belief that what readers believe about reading and reading instruction affects their use of reading strategies. These beliefs need to be considered as you design instruction. The Interview is designed to help you understand to which of three models of reading instruction the reader has been exposed. The models are described below.

The Subskills Model is based on the belief that reading is learned from parts to wholes in a highly prescribed sequence that begins instruction with letter/sound relationship, then moves to word recognition, and then to vocabulary. Errors are discouraged.

The Skills Model is based on an eclectic view of reading instruction that is found in most basals. Instruction takes a balanced approach to phonics skills, vocabulary building, and comprehension. Reading is thought of as a set of hierarchical skills that must be taught in a simplified fashion.

The Holistic Model of reading instruction is based on the belief that readers learn best when the language cueing systems and the reading strategies are integrated. In order to construct meaning, the reader must use all of the language systems.

A reader's answers to questions in the interview can give you considerable insight into which of the three reading models described briefly above have influenced the reader's thinking. For example, consider different responses to the question, "When you are reading and come to something you don't know,

what do you do?" If the response is "I sound out words," you can suspect that the subskill model is in operation. A response such as, "I try to go back and remember what a word means" would be indicative of a skill model. A response such as, "I will think of all the words I know that could fit there" or "I will read on to see if I can make sense" would indicate a more holistic orientation.

The Interview consists of ten questions. Each question is explained in terms of the rationale for asking that question. Examples of the responses of three children are offered to assist you in interpreting the responses you get from readers.

The RMI manual has very helpful chapters on holistic curriculum and the implications of the RMI for instruction. Several clear examples are offered for each of the alternative procedures, which facilitates understanding the difference between the procedures. The manual includes appendices that contain blank forms, the original Reading Miscue Inventory Questions, and the Goodman Taxonomy of Reading Miscues.

How Does the *Reading Miscue Inventory* Inform Instruction?

In using the RMI to plan instruction, it is useful to look at the strategies the child has in place and how he/she is applying these strategies. If needed, you may decide to model or demonstrate the use of a specific strategy to either an individual, a small group, or sometimes to a whole class in the form of a mini-lesson. You may often discover that these strategy demonstrations help even your best readers as they encounter new forms or materials in which they need the strategy.

SPED Kids You will find that because the RMI is time consuming you may not wish to use it with each of your learners. You will probably want to select those learners about whom you are most puzzled as readers. Information from the RMI will permit you to place children in instructional groups for work on use of the cueing systems, metacomprehension, and strategy instruction.

What Are the Advantages of the *Reading Miscue Inventory?*

The RMI is an exceptionally comprehensive guide to both the theory underlying miscue analysis and the procedures for conducting it. As a classroom teacher, reading specialist, or researcher, you will find all the information you need to begin miscue analysis.

The theoretical chapters in the RMI are well-written, well-documented, and provide a solid foundation for understanding miscue analysis. There is an extensive list of references that includes resources cited within the text as well as additional reading.

Procedure I is clearly the most complex and yields the most complete picture of the reader's behavior. This procedure should probably be used with the most challenged readers— those about whom you or the reading specialist are the most puzzled.

What Are the Disadvantages of the *Reading Miscue Inventory?*

The single greatest disadvantage of the RMI is that it requires a very knowl-

edgeable teacher. While a knowledgeable teacher is never, in itself, a disadvantage, the process of interpreting miscues requires a solid knowledge base. In order to become proficient at miscue analysis, you have to carefully study it and practice it.

The Alternative Procedures II–IV focus attention on the sentence rather than on individual miscues. While this can yield very helpful information, the process of analyzing self-corrections is not included. Self-corrections (and the discussion of them with the reader) are powerful sources of information about how the reader is engaged in metacomprehension activity.

All of the forms, with the exception of Alternative Procedure IV, are quite time consuming. While the time may be well spent, it will be a challenge for the busy classroom teacher to find time to use the forms other than IV.

Where Do I Get More Information About the *Reading Miscue Inventory?*

Goodman, Y. M., Watson, D. J., & Burke, C. L. (1987). *Reading miscue inventory: Alternative procedures.* Katonah, NY: Richard C. Owen Publishers.

Goodman, Y. M., & Burke, C. (1980). *Reading strategies: Focus on comprehension.* Katonah, NY: Richard C. Owen Publishers.

Marek, A.M. (1991). Retrospective miscue analysis: An instructional strategy for revaluing the reading process. In Goodman, K. S., Bird, L. B., & Goodman, Y. M. (Eds.), *The whole language catalog.* New York: American School Publishers, Macmillan/McGraw-Hill.

Watson, D. (1987). Reader-selected miscues. In Watson, D. (Ed.), *Ideas and insights: Language arts in the elementary school*. Urbana, IL: National Council of Teachers of English.

Reading Inventory for the Classroom

Third Edition

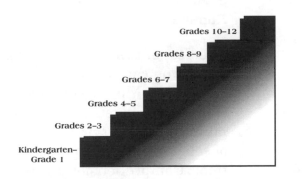

Level:

Preprimer

through

Grade 12

Year Published: 1998

What Is It?

The *Reading Inventory for the Classroom* (RIC) is an informal reading inventory developed by authors who say that their view of learning is drawn from transactional theory—a belief that the reader, the text, and the social-situational context are linked and transformed as a result of the reading act. They argue that in their process-oriented and holistic view of the reading process assessment should "offer the teacher insights into student interests, attitudes, and motivation (affective considerations), background knowledge, types of text that students may have difficulty reading, and learning or teaching situations that may be problematic" (Flynt & Cooter, 1998. p. 1).

The authors make the point that many teachers may be in transition between traditional methods and more process-oriented methods. Therefore, the RIC retains some traditional methods and descriptions. The RIC is designed to assess background knowledge and the reader's ability to decode and comprehend narrative and expository texts.

The inventory consists of four forms. Form A and Form B are narrative passages from preprimer through Level 9. Form C is expository passages Level 1 through Level 9. Form D is expository passages Level 10–Level 12. The graded passages were written or adapted by the authors.

The process of administering the RIC involves a four-step process. These steps are described below.

Step One: Interest/Attitude Interview

Two forms are offered. One is for grades one and two and the other is for grades three through twelve. The interview questions are intended to be springboards to discussion of interests, attitude and habits. The purpose is to help you select materials that are of interest to learners and to make suggestions to parents for support from home.

Step Two: Initial Passage Selection Sentences

The manual suggests that you begin having students read the passage selection sentences two grade levels below the child's current grade placement. The highest level of placement sentences read with zero errors is the level at which you enter the reading passages.

Step Three: Oral Reading Passages

First you have the student read passages orally and retell what they can. Then you use the comprehension questions to inform your aiding of the retelling, if necessary. Next, you have the student read part of the passage orally. You code the miscues while they read. A 100-word sample is reprinted on the Assessment Protocol. If you code the oral reading miscues on this sample you can use the Miscue Grid to analyze the miscues. Miscues are analyzed in terms of: mispronunciation, substitution, omission, insertion, teacher assistance, and self-correction. The grid also provides a place for you to indicate that a meaning disruption occurred. This is in recognition of the fact that not all miscues result in a disruption in meaning.

You analyze the performance on each passage in terms of oral reading accuracy and silent reading comprehension. Performance is rated as *easy, adequate,* or *too hard.* The descriptions of these levels of performance compare closely to the traditional independent, instructional and frustration levels used in the typical informal reading inventory.

Once you have discovered the level that is too hard for the student to read, you determine the listening comprehension level by reading passages to the student and asking the comprehension questions. The highest level at which the student can answer 75% of the comprehension questions is consid-

ered to be that student's listening comprehension level.

Step Four: Completing the Student Summary

The Student Summary is a form on which you can draw all of the data together. The Miscue Summary Chart shows an analysis of the number of miscues of each type with the number of self-corrections and meaning disruptions. Comprehension Response Summary Charts display either story grammar elements or expository grammar elements analyzed in terms of unaided recall, aided recall, and elements not recalled. The summary contains a checklist of oral reading skills and places for you to summarize abilities and needs in both oral reading and reading comprehension, as well as what you learned from the Interest/Attitude Interview.

How Does the *Reading Inventory for the Classroom* Inform Instruction?

You will be able to determine students' independent, instructional and frustration reading levels for both narrative and expository texts using this tool. You will have insights into the student's interests and attitudes related to both home life and school life from the interviews. You will be able to make some instructional decisions regarding help that is needed in retelling. It will be possible for you to identify the narrative or expository grammar elements that a child is not able to include in retellings. This will inform your instruction.

The miscue analysis is primarily quantitative. You will have information about the number of each type of miscue the child made. There is a table of selected common miscues and intervention strategies. Using this information, you will be able to plan interventions for some miscues.

The authors make an important point about intervention. They suggest that after collecting inventory data that you take a couple of weeks working on what students know and are able to do. They suggest that you use this time to collect more descriptive information about the student as a reader. They say, " . . . we feel that this process should help the teacher and examiner learn more about the student's reading abilities, confirm or reject initial findings drawn from this inventory, and discover ways of helping students continue to grow as successful readers" (Flynt & Cooter, 1998, p. 10).

What Are the Advantages of the *Reading Inventory for the Classroom?*

If you take a process view of reading rather than a subskills view, you will find this inventory very consistent with your views. The manual is well-written and offers helpful explanations, directions and forms. The Initial Passage Selection Sentences are a refreshing departure from the traditional graded word lists which are usually used to determine the entry point in graded passages. The sentences consist of words drawn from the accompanying reading passages. The sentences are

much more like the reading act than is the decoding of decontextualized word lists.

The authors have attended to the research on emergent literacy. Special consideration has been made for working with emergent readers. The inventory includes a method for assessing prereading capabilities using holistic instructional procedures. At the preprimer level students are shown a wordless picture story. After making a background statement, you ask the student to tell the story from the pictures. Checklists are provided for evaluating performance at the preprimer and primer levels.

What Are the Disadvantages of the *Reading Inventory for the Classroom?*

The authors missed a wonderful opportunity to drawn on their process-oriented philosophy in the analysis of miscues. The manual does not provide for a miscue analysis that examines the cueing systems on which the reader was drawing in making the miscue. The miscues are simply counted and rated as disrupting meaning or not. This overlooks a very rich data source.

Where Do I Get More Information About the *Reading Inventory for the Classroom?*

Flynt, E. S., & Cooter, R. B. (1998). *Reading inventory for the classroom. Third edition.* Upper Saddle River, NJ: Merrill.

Reading Style Inventory

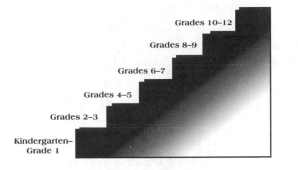

Grades 10–12
Grades 8–9
Grades 6–7
Grades 4–5
Grades 2–3
Kindergarten–
Grade 1

Level:

Primary

through

Adult

Year Published: 1994

What Is It?

The *Reading Style Inventory* (RSI) is a 68-item, untimed inventory of reader preferences that assesses the preferred learning styles for reading in grade one through adult. There are three forms available: RSI-P for grades one and two, RSI-I for grades three through eight, and RSI-A for grade nine through adult. Young children must mark answers in the inventory booklet for RSI-P. At the other levels, students may mark answers on an answer sheet or by using a computer.

The RSI is based on the learning style work of Rita and Kenneth Dunn. The Dunns have identified at least twenty-one elements of learning style that group into the following five categories assessed with the RSI: environmental stimuli, emotional stimuli, sociological stimuli, physical stimuli, and psychological stimuli. Carbo (1994) makes the following claim about the diagnosis of reading style: "Diagnosis of a child's unique reading style does not describe what the child knows but, rather, it provides impor-

tant information about *how* a particular student learns best. Reading style diagnosis has enabled teachers to select appropriate reading method(s) and materials for a child, and has eliminated much of the time wasted on trial-and-error teaching procedures that contribute to early reading failure" (p. 3).

The author, Marie Carbo, recommends administering the RSI individually or in small groups of two to six children until the end of second grade. The inventory is untimed, and should be administered to first and second grades over three to four sittings. Permission is granted to make overhead transparencies of the RSI-P student test booklet to facilitate administration. She suggests that by the end of second grade the RSI may be administered to large groups, as well as individuals. Students who cannot read at a beginning fourth grade level should have the RSI read to them.

The RSI may be computer scored. Responses are analyzed along the following dimensions: global/analytic tendencies, perceptual strengths, preferred reading environment, emotional profile, sociological preferences, and physical preferences. For each diagnosis category, the Individual Reading Style Profile indicates strengths and preferences. For each strength or preference listed, there are recommended strategies for teaching reading and references to the RSI Manual. For example, on an eleventh grade student's profile, the diagnosis under Global/Analytic Tendencies was "strong analytic tendencies." The recommended strategies were "Give routines, rules, directions, details." For the same student, the Emotional Profile diagnosis said, in part, "peer-motivated," and the accompanying recommended strategy was "encourage sharing reading interests with peers."

In addition to the "Individual Reading Style Profile," you can have the computer print "Reading Method Recommendations" and "Reading Materials Recommendations" for each student. These recommendations are grouped under headings such as "highly recommended, recommended, acceptable, special modifications, and not recommended."

The teacher's guides are clearly written and easy to follow. The Diskette Operating Manual "For People Who Hate to Read Manuals" is clear and easy to follow and the program is user friendly. In addition to the reports discussed above, the program yields four different kinds of RSI Group Profiles, a Parent Profile, and a Parent Letter. The materials that accompany the RSI are helpful in interpreting the data and placing your students in the appropriate materials and approaches to reading instruction. There is an extremely helpful Checklist of Equipment, Materials and Supplies in the RSI Manual.

The validity of the RSI is established by the author based on the construct validity of the learning styles work of the Dunns. If their conceptualization of learning styles is valid, then the RSI is a valid measure of learning style. The content validity was assessed by 87 educators in 23 states who were asked to comment on the degree to which the RSI measured the elements of reading style in an accurate and appropriate fashion. Ninety-three percent of the panel gave the RSI a favorable rating. Another review of the RSI by experts in the field resulted in the instrument being selected by the National Center for the Study of Learning/Teaching Styles for inclusion in the *Learning Styles Network's Instruments Assessment Analysis*. The validity of the RSI seems to be effectively established.

The reliability of the RSI is reported in the manual through various studies conducted with each of the three forms. The first test-retest reliability study was conducted in 1981, and the second in 1988, with samples drawn from both inner-city and suburban schools in New York. The 1981 reliability coefficients on 293 subjects in grades two, four, six, and eight ranged from .67 to .77. RSI items were refined between 1981 and 1983. The 1988 coefficients on 87 second graders ranged from .69 to .83, and averaged .74. A third study that was conducted in 1992 with 210 students drawn from five states in grades three, five, and six is reported in the RSI Manual. The reliability coefficients for the RSI subscales ranged from .63 to .87, and averaged .76. The reliability data on the RSI establish reliability at an acceptable level.

How Does the *Reading Style Inventory* Inform Instruction?

Teachers familiar with the RSI suggest that if your students have not had experiences with the language and concepts of the inventory that you structure situations to make the language familiar before using the inventory. For example, one of the questions asks if tracing a word helps you learn it. You might need to help children understand what "tracing a word" means by doing that with them and discussing it in a lesson before they take the inventory. You might arrange a place where children can read by lamplight rather than the usual bright lights of a classroom. You might set up a place where children can experience reading with quiet music playing in the background. You could have children experience reading sitting at a table on a hard chair and on softer seating. Experiences like these develop understandings in the students that permit them to better relate to the questions in the RSI.

Some teachers prepare students for responding to the RSI by sharing a book called *Rose and Tulip*, a Reading Styles Institute publication, which highlights differences in the way we learn. Transitioning from this book to finding out about children's learning styles is easy and natural. Giving children these experiences prior to taking the RSI probably increases the reliability of the data you get from the tool.

Bonnie Bergstrom, a teacher who uses the RSI, goes through the data and gets a mental picture of what each of her students needs. Then, working in groups of six, she goes over the information with each child in the group. As a group they discuss each child's learning needs, and talk about similarities and differences within the group. Their discussion focuses on what they can do with the results. The children are encouraged to share this information with their parents. Bonnie encourages the children to take control of their own learning by creating situations that best fit their styles whenever possible. She says this information empowers students. For example, if a child understands that he or she prefers dim light and warmth when reading, then it is sometimes possible for that child to create or get into the kind of environment that is most preferred.

Bonnie shares the information from the RSI with parents at the fall conference. She talks with parents about how they can best accommodate their child's preferred learning styles at home. She has developed a set of handouts that she gives to parents to help them understand how to help. For example, if a child is shown to be a very tactile learner, Bonnie will give the parents a handout on the Fernald Technique, which they can use with their child at home.

The information from the RSI also helps Bonnie at times to defuse the debate over phonics instruction that is of concern to many parents. If a child is not an auditory and visual learner, Bonnie can show the parent how phonics instruction will not be of particular help to the child. Conversely, if the child is a strong auditory and visual learner, Bonnie can show the parents how she will meet the need for visual and auditory learning as she works with the child.

The RSI has informed instruction in Bonnie's room in other important ways. For example, she has increased the kinesthetic and tactile materials for children to use. Bonnie makes recorded books which most of her students use to read along silently, following print with their finger, giving them a tactile component in learning. She records the books on five- to seven-minute tapes, reading slowly. This practice has become an important part of her reading program. She also stops at a nearby bakery each day and brings day-old round-loaf bread to school. Children who wish to can snack on this bread during class. Bonnie says, "This one small thing makes such a big change in the affect of the students. They then are willing to believe that this teacher understands my learning needs and will do whatever she can to accommodate them."

Bonnie has seen another important affect of the RSI. One of the theories behind reading styles work, she explains, is that if children are matched to instruction and materials that are consistent with their reading styles, behavior problems will subside. Bonnie finds herself managing materials and instruction rather than behavior because the children's learning needs are met.

What Are the Advantages of the *Reading Style Inventory?*

The RSI is a valid and reliable instrument for assessing the individual learning styles of your students. Once you know these preferences, the RSI reports and manual are helpful in matching instructional materials and strategies to the learning styles of your students. Carbo has reported impressive research results indicating gains

in reading achievement when instruction is matched to learning style.

The administration and scoring of the RSI are very easy with the computer-scored format. This is a great improvement over procedures of the past, when teachers had to send the score sheets to the publisher for scoring. There is one kind of group report available that could be very helpful in identifying groups of students for whom certain instructional strategies and materials are appropriate. The RSI Group Names Report lists the names of your students grouped for each of the five reading style elements under the headings indicating their degree of preference. You can quickly see the group of your students, for example, who have very strong global tendencies and who would benefit from connecting the reading program to real-world resources such as articles, interviews, and news events.

What Are the Disadvantages of the *Reading Style Inventory?*

The RSI manual offers no concurrent validity data in comparison to other measures of learning style. Faith in the RSI is placed almost exclusively in the work of Dunn and Dunn and the panel of educators who evaluated the RSI for validity.

Subjects are self-reporting the information from which interpretations of reading styles are made. It is possible that students will not provide accurate information. Corkill (1992), in reviewing the RSI, suggests that older students beyond seventh or eighth grade may find the statements in the RSI too simplistic. If this were the case, a valid measurement of reading style with older learners would be in question.

Where Do I Get More Information About the *Reading Style Inventory?*

Benson, J. (1992). Review of the Reading Style Inventory. In Kramer, J. J., & Conoley, J. C. (Eds.), *The eleventh mental measurement yearbook.* Lincoln, NE: University of Nebraska Press.

Carbo, M. (1994). *Reading style inventory manual.* (4th ed.). Syosset, NY: National Reading Styles Institute.

Carbo, M., Dunn, R., & Dunn, K. (1986). *Teaching students to read through their individual learning styles.* Englewood Cliffs, NJ: Prentice Hall.

Corkill, A. J. (1992). Review of the Reading Style Inventory. In Kramer, J. J., & Conoley, J. C. (Eds.), *The eleventh mental measurement yearbook.* Lincoln, NE: University of Nebraska Press.

Dunn, R., & Dunn, K. (1978). *Teaching students through their individual learning styles: A practical approach.* Reston, VA: Reston Publishing Company.

Weaver, C. (1994). *Reading process and practice: From socio-psycholinguistics to whole language.* Portsmouth, NH: Heinemann.

Stanford Diagnostic Reading Test

Fourth Edition

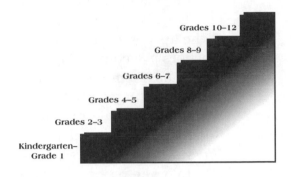

Grades 10–12
Grades 8–9
Grades 6–7
Grades 4–5
Grades 2–3
Kindergarten–
Grade 1

Level:

End of Grade One

through

First Semester of College

Year Published: 1995

What Is It?

The *Stanford Diagnostic Reading Test - Fourth Edition* (*SDRT-4*) is a norm-referenced test designed to identify the strengths and weaknesses in reading performance in students from the second half of first grade through the first semester of college. It is the 1995 update of a test first published in 1966.

The authors of the *SDRT-4* view reading as a developmental process that encompasses four major components: decoding, vocabulary, comprehension and scanning. There are six levels of the test. Each of the levels and its testing objectives are described below.

Red Level: Intended for use in the second half of grade one and the first half of grade two. It measures phonetic analysis of consonants (single, blends, digraphs) and vowels (short and long). It measures vocabulary with word reading and listening vocabulary. Comprehension is measured through sentences, riddles, cloze, and short paragraphs with questions.

Orange Level: Intended for use in the second half of grade two and the first

half of grade three. It measures phonetic analysis of consonants and vowels. Vocabulary is measured through listening vocabulary and reading vocabulary (synonyms and classification). Comprehension is measured through cloze, paragraphs with questions, and by type of text (recreational reading, textual reading, and functional reading)

Green Level: Intended for use in the second half of grade three and the first half of grade four. It measures phonetic analysis of consonants and vowels (long, short and other). Vocabulary is measured through listening vocabulary and reading vocabulary (synonyms and classification). Comprehension is measured through paragraphs with questions, by type of text (recreational, textual, functional), and by mode of comprehension (initial understanding, interpretation and critical analysis and reading strategies).

The testing objectives of the remaining three levels are the same across all levels. The *Purple Level* is intended for use in grades 4.5–6.5; the *Brown Level* is intended for use in grades 6.5–8.9; and the Blue Level is intended for use in grades 9.0–12.9. Reading vocabulary is assessed with synonyms, classification, word parts and content area words. Comprehension is assessed through paragraphs with questions, by type of text (recreational, textual, functional), and by mode of comprehension (initial understanding, interpretation, critical analysis, and reading strategies). Scanning ability is also assessed.

In addition to the norm-referenced subtests described above, the SDRT-4 makes available three informal teacher-administered and teacher-scored assessment. The *Reading Strategies Survey* is designed to determine which reading strategies students use in various reading situations. Students respond "yes" or "no" to a series of statements—some describing desirable reading strategies and some describing inefficient reading behaviors. You will be able to assess which before-, during-, and after-reading strategies your children use with this instrument which can be individually- or group-administered. The manual offers administration and scoring guides, as well as implications for instruction and instruction suggestions for teaching some effective reading strategies.

The *Reading Questionnaire* is designed to assess some of the abilities or knowledge, other than comprehension skills and strategies, that a student brings to the Reading Comprehension subtest of the SDRT-4. The questionnaire is to be administered prior to the Reading Comprehension subtest to measure students' attitudes toward reading, reading habits and interests, and knowledge of topics and concepts critical to success with the Reading

Comprehension subtest. Data from this informal instrument may be useful to you in interpreting performance on the Reading Comprehension subtest.

The *Story Retelling* is provided out of the author's recognition that many teachers are combining formal and informal assessment tools to gain greater understandings of their students. When used as a supplement to the Reading Comprehension subtest, the *Story Retelling* offers you the opportunity to make process-oriented, qualitative evaluation of both the student's recall ability after silent reading or narrative text, understanding of story grammar, and the use of comprehension strategies.

The *Story Retelling* assessment may be used as an oral retelling one-on-one, or as a written retelling when group administered. There are three levels of *Story Retelling* available. Level I corresponds to the Red and Orange Levels, Level II corresponds to the Green and Purple Levels, and Level III corresponds to the Brown and Blue Levels.

Test items were selected after a review of literature in the reading education field, recent state and district school curricula and objectives, teacher surveys, as well as consultation with reading specialists, the National Council of Teachers of English, and the International Reading Association.

Raw scores on the SDRT-4 may be converted to percentile rank, stanine, grade equivalent and scaled scores. The development of the test and the national standardization process were ambitious. The collection of normative data took place during the fall of 1994 and the spring of 1995. Approximately 33,000 students from 400 school districts participated in the fall standardization program, with another 7,000 in the three equating programs. The spring standardization involved an additional 20,000 students. The *1995 Multilevel Norms Book and Technical Information* provides thorough information on the demographics of the norming sample, as well as clearly establishing the reliability and validity of the SDRT-4.

How Does *Stanford Diagnostic Reading Test-4* Inform Instruction?

The best use of this tool is with students about whom you are puzzled as readers. When you identify children who are not making the progress that you would expect, you are not getting adequate diagnostic data from the informal tools you are using, or when you want normative data on a student's use of specific skills, the test will be very useful to you.

At the early levels (Red, Orange Green) you can get very detailed information about the reader's strengths and weaknesses in phonic skills. Combining this data with your own observations and information from running records, for example, will provide you with rich information for instructional planning.

Knowledge of word meanings is a critical aspect of reading. The vocabulary subtests at the early levels will permit you to compare word reading ability with listening vocabulary. Children who score well on the listening vocabulary and poorly on word reading will be subjects for further diagnosis. The breakdown of the Reading Vocabu-lary subtests will help you identify specific skill areas of weakness.

The comprehension measures will permit you to make inferences about the type of texts on which a reader is successful or struggling. If scores are higher on, for example, textual reading than functional reading, you will know that you need to increase instructional attention to functional reading activities such as reading posters, directions, and advertising.

By taking advantage of the three informal assessments, you will be able to make more informed instructional decisions. It will be very helpful to identify the attitudes towards reading of those struggling readers. The literature on reading education now places as much emphasis on teaching strategies as it does on teaching skills. The Reading Strategies Survey will be a useful source of information for planning strategy instruction, especially when you combine that data with information you get from running records and retrospective miscue analysis.

You will have a great deal of information about a reader's comprehension performance when you compare performance on the comprehension subtests with the story retelling. The performance on the comprehension subtests will give you normative information broken down by both types of text and modes of comprehension. This will be greatly enriched with the story retelling data which guides you through analyses of both the reader's understanding of story elements (introduction, setting, characters, problem, plot/events, resolution, theme, sequence) and the reader's use of some important aspects of the reading process.

What Are the Advantages of the *Stanford Diagnostic Reading Test-4?*

The SDRT-4 offers a well designed, carefully and thoroughly normed test that is consistent with current thinking about the reading process. It will provide you with sufficient information to make informed decisions about ways to help struggling readers. The combination of formal and informal instruments within the total battery will greatly enhance your ability to make instructional decisions.

What Are the Disadvantages of the *Stanford Diagnostic Reading Test-4?*

The author's success in creating helpful informal measures to supplement the formal assessment is laudable. However, neither the *Story Retelling* nor the *Strategies Survey* offer ways in which you can make informed decisions about the student's ability to monitor his or her use of the reading process. Nowhere can you get information about the student's monitoring of the reading process through such questions as "Does it look right? Does it sound right? Does it make sense?" This means that you will probably wish to supplement data on the SDRT-4 with information from running records, or other forms of miscue analysis and retrospective miscue analysis.

Where Do I Get More Information About the *Stanford Diagnostic Reading Test-4?*

Engelhard, G. (1998). Review of the Stanford Diagnostic Reading Test, Fourth Edition. *The thirteenth mental measurement yearbook.* Lincoln, NE: University of Nebraska Press.

Karlsen, B., & Gardner, E. F. (1995). *1995 Multilevel Norms Book and technical information.* San Antonio, TX: Harcourt Brace Educational Measurement.

Karlsen, B., & Gardner, E. F. (1995). *Stanford diagnostic reading test, fourth edition, directions for administering.* San Antonio, TX: Harcourt Brace Educational Measurement.

Swerdlik, M. E., & Bucy, J. E. (1998). Review of the Stanford Diagnostic Reading Test, Fourth Edition. *Thirteenth mental measurement yearbook.* Lincoln, NE: University of Nebraska Press.

The Stieglitz Informal Reading Inventory

Second Edition

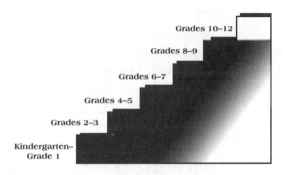

Grades 10–12
Grades 8–9
Grades 6–7
Grades 4–5
Grades 2–3
Kindergarten–Grade 1

Level:

Emergent Reader

through

Eighth Grade

Year Published: 1997

What Is It?

The Stieglitz Informal Reading Inventory (SIRI) contains graded word lists in context, graded word lists in isolation, practice passages and graded reading passages, and a variety of assessment and evaluation strategies. The purposes of the informal reading inventory are to place students appropriately in reading material for instruction and to analyze reading difficulties in order to design instruction. The inventory's components are described below.

Graded Words in Context Test

In this test ranging from preprimer through eighth grade, target words are presented in sentences. The reading of these sentences is scored only on the target words. Performance on the graded words is used to determine where to begin a student in the reading of the graded passages.

Graded Words in Isolation Test

This test is offered as a diagnostic option. Graded word lists are presented in isolation for the purpose determin-

ing how well students recognize words without the benefit of context. Inferences about level of sight vocabulary and decoding ability may be drawn from this test.

Dictated Story Assessment Strategy

Instead of offering graded passages at the preprimer and primer levels, the SIRI assesses reading achievement of children reading below the first-grade level with a dictated story assessment strategy. Ten photographs are included in the material. The photographs are used to stimulate discussion. You ask the student to select a photograph to talk about. You then engage the child in discussion about the photograph, and finally you take their dictation about the photograph. This dictated "story" is then used to assess the performance of emergent readers.

Graded Reading Passages

Graded passages of both expository and narrative text are assembled from grade one through grade nine. Expository passages include science, social studies, and consumer education texts. Narrative passages include descriptive text, tales, humor, and mystery texts. Word recognition and comprehension scores are derived from the graded reading passages. Word recognition miscues that disrupt meaning are counted as one error. Miscues that do not disrupt the intended meaning are counted as one-half error. Repeated substitutions and repeated errors on the same words are all counted as only one error. Miscues that are cultural, regional, dialectical, self-corrections, hesitations and ignoring of punctuation are not counted as errors. Summary sheets are provided for recording and analyzing miscues.

Comprehension is measured by asking six questions for each passage. Questions are designed to tap literal, interpretive, and critical/creative thinking. As an alternative or additional measure of comprehension, the SIRI offers the opportunity to evaluate free and aided retellings of the readings. Very detailed forms are offered for the analysis of retellings.

How Does *The Stieglitz Informal Reading Inventory* Inform Instruction?

The inventory will be useful to you especially if you are teaching reading in a literature-based program and wish to know the instructional level of each of your learners. By analyzing the miscues made on the graded passages, you can gain insight into the extent to which the student is reading for meaning. Examining performance on the comprehension questions across passages will permit you to make infer-

ences about the kinds of questions the student is able to answer and the kinds of thinking about reading that are challenging. For example, if you see a pattern of accurate responses to literal questions but limited accuracy on inferential questions, this may indicate a need for instruction in drawing inferences. You can use the retelling feature to gain further insights into comprehension ability.

What Are the Advantages of *The Stieglitz Informal Reading Inventory?*

The Graded Words in Context are much more like real reading activity than the decontextualized word lists that are often included in informal reading inventories. This is an improvement.

The reading passages are of adequate length and are interesting. Especially useful is the comprehension check which not only helps you analyze the kinds of thinking the student can do in response to reading, but also guides your evaluation of retellings.

The Dictated Story Assessment Strategy is a more reasonable assessment of emergent reading behavior than the typical informal reading inventory use of text selections at the preprimer and primer level. Especially useful is the Dictated Story Assessment Strategy Record Form which offers support in evaluating the performance.

The manual is clearly written, well organized, and makes it easy to do the mathematical calculations.

What Are the Disadvantages of *The Stieglitz Informal Reading Inventory?*

While the authors are to be commended for recognizing that not all oral reading miscues should be counted with equal weight, the inventory falls short in miscue analysis. You are encouraged to record (count) the miscues that receive full credit and half credit, but this can only lead to an assessment of the reader's efforts at trying to make meaning. There is no provision for analyzing miscues in terms of the reader's use of the cueing systems—a significantly important aspect of miscue analysis.

Where Do I Get More Information About *The Stieglitz Informal Reading Inventory?*

Stieglitz, E. L. (1997). *The Stieglitz informal reading inventory: Assessing reading behaviors from emergent to advanced levels.* Boston: Allyn and Bacon.

Test of Early Reading Ability–2

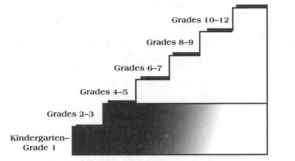

Grades 10–12
Grades 8–9
Grades 6–7
Grades 4–5
Grades 2–3
Kindergarten–Grade 1

Level:

Age 3

through

Age 9

Year Published: 1989

What Is It?

The *Test of Early Reading Ability–2* (TERA–2) is a norm-referenced test of very early reading achievement. The test is based on the work of many researchers and theorists in emergent literacy from the late 1960s to the present. The authors, Reid, Hresko, and Hammill, have rejected old ideas of reading readiness, and have designed the test based on our current understandings of the early conceptions children have about reading. These early conceptions include understanding some of the functions of print, handling books, learning about structures in written language, identifying letters and numerals, syllabic awareness, and phonemic awareness.

The test is intended to help you detect early reading difficulties so that children can be helped to avoid later reading failures. The stated purposes of the test are: to identify those children who are significantly different from their peers in the early development of reading, to document children's progress in learning to read, to serve as a measure in research projects, and to

suggest instructional practices (Reid, Hresko, & Hammill, 1989, p. 5).

Many aspects of TERA–2 are similar to the book handling tasks and concepts of print procedures described elsewhere in this Handbook (see Book Handling Tasks on pp. 31–34 and An Observation Survey of Early Literacy Achievement on pp. 231–235). All of these tools measure three components of reading that are discovered by most children during the preschool years: children's efforts at constructing meaning from print, to learn and make use of the alphabet, and to discover conventions in reading and writing English.

TERA–2 approaches assessing understanding of the construction of meaning in three ways: ability to read signs, logos, and other common environmental print; knowledge of relations among vocabulary items; and awareness of print in connected text.

TERA–2 approaches assessing knowledge of the alphabet through letter naming and oral reading. Knowledge of the conventions of written language is measured through book handling tasks, understanding of punctuation, left-to-right orientation, the understanding of how a story is spaced on the page, and proofreading.

In creating the second edition of the TERA, Reid, Hresko and Hammill drew items from the first edition and created new items based on the emergent literacy research. Proposed items for the second edition were submitted to a panel of experts who were asked to assign the items to one of the three foundational theoretical constructs: constructing meaning, knowledge of the alphabet, and print conventions.

You administer the test by showing the child pages in the "Picture Book" and then scoring their responses (correct or wrong; 1 or 0) on the "Profile/Examiner Record Form." The two equivalent forms each consist of 46 items. Each page of the "Picture Book" contains text or pictures. You are asked to cut pictures or logos from local newspapers and magazines and glue them into the book for items that would be unique to your locale. Examples of this include fruit drink logos and toothpaste logos. The test is untimed and usually takes 15 to 30 minutes to administer depending on the age of the child.

The TERA–2 yields four kinds of scores and a rating. In addition to the raw score, the derived scores are: percentile rank, normal curve equivalent (NCE), and a reading quotient (RQ). The normal curve equivalent and reading quotient are standard scores. The NCE ranges from 1 to 99 with a mean of 50 and a standard deviation of 21.06. The RQ ranges from less than 70 to greater than 130 with a mean of 100 and a standard deviation of 15. The ratings are derived from both the reading quotient and the normal curve equivalent scores. Ratings range from "very poor" to "very superior."

In addition to the scores and ratings described above, the TERA–2 yields an assessment of "Instructional Target Zone." The Record Form contains a chart listing the test items that pertain to each of the three constructs: meaning, alphabet, and conventions. You are instructed to mark a slash through all of the numbers corresponding to items passed. Unslashed items immediately above the slashed, passed items constitute what the authors call the "instructional target zone." They suggest that "these items are probably representative of the kinds of items the child is ready to be taught" (p. 16).

The TERA–2 was standardized on a sample of 1,454 children from age three to age nine in 15 states. The demographic characteristics of the sample are comparable to the percentages reported for the population of the United States in the Statistical Abstract of the United States (1985). There was an almost equal proportion of males and females. The locations included urban and rural sites in the Northeast, North Central, South, and West. It is difficult to determine the exact ethnicity of the sample because the authors report small percentages of American Indian, Hispanic, and Asian, and then a very large percentage (90–91) of "other."

Internal consistency coefficients for all of the children in the norming sample ranged from .80 to .90. Eighty-six percent of the subjects exceeded the .80 alpha and 64 percent exceeded the .90 alpha. These data indicate sufficient internal consistency. Stability of the test was assessed through test-retest with alternate forms, with a correlation coefficient of .89. Reliability of the TERA–2 is acceptable. The TERA–2 appears to have adequate content validity in light of the match between test items and components of the emergent literacy conceptualizations described earlier.

How Does the *Test of Early Reading Ability-2* Inform Instruction?

The primary reason to use the TERA–2 is to have normative data on the emergent reading performance of your learners. If your program evaluation plan includes measuring performance across time, the Normal Curve Equivalent scores on the TERA–2 will be useful to you.

You will be able to make some instructional decisions by attending to the items on which individual children performed below expectations. Some teachers feel that two of the strengths of the test are the use of environmental print that children are asked to recognize, and the information obtained about how the reader tracks down the page and indicates knowledge of left to right directionality.

If you are considering using the TERA, I recommend that they prepare in advance. For example, you must find your own environmental print to use in the test and some of the items have more than one page in the easel booklet, so one must be familiar with the test.

What Are the Advantages of the *Test of Early Reading Ability-2?*

For teachers interested in discovering what young learners know about print

and book handling, it is much easier to obtain the TERA–2 than to create your own measures. The authors have recognized the importance of locale in assessing awareness of environmental print. They have accommodated regional trademarks and logos in creating these items.

The TERA–2 manual is easy to read and use. The authors have taken pains to provide solid information about the appropriate uses of the test, and have offered wise cautions in interpreting the data. About supplementing test data, the authors say, "The user must understand that TERA–2 items, because they are present in a formal testing format, are necessarily decontextualized and do not capture children's knowledge in the same way as naturalistic observation of literacy events. . . . Consequently, users might wish to supplement TERA–2 data with observational information. . . . " (p. 4).

The authors of the TERA–2 are to be commended for following the guidelines of the International Reading Association and the American Psychological Association in choosing not to use age and grade norms for the test. However, their recommended use of "reading quotients" bear a close resemblance to grade scores.

What Are the Disadvantages of the *Test of Early Reading Ability-2?*

It is curious that while the authors wisely chose not to use age and grade equivalents, they have chosen to use Reading Quotient scores, which look remarkably like intelligence quotient scores (mean of 100, standard deviation of 15). In the Instructional Target

Zone analysis you are instructed to use "mental age" equivalents listed along the margins to determine which test items indicate next learning goals. This rejection of age equivalents and use of mental age equivalents seems contradictory.

The authors used an 11-member panel of experts to assign test items to the three over-arching constructs: meaning, alphabet, and conventions. They state that where there was at least 85% agreement in the panel's categorization, an item was retained. The classification of some items is curious. For example, reading a sentence aloud is called an alphabet item, while matching an upper-case letter to its lower-case equivalent is classified as convention.

While the desire to include environmental print indigenous to the child's world is commendable, the task of locating the appropriate-sized logos and labels in your local newspapers and magazines, cutting them out, and gluing them into the Picture Book will be time-consuming and take effort. Of even greater concern about this practice is the fact that the TERA–2 is a normed-referenced test and yet these test items vary by locale.

Where Do I Get More Information About the *Test of Early Reading Ability–2?*

Beck, M. D. (1992). Review of the Test of Early Reading Ability–2. In Kramer, J. J., & Conoley, J. C. (Eds.), *The eleventh mental measurements yearbook*. Lincoln, NE: University of Nebraska Press.

Hiltonsmith, R. W. (1992). Review of the Test of Early Reading Ability–2. In Kramer, J. J., & Conoley, J. C., (Eds.), *The eleventh mental measurements yearbook*. Lincoln, NE: University of Nebraska Press.

Reid, D. K., Hresko, W. P., & Hammill, D. D. (1989). *Test of early reading ability, second edition, Examiner's manual*. Austin, TX: Pro-ed.

Test of Phonological Awareness

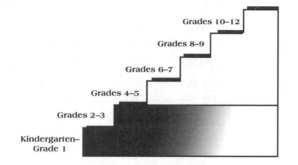

Grades 10–12
Grades 8–9
Grades 6–7
Grades 4–5
Grades 2–3
Kindergarten–Grade 1

Level:

Kindergarten
through
Second Grade
(Normed between the ages of
5 years 0 months and 8 years 11 months)

Year Published: 1994

What Is It?

The *Test of Phonological Awareness* (TOPA) is a standardized, norm-referenced test of children's sensitivity to, or explicit awareness of, the phonological structure of words in language. It can be administered to whole-class groups in about 15–20 minutes. The authors recommend administration to groups of six to eight students who are either very young, or have difficulties following instruction or other behavioral problems.

Reading teachers and researchers have developed a growing appreciation of the important role played by phonological awareness in success in early reading instruction. The 1998 National Research Council report entitled *Preventing Reading Difficulties in Young Children* reviewed dozens of studies that have confirmed a close relationship between phonological awareness and reading ability, not only in beginning reading but beyond.

There are two versions of the TOPA: Kindergarten and Early Elementary. The Kindergarten version contains two subtests. Each subtest is comprised of ten items. Subtest I tests children's ability to hear which initial sounds in spoken words are the same. For example, children might be shown a picture of a cat followed by pictures of a dog, a horn and a cow. The examiner would say, "The first picture is cat. The other pictures are dog, horn, cow. Mark the one that begins with the same sound as cat." Children are to make an x on the picture of the cow. Subtest II asks children to identify the picture that has a different first sound than the other three.

The Early Elementary version of the TOPA is formatted exactly the same as the Kindergarten version except that children are asked to deal with ending sounds rather than beginning sounds. Each subtest contains ten items. In Subtest I they are asked to identify the picture corresponding to a word that ends with the same sound as the stimulus word. In Subtest II they are asked to identify the picture corresponding to a word that ends with a different last sound than the other words.

Raw scores may be converted to a variety of derived scores. These derived scores are TOPA Quotient (the mean is 100), Normal Curve Equivalent Score (percentile ranks statistically transformed into a scale of equal units ranging from 1 through 99, suitable for computing averages), percentile rank, stanine, W-Scale Score, T-Score and z-Score. The Normal Curve Equivalent, percentile rank and stanine scores are likely to be the most useful.

The standardization group for the kindergarten version was 857 students. For the early education version it was 3,654 students. Reasonable care was given to even distributions across geographic regions, gender and ethnic groups.

How Does the *Test of Phonological Awareness* Inform Instruction?

The authors of the TOPA suggest that children scoring below the 25th percentile on the TOPA at the beginning of the second semester of kindergarten are at risk for difficulties in learning to read because of delayed development of phonological awareness. Children scoring below the 15th percentile in first and second grades are likely to be struggling in learning to read as a result, at least in part, due to difficulties in processing the phonological features of words or a lack of awareness of the phonological structure of words.

The authors suggest that if the TOPA is to be used to identify children most in need of phonological training that all children should be tested as close to the same time in the school year as possible. While the test can be given at any time during the school year, the authors recommend giving the Kindergarten version during the second half of the year.

Kindergarten children scoring below the 25th percentile will benefit from instruction in phonological awareness before formal reading instruction. Children in first and second grade scoring below the 15th percentile will benefit from instruction in phonological awareness as a supplement to regular reading instruction.

What Are the Advantages of the *Test of Phonological Awareness?*

The greatest advantage of the TOPA is that you can quickly evaluate the phonological awareness of a whole class of children—if your students are able to handle the test in a whole group. It could be highly beneficial to be able to identify which of your students are most in need of phonological awareness instruction.

The Examiner's Manual for the TOPA effectively establishes test-retest reliability, content validity, predictive validity and construct validity for the test. The Kindergarten version was standardized on 857 students in ten states. The Early Elementary version was standardized on 3,654 students in 38 states. Adequate geographic and ethnic balances were achieved within the norming sample.

The Examiner's Manual is well written with clear explanations for administering and interpreting the test. It contains helpful suggestions for sharing test data with others and provides references to resources for phonological awareness teaching.

What Are the Disadvantages of the *Test of Phonological Awareness?*

The greatest disadvantage of the TOPA is that it measures a relatively narrow aspect of phonological awareness—the ability to hear differences in beginning and ending sounds in words. A more sophisticated aspect of phonological awareness is the ability to segment words by their phonemes or to synthesize individually presented phonemes together to make a word. While such phonological activity is too difficult for most kindergarten children, you may need a more sophisticated measure with older children than provided by the TOPA.

Most classroom teachers and reading specialists do not need the normative data available on the TOPA. The real purpose of the test is to identify those children with the most limited phonological awareness. Normative data is not necessary to making this determination.

The TOPA is administered with live voice. This means that a teacher with a dialect different from the students should not administer the test to those students. This may be problematic in some classrooms, especially where the ethnic diversity is high.

Where Do I Get More Information About the *Test of Phonological Awareness?*

Long, S. H. (1998). Review of the Test of Phonological Awareness. *The thirteenth mental measurement yearbook.* Lincoln, NE: University of Nebraska Press.

McCauley, R. (1998). Review of the Test of Phonological Awareness. *The thirteenth mental measurement yearbook.* Lincoln, NE: University of Nebraska Press.

National Research Council (1998). *Preventing reading difficulties in young children.* National Academy Press, Washington, D.C.

Torgesen, J. K., & Bryant, B. R. (1994). *Test of phonological awareness, Examiner's manual.* Austin, TX: pro-ed.

Test of Reading Comprehension

Third Edition

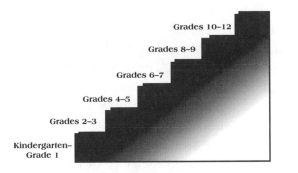

Grades 10–12
Grades 8–9
Grades 6–7
Grades 4–5
Grades 2–3
Kindergarten–Grade 1

Level:

Primary

through

High School

Year Published: 1995

What Is It?

The *Test of Reading Comprehension, Third Edition* (TORC), is a norm-referenced, silent reading test designed to evaluate the ability of subject's aged 7-0 through 17-11 to comprehend printed text. The authors view *reading* and *reading comprehension* as synonymous. They take a constructivist view that reading is the ability to both construct meaning from graphic symbols and to project meaning onto those symbols. They draw on the work of Chomsky to make the case that the syntax of the language, rather than phonics, is the basis upon which readers make semantic interpretations and phonological translations.

The authors further view reading as an interaction between the reader and the text. They articulate the role of the reader's expectations, the reader's language and the reader's ability to process text. Their views of the reader's processing of text are essentially their *operational* definition of *comprehension*. Four mental operations used by readers in processing text are described in the manual. One, *prior knowledge*, refers to the reader's ability to draw on background knowledge to create meaning with text. Two, *skills in determining logical relationships*, refers to the reader's ability to choose information in the text selectively and to relate critical information to prior knowledge or other elements of the text. Three, *systematic integration of the total text*, refers to the reader's ability to build overall meaning as they read, with each new piece of text adding to the understanding of the whole text. Four, *active processing*, refers to the notion that reading is an active process in which readers are generating meaning while they are reading. The manual implies that the four mental operations described above are measured by the test. We will return to this issue later.

The test consists of a General Reading Comprehension Core and Diagnostic Supplements. The General Reading Comprehension Core consists of four subtests. Subtest One, General Vocabulary, measures the reader's ability to read three stimulus words that are related in some way and then choose two from four words that are closely associated with the three stimulus words. In this way the subtest measures the reader's understanding of sets of vocabulary items that are all related to the same general concept. For example, the three stimulus words might be *stand, run, walk* and the four choices are *crawl, fast, leap, arm*. Correct responses would be *crawl* and *leap* because they are most closely associated, conceptually, with the stimulus words.

Subtest Two, Syntactic Similarities, measures the reader's ability to identify meaningfully similar, but syntactically different sentence structures. Here the reader is given five sentences and must select the two that most closely convey the same meaning. The following example is used in the manual.

A. Sam plays.

B. Sam will not play.

C. Sam has played.

D. Sam is playing.

E. Sam is going to play.

The correct response is that A and D are the most alike.

Subtest Three, Paragraph Reading, asks readers to answer questions relating to theme, recall of details, drawing inferences, and identifying a negative inference—a sentence that could not go with the story.

Subtest Four, Sentence Sequencing, measures the ability to order five sentences into meaningful short paragraphs.

In addition to the General Reading Comprehension Core, the test consists of four subtests that comprise the Diagnostic Supplements. Subtests Five through Seven measure the reader's understanding of vocabulary associated with mathematics, social studies and science. Like Subtest One, General Vocabulary, these subtests give the reader three stimulus words and the reader then chooses two of the four response words that are most closely associated, conceptually, to the stimulus words. Subtest Eight measures the young and remedial readers' understanding of written directions commonly found in schoolwork.

One way to determine the validity of the TORC is to examine the extent to which the test items tap into the four mental operations described above as text processing ability. Let's consider each of the operations in light of the subtests of the General Reading Comprehension Core. Table One illustrates where each of the mental operations is tested.

The data in Table One suggest that the four mental operations thought to make up the ability to process text are measured across the four subtests. Each of the subtests calls for the use of prior knowledge, logical relationships, and active processing. The paragraph reading and sentence sequencing subtests additionally call for the integration of the total text.

The test has adequate content validity based upon this analysis. The authors establish adequate concurrent validity with four other widely used and accepted tests. Test-retest reliability coefficients ranged from .79 to .80 across the subtests, and demonstrate a high degree of reliability for the TORC.

The TORC was normed on a sample of 1,962 persons in 19 states in the fall of 1993 and the winter of 1994. While this norming sample is small, the demographics of the sample are

Table 1   Presence of Text Process Operations in Subtests

	General Vocabulary	Syntactic Similarities	Paragraph Reading	Sentence Sequencing
Prior Knowledge	X	X	X	X
Logical Relationships	X	X	X	X
Integration Total Text			X	X
Active Processing	X	X	X	X

representative of the population of the United States according to the 1990 census. Adequate information about the normative sample in terms of geographic region, gender, residence, race, ethnicity, and disabling conditions are reported.

Raw scores on the TORC may be converted to grade equivalents, age equivalents, percentiles, subtest standard scores, and the composite Reading Comprehension Quotient (RCQ). The RCQ scores range from below 70, "very poor" to above 130, "very superior." The manual encourages you to carefully examine the subtest scores when a student's RCQ is below 90.

How Does the *Test of Reading Comprehension* Inform Instruction?

Data from the TORC should be carefully analyzed from several perspectives. First, the overall performance as described by the RCQ should be examined to see how it compares with your personal evaluation of the reader's performance on other texts. Does this test performance confirm your professional view of this student as reader?

Second, look at the scores on the subtests of the General Reading Comprehension Core. Is performance across subtests consistent? If performance on one of the subtests is lower than performance on the rest of the subtests, you will need to analyze why this has happened. If, for example, performance on Sentence Sequencing was much lower than other subtests, you will need first to discover whether or not the student understood the directions. You can do this by designing an instructional activity that requires the same kind of sequencing behavior. If the student requires instruction in how to do the task, you can conclude that the directions were not understood. If however, you are sure the directions are understood, but performance was low, you may conclude that instruction and practice in sentence sequencing and thinking about the message of the whole text are required.

Third, compare performance on the General Reading Comprehension Core with performance on the Diagnostic Supplements. If performance on the Core is higher than on the Diagnostic Components, you can safely conclude that performance on the school directions subtest is due to lack of familiarity with such directions rather than generally poor comprehension ability.

What Are the Advantages of the *Test of Reading Comprehension*?

The TORC is an interesting and innovative approach to the testing of comprehension. The designers have attended to the knowledge base that undergirds constructivist views of reading comprehension and have designed a reasonable alternative to traditional tests of reading comprehension.

The manual is unusually well written and clearly documents the rationale and design of the test as well as the norming process, administration, scoring and interpretation. The manual also offers suggestions for instructional resources.

The third edition of the TORC presents several improvements over the second edition. Key among these are new norms established in 1993–1994 on a clearly described sample stratified by age. Reliability and validity are clearly established and carefully explained in the manual.

The authors provide data to derive grade scores, but state their reluctance to do so. They also warn users throughout the manual of the limitations of grade scores.

What Are the Disadvantages of the *Test of Reading Comprehension*?

While the general vocabulary, syntactic similarities and sentence sequencing subtests present innovative ways to test aspects of text processing, the paragraph reading subtest offers the reader very short passages. The shortest is thirty words, and the longest 120 words. This subtest is significantly different from the whole texts that students are asked to read with good comprehension in daily school activities. Therefore, performance on this test must be compared carefully to performance on daily activities. If a student's performance in literature discussion groups, guided reading activities, or on running records is better than performance on the TORC, this discrepancy between daily work and test design may be the explanation. This bears careful analysis by you.

The title of the "General Vocabulary" subtest is misleading. It does not measure general vocabulary, but instead measures the ability to make analogies. Understanding analogies may not be a regular part of the curriculum in many schools. Students may have difficulty with this subtest, not because their general vocabulary is low, but because of the way it was assessed here.

Where Do I Get More Information About the *Test of Reading Comprehension*?

Brown, V. L., Hammill, D. D., & Wiederholt, J. L. (1995). *Test of reading comprehension, third edition, Examiner's manual*. Austin, TX: Pro-ed.

Green, F. J. (1998). Review of the test of reading comprehension, third edition. *Thirteenth mental measurement yearbook.* Lincoln, NE: University of Nebraska Press.

Perlman, C. (1998). Review of the test of reading comprehension, third edition. *Thirteenth mental measurement yearbook.* Lincoln, NE: University of Nebraska Press.

Test of Written Language–3

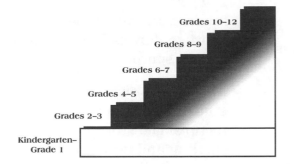

Grades 10–12
Grades 8–9
Grades 6–7
Grades 4–5
Grades 2–3
Kindergarten–
Grade 1

Level:

Age 7 years 0 months

through

17 years 11 months

Year Published: 1996

What Is It?

The *Test of Written Language–3* (TWL–3) is a norm-referenced test designed to evaluate abilities in written language production. The first edition of the TWL was introduced in 1978. Each successive revision of the test has been in response to criticisms of the existing edition. Significant changes were made in TWL–2. The changes that have been made in TWL–3 include shortening the time required to administer and score the test; adding easier items and dropping some of the more difficult items; entirely new normative data have been collected; and the norming sample has been carefully studied to be representative of gender, residence, geographic region, race, handicapping conditions, income of parents, and education of parents.

The TWL–3 requires a knowledgeable administrator. The authors, Hammill and Larsen, suggest that most persons who have completed college have sufficient understanding of writing to administer and score the test. They suggest that, in order to successfully use the test, you will need knowledge of the nature of written language, the components of writing, the testing formats that are useful in assessing writing, and a model for assessing writing. The well written manual reviews the pertinent background information.

The authors review the research on the nature of written language in identifying the components of written language. They conclude that the three components of written language are the conventional component, the linguistic component, and the cognitive component. Each of these three components is defined below.

The *Conventional Component* is the ability to make use of the rules established for punctuation, capitalization, and spelling. These rules must be understood by students before they can write efficiently and accurately.

The *Linguistic Component* is the ability to make use of syntactic and semantic structures—the grammar and meaning-communication components of writing. Writers must be able to select suitable words, tenses, plurals, subject-verb cases and correspondences.

The *Cognitive Component* is the ability to write logically using coherent and properly sequenced structures. Regardless of content, what we write must be structured in a way that a reader can create meaning.

Hammill and Larsen (1996) argue that in order to be usable, a writing test must yield a profile of a writer's strengths and weaknesses regarding specific components of writing and how that writer is able to combine those components in everyday writing. They suggest that the most common ways of assessing these abilities is through both contrived and spontaneous writing formats. They recognize that "written language has a deep, complex, and multidimensional nature and that the content of the TWL–3 is both selective and limited," and they go on to argue that the content of the TWL–3 is not "superficial, shallow or unrepresentative" of real writing (p. 69).

The three writing components and the two writing formats described above form the rationale for the structure of the TWL–3. The subtests of the TWL–3 assess the conventional, linguistic, and conceptual components of writing through both contrived and spontaneous formats. The eight subtests are described below. Subtests 1 through 5 are structured with contrived formats.

Subtest 1: Vocabulary   The student writes a sentence using a stimulus word.

Subtest 2: Spelling   The student writes dictated sentences, being careful to use spelling rules.

Subtest 3: Style   The student writes dictated sentences, being careful to use punctuation and capitalization rules.

Subtest 4: Logical Sentences   The student edits sentences to remove something that is illogical.

Subtest 5: Sentence Combining   The student combines the meanings of two short sentences into one grammatically correct sentence.

Subtest 6: Contextual Conventions   The student writes a story in response to a picture. The story is evaluated for spelling and adherence to rules governing punctuation and capitalization.

Subtest 7: Contextual Language   The student's story is evaluated for the quality of its vocabulary, grammar, and syntax.

Subtest 8: Story Construction   The student's story is evaluated for the quality of its composition—particularly prose, plot, and organization.

The TWL–3 is normally administered one-on-one in an untimed situation. The authors state that the entire test can be administered in approximately 1.5 hours, and usually can be completed in one testing session. The manual offers suggestions for group administration. There are two equivalent forms of the test, Form A and Form B.

Each subtest is scored to yield a raw score, a percentile score, and a standard score. A percentile score, on a scale of 100, indicates the proportion of the norming sample that scored at or below your student's score. The standard scores on the TWL–3 are set to range from 1 to 20 with a mean of 10 and a standard deviation of 3. Interpretations of the standard scores range from "very poor" to "very superior."

In using the "Profile/Story Scoring Form," you first calculate the scores for each of the separate subtests and then use that data to compute composite scores. One composite score is calculated for the contrived writing subtests and one is calculated for the spontaneous writing subtests. From these you calculate Composite Quotients for each of the formats and the test overall. The authors state that a Composite Quotient is "useful because it allows the examiner to estimate a student's overall writing competence and to document any preference for contrived or spontaneous testing formats" (p. 36). The Quotient Scores are constructed, like intelligence quotients, to have a mean of 100 and a standard deviation of 15. On the TWL–3, Quotient Scores range from 35 to 165 and are rated from "very poor" to "very superior." The manual offers advice on ways to interpret the Composite Quotients. Additionally, the manual offers an excellent chapter on ways to collect additional assessment data and implement programs for those who need special writing instruction.

In addition to the scores discussed above, the TWL–3 provides age and grade equivalents. The authors recommend that these scores should be interpreted with caution because interpolation, extrapolation, and smoothing were used to create these equivalents.

The TWL–3 was normed using a sample of 2,217 persons residing in 25 states. The data were collected in the first six months of 1995. The first 970 students tested were living in the four major geographic regions as defined by the U. S. Census Bureau. All students tested were in general classes, including those with disabilities. The remaining 1,247 students in the sample were at sites randomly selected using the publisher's customer files. Test administrators identified in this manner lived in all 50 states. The characteristics of the sample are comparable to those in the 1990 Statistical Abstract of the United States. The sample appears to be representative of students in the United States.

Reliability coefficients are reported for internal consistency, test-retest stability, and interscorer reliability. These coefficients range from .82 to .95 and verify the reliability of the test. The validity of the test is well established through presenting a solid rationale for the subtests and the results of item analysis procedures. Content validity was established in building the rationale for the design of the test on the research on writing. Concurrent validity was established by correlating results on the TWL–3 with the Comprehensive Scales of Student Abilities (CSSA), a teacher rating scale that assesses a range of school-related abilities, including writing. Correlation coefficients ranged between .50 and .53 with statistical significance at the .05 level. These coefficients represent a moderate relationship between the two tests.

The authors establish construct validity on the basis of the relationship between the subtests of the TWL–3 and the identified components of writing. Further construct validity is adequately documented in studies of subtest interrelationships, group differentiation, item validity, factor analysis, and the relationship of the TWL–3 to other measures of school achievement. However, Hansen (1998) in his review of the test points out some validity data render the test "relatively useless" for primary grade students.

Overall, the TWL–3 appears to be a reliable and valid test of writing ability. The manual is extremely helpful in providing detailed information about administration, scoring, and interpretation of the test, as well as useful recommendations for planning instruction. The authors appropriately recommend against the use of age and grade equivalents.

How Does the *Test of Written Language–3* Inform Instruction?

You may find that the best use of the TWL–3 is in program evaluation. Giving the test in the fall and again in the spring would provide normative data on student growth in your writing curriculum. However, some teachers have questioned the value of this information in light of the time required to administer, score and interpret the test.

Other teachers have found the TWL–3 useful in gaining insight into the writing performance of children who are struggling. Giving this test permits them to make instructional decisions in the areas of writing conventions, semantics, syntactics, and coherence. Some teachers use the subtests on conventions to determine which conventions they need to focus on in their whole group instruction, and which children might need help on an individual basis. You might follow the test with a writing conference in which you and the student review the data and add to his or her "goals as a writer" list.

You might find it useful to keep a master list of the conventions children

need to work on and focus on the instruction needed by most of your students first.

Teachers have found that the TWL–3 is very helpful in explaining a child's needs and goals to parents. In sharing the information from the test with parents, you can encourage them to foster the writing experiences of students at home.

What Are the Advantages of the *Test of Written Language–3?*

One of the greatest advantages of the TWL–3 is that it is grounded in research on the nature of writing. The subtests accurately reflect many of the components that contribute to effective writing. The fact that this test combines both contrived and spontaneous formats is a further advantage. While these formats are widely accepted measures of writing ability, it is helpful to have them both used in this one test. The manual is well written to be both comprehensive and thoughtful.

The cautions on test interpretation and the recommendations for implementing writing instruction are extremely helpful. The clearly articulated rationale for the design of each of the subtests is useful in helping understand why the test tests what it tests. The scoring of the contrived subtests is quite simple—not a claim that can be made for the spontaneous subtests. The data on the establishment of reliability and validity are extremely complete.

What Are the Disadvantages of the *Test of Written Language–3?*

On a practical level, one of the disadvantages of the TWL–3 is the amount of time required for administration and scoring. You will probably need to select as testing subjects only those students about whom you are most puzzled as writers. The scoring of the spontaneous subtests takes both a good deal of linguistic knowledge and time. The authors do, however, present an impressive list of references from which you can draw to update your knowledge.

Many teachers today appreciate the importance of students' sense of audience and purpose in writing. The TWL–3 asks students to write a story, but no consideration is given to either audience or purpose.

Most of the analysis of writing in the test is at the sentence level or smaller. Only in the analysis of the story do we see an evaluation of longer discourse, and then there is little opportunity for you to evaluate the thinking the student put into planning the overall structure of the piece.

It is unfortunate that Hammill and Larsen have succumbed to pressure from those who wish to have age or grade equivalent data on norm-referenced tests. This decision flies in the face of strongly stated recommendations against such scores from both the International Reading Association and the American Psychological Association. When we know that a kind of score is likely to be misunderstood, misleading, and unreliable, it is incumbent on test designers to take the lead in the elimination of such scores.

Where Do I Get More Information About the *Test of Written Language–3?*

Bucy, J. E. (1998). Review of the Test of Written Language, Third Edition. *Thirteenth mental measurement yearbook.* Lincoln, NE: University of Nebraska Press.

Deno, S. L., Marston, D., & Mirkin, P. (1981). Valid measurement procedures for continuous evaluation of written expression. *Exceptional Children, 48*, 368–370.

Hammill, D. D., Brown, L., & Bryant, B. R. (1992). *A consumer's guide to tests in print* (2nd ed.). Austin, TX: Pro-ed.

Hammill, D. D., & Larsen, S. C. (1996). *Test of written language examiner's manual.* (3rd ed.). Austin, TX: Pro-ed.

Hansen, J. B. (1998). Review of the Test of Written Language, Third Edition. *Thirteenth mental measurement yearbook.* Lincoln, NE: University of Nebraska Press.

McCutchen, D., & Perfetti, C. A. (1983). Local coherence: Helping young writers manage a complex task. *The Elementary School Journal, 84*, 71–75.

Test of Written Spelling–3

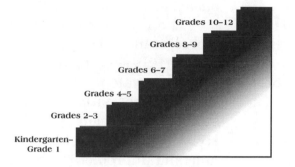

Grades 10–12
Grades 8–9
Grades 6–7
Grades 4–5
Grades 2–3
Kindergarten–Grade 1

Level:

Grade One

through

Twelve

Year Published: 1994

What Is It?

The *Test of Written Spelling–3* (TWS–3) is a norm-referenced spelling test for use in grades one through twelve. It contains one hundred words, fifty words that are considered "predictable" in their spelling and fifty words considered "unpredictable."

The authors, Larsen and Hammill, have carefully reviewed the research on spelling, dating from the mid-sixties, in forming the rationale for the TWS–3. This history is well reviewed in the Examiner's Manual. In tracing the history of spelling research, they begin with a review of the early work that assumed English orthography was highly irregular and that most words learned in school had to be memorized. They end with a review of the work of researchers who demonstrated that English orthography is not chaotic, but is essentially rule-governed. Some words have highly predictable spellings based on dependable generalizations. The spelling of other words does not conform to any rules. Larsen and Hammill have deemed these rule-governed spellings "predictable words" and

the non-conforming spellings "unpredictable words." Therefore, the TWS–3 has a list of 50 predictable words and a list of 50 unpredictable words. The rationale for the test design is clearly supported with research evidence. The test uses a dictated-word test procedure that measures how a student actually spells the words, rather than a procedure in which students are asked to select a misspelled word from a group of words—an editing task.

The authors identify four purposes for the TWS–3: to identify students who score significantly below their peers and might need remediation; to determine areas of relative strength and weakness in spelling; to document overall progress as a result of teaching; and to serve as a research measure.

The manual is well written and very helpful. The Preface traces the history of the TWS since 1976 and identifies the improvements made with each new edition in light of critical reviews. The first chapter of the manual reviews the history of spelling instruction and the design of the TWS–3. The authors are very frank about what the test can and cannot do. An important caveat is offered that the TWS–3 should never be used for instructional planning. The authors state: "The reason for this is straightforward. To prepare an instructional plan, the examiner needs to know which words the student cannot spell. Can he or she spell functional, everyday words? Which spelling generalizations has the student mastered? Which have not been mastered? Answers to such questions require information that is beyond standardized tests' capacity to provide. Informal teacher-made tests and criterion-referenced tests are much more useful for gleaning data to use in planning individual spelling programs" (Larsen & Hammill, 1994, p. 4).

You begin the test at entry levels determined by the grade level of the student(s) you are testing. Then basal and ceiling levels are determined. The basal level is the lowest point at which the student gets five consecutive correct spellings. All words before that point are considered correctly spelled. The ceiling level is the highest point at which five consecutive words are misspelled. All of the words beyond that point are assumed to be incorrectly spelled. The test is administered by saying the word, then saying a sentence that contains the word, and then repeating the word in isolation.

The original test words in grades one through eight were selected from ten of the most frequently used basal spelling series. Only words that appeared in all ten series were selected. In selecting new words for lower levels and words for the grades above eighth, the authors selected words from the EDL Core Vocabularies in Reading, Mathematics, Science, and Social Studies (Taylor, Frackenpohl, White,

Nieroroda, Browning & Birsner, 1979). Relevance of the words in TWS–3 was established by checking that they were present in five current leading spelling basal series and the EDL list.

The TWS–3 yields five scores: raw scores, standard scores (SS), percentile scores (PS), spelling ages (SA), and grade equivalents (GE). The standard scores are set with a mean of 100 and a standard deviation of 15. A standard score is determined for both predictable and unpredictable words. The standard scores are interpreted on a range from "very poor" to "very superior." The percentile scores for the two lists indicate the percentage of the distribution of the norming sample that performed at or below the performance of the student under consideration.

The authors describe the calculation of the spelling age scores and grade equivalent scores as follows: "Spelling ages and grade equivalents are derived by calculating the average score of students in the normative group at each age interval and at each school grade. Through a process of interpolation, extrapolation, and smoothing, spelling ages or grade equivalents are generated for each raw score point achieved on the TWS–3 subtests and total score" (p. 13). The SA and GE scores were included in the first edition of the test, dropped from the second edition, and added to the third edition. The authors acknowledge the arguments against these scores and, in fact, say that the criticism of these scores is what led them to eliminate them from the second edition. Of their inclusion in the third edition, the authors state: "In spite of all the negative criticisms directed at these scores, practitioners continue to use them and demand that publishers provide them. In many instances, state agencies and local schools mandate their use in discrepancy formulas, diagnostic evaluations, and preparation of written reports and, therefore, purchase only tests that offer those kinds of scores. For these reasons, we have restored spelling ages and grade equivalents to the TWS–3. We do so, however, with great reluctance. . . . We prefer that TWS–3 users employ standard scores or percentiles when possible" (p. 13).

The norming sample consists of 3,805 students whose scores were used to norm the second edition in 1986 and an additional 855 students tested in 1993 for the third edition. The 4,660 students in the norming sample resided in 23 states. The characteristics of the sample are comparable to those in the 1990 Statistical Abstract of the United States. The sample appears to be representative of students in the U.S. Reliability coefficients are reported for internal consistency, test-retest stability, and interscorer reliability. These coefficients range from .97 to .99, and establish the reliability of the test. The validity of the test is well established through presenting a solid rationale for the subtests and the results of item analysis procedures. Concurrent validity was established by correlating results on the TWS–3 with the spelling subtests of four other tests. The mean coefficient for the predictable words subtest is .88; for the unpredictable words subtest the coefficient is .92.

How Does the *Test of Written Spelling–3* Inform Instruction?

Teachers who use the TWS–3 appreciate that it is a test which requires that students actually spell test items rather than recognizing misspelled words as is done in some group-administered spelling tests. Schools typically use the TWS–3 as a school-wide screen instrument beginning in about second grade. Commonly, the test is given in the fall to collect baseline data and again in the spring to evaluate the effectiveness of the spelling component of the curriculum. This has proven especially useful in schools where spelling is taught as an integral part of the writing curriculum rather than in isolation with a published program.

Results from the test may be helpful in making some decisions about the nature of spelling instruction. For example, those children who achieve high scores might participate in accelerated spelling instruction that focuses on irregular words, challenging patterns and moves at a rapid pace. Their program might include words from the literature being read, as well as words from their own writing. Those students who score on the lower end of the exam may be enrolled in a developmental spelling program which stresses phonological rules and patterns and proceeds in a highly structured, sequential order. There would be overlap in these two approaches; the basic difference would be the pacing.

What Are the Advantages of the *Test of Written Spelling–3?*

The TWS–3 is truly a spelling test rather than an editing test. This lends considerable validity to the test. The research-driven design of the test is a further advantage. The manual is well written and the directions are easy to follow. The manual is also responsibly done in terms of recommendations for sharing the test results. Larsen and Hammill argue that the results should be shared following three guidelines: the person sharing the results should have a thorough understanding of the rationale, purposes, content and construction of the test; when test results are shared, they should always be accompanied by a personal interpretation from the examiner; and that test results should be shared with students who have taken the test.

The TWS–3 appears to measure what it was supposed to measure efficiently and consistently. The test is well-constructed, easily administered, and apparently useful in identifying students who are having difficulty in spelling.

The manual offers a complete set of references for those who wish to read the original research that was used in establishing the rationale for the test.

What Are the Disadvantages of the *Test of Written Spelling–3?*

The use of age scores and grade equivalents is clearly a disadvantage of the third edition of this test. Reviews of the first and second editions were highly positive, and the authors did a good job of modifying the test at each revision to account for criticisms. Their decision to eliminate age and grade scores from the second edition was a correct decision. It acknowledged the expertise of the membership of the International Reading Association which directed the President of the Association to write to test publishers requesting that age and grade scores be eliminated from norm-referenced tests. The decision to reintroduce age and

grade scores in the third edition because "practitioners continue to use them and demand that publishers provide them" (p. 13) is unfortunate. This wrong decision is not counter-balanced by the authors' statement that "We prefer that the TWS–3 users employ standard scores or percentiles when possible" (p. 13).

Suen (1998) was critical of the lack of supportive evidence for the purposes the authors claim for the test. Suen says, ". . . the usefulness of the TWS–3 remains unclear." In sum, the TWS–3 is a psychometrically excellent test in search of a useful, practical function. Perhaps this criticism should be factored into your evaluation of the instrument.

Where Do I Get More Information About the *Test of Written Spelling–3?*

Erickson, D. B. (1985). Review of the Test of Written Spelling—revised edition. In Mitchell, J. V. (Ed.), *The ninth mental measurement yearbook*. Lincoln, NE: University of Nebraska Press. (Note that this review is for the second edition).

Hammill, D. D., & Bartel, N. (1990). *Teaching students with learning and behavior problems*. Boston: Allyn and Bacon.

Hammill, D. D., Brown, L., & Bryant, B. R. (1992). *A consumer's guide to tests in print,* (2nd ed.). Austin, TX: Pro-ed.

Larsen, S. C., & Hammill, D. D. (1994). *Test of written spelling, third edition, Examiner's manual.* Austin, TX: Pro-ed.

Longo, A. P. (1998). Review of the Test of Written Spelling, third edition.

Thirteenth mental measurement yearbook. Lincoln, NE: University of Nebraska Press.

Suen, H. K. (1998). Review of the Test of Written Spelling, Third Edition. *Thirteenth mental measurement yearbook.* Lincoln, NE: University of Nebraska Press.

Woodcock Reading Mastery Tests–Revised

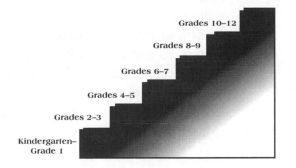

Grades 10–12
Grades 8–9
Grades 6–7
Grades 4–5
Grades 2–3
Kindergarten–Grade 1

Level:

Kindergarten to College Senior and
Adult to Age 75

Year Published: 1987, renormed in 1998

What Is It?

The *Woodcock Reading Mastery Tests—Revised* (WRMT–R) is a comprehensive battery of tests that measures an array of aspects associated with success in reading. The test comes in two forms, G and H, and includes an Easel-Kit to display test items (set up between you and the subject so that you can see examiner and subject pages simultaneously), a comprehensive examiner's manual, and test records for recording responses and scores and profiling results.

Form G contains the complete test battery, which consists of four tests of reading achievement (word identification, word attack, word comprehension, and passage comprehension); a readiness section containing two tests, visual-auditory learning and letter identification; and a two-part supplementary letter checklist. Form H does not contain the readiness section or the supplementary checklist. A microcomputer scoring program is available and so is a Report to Parents.

The WRMT–R is the 1987 revision of the 1973 original. The readiness section and the extension to college and adult populations are new features of the revised edition. Other major changes in the revision include an expansion of the word comprehension test to include antonyms and synonyms as well as analogies, the number of sample items has been increased, and a "Short Scale" Total Reading score using only the word identification and passage comprehension subtests has been made available.

Each of the six subtests is described below.

Test 1: Visual-Auditory Learning

This test consists of teaching the subject a vocabulary of rebus forms that are said to represent real, oral words. The subject is then asked to "read" these rebuses in strings representing sentences.

Test 2: Letter Identification

Here the subject is asked to respond by either the name or common sound to a set of letters varying in font size and style. The fonts include Roman, italic, bold, serif and sans-serif type styles, cursive characters, script, and decorative styles. A Supplementary Letter Checklist presents letters in a style common to many beginning reading materials.

Test 3: Word Identification

This test requires the subject to decode isolated words. It is not necessary to know the meaning of the words. As you move through this test, the words decrease in the frequency with which they appear in written English. In Subtests 3 and 4, it is important that you know the correct pronunciation of each test word. Pronunciation keys are provided, as well as an audio cassette tape on which the pronunciations are modeled.

Test 4: Word Attack

This test requires the subject to decode either nonsense words or words that have very low frequency of occurrence in English. The test is said to cause the subject to apply phonic and structural analysis skills in order to pronounce the words. Nonsense words are used here to assure that the subject has to apply word attack skills in decoding the word. Real words might be familiar or recognized by the subject.

Test 5: Word Comprehension

This test consists of asking the subject to identify an antonym, synonym, or analogy for the test words. Various subsets of the test items may be scored to reflect the subject's ability to comprehend words across four special vocabularies: general reading vocabulary, science-mathematics vocabulary, social studies vocabulary, and humanities vocabulary.

Test 6: Passage Comprehension

This subtest consists of two- and three-sentence passages from which a word has been eliminated. The subject is asked to supply the missing word in this modified cloze procedure. The test passages are drawn from textbooks, newspapers, and typical household and business documents. Some items have illustrations that aid in identifying the missing word.

Richard Woodcock, the author of the WRMT–R, has recommended clustering scores from groups of the subtests for increased validity and generalizability of the scores. In this way, more than one reading component is used in determining a score that is then used for interpretation. The five cluster scores are: Readiness Cluster, Basic Skills Cluster, Reading Comprehension Cluster, Total Reading–Full Scale, and Total Reading–Short Scale.

Woodcock suggests that the WRMT–R may be used for a variety of purposes. The most frequent use of the test is probably clinical assessment and diagnosis for subjects in school. The results of the test may be used in planning instructional goals for an Individual Educational Plan. Some schools use the test for determining instructional placement for new students or instructional grouping of students. The results of the test may be used to help an individual understand his or her current ability as a reader, for measuring growth, for program evaluation, or as a research tool.

The Examiner's Manual, revised in 1998, contains clear and highly useable instructions for preparing to administer the test. Because the interpretation of the results is very complex, you may need to engage in some training before using the test. The manual includes suggestions for examiner training and a helpful Checklist for Examiner Training Activities (p. 15) and a checklist for observations of practice testing sessions (p. 16).

The manual states that the first four subtests usually take about five minutes each; the last two usually take about ten minutes each. An experienced examiner can give the entire battery in about 40 to 45 minutes.

The interpretation of the WRMT–R permits you to do an error analysis, to describe the subject's developmental status, to describe the quality of the subject's performance, and to compare performance with other subjects at the same grade level or age. This is done using a variety of scores that are described below.

W Scores are used in the completion of the score summaries for subtests and clusters. They range from 338 to 608 and are designed so that you do not have to use negative numbers in calculations. Grade Equivalent Scores (GE) reflect the subject's performance in terms of the grade level in the norming sample where the median score is the same as the subject's score. Woodcock recognizes the criticism of Grade Equivalent Scores and responds to it with the following statement: "This problem with grade equivalent scores is eliminated when the items in a test are distributed uniformly over a wide range of difficulty and when the test has been normed on an appropriately selected sample of students across a wide range of grades. With the WRMT–R and other individually administered tests of this design, grade

equivalent scores *do* represent the level of task difficulty that the subject can perform and *are* properly used as an aid in instructional planning" (p. 39).

The WRMT–R uses what Woodcock calls an "extended grade equivalent scale" (p. 39). This extended grade score is used with subjects who score below the average obtained by beginning kindergartners or above the average obtained by college seniors at the end of the senior year. These extended grade scores are expressed with a decimal point, as grade scores typically are, but here a percentile post-script is added. For example, if the subject's score was equivalent to the 50th percentile for subjects in the ninth month of the senior year of college, the GE would be written 16.9^{50}.

Age Equivalent Scores are used to express the subject's performance in terms of the age level in the norming sample where the median score is the same as the subject's score.

Relative Performance Indexes (RPI) are used to represent the percent of mastery demonstrated by a subject where the average performance would be expected to yield a score of 90 percent. For example, an RPI of 68/90 means that the subject would perform tasks with 68 percent mastery that average persons of his or her age or grade would perform with 90 percent mastery. RPIs are intended to indicate relative quality of performance, not relative standing within a group.

Instructional Ranges (IR) are used to estimate the range between the subject's independent and frustration reading levels. The purpose is to guide you in determining the level of instruction that would be easy and the level that would be difficult for the subject. The easy level is defined as an Relative Performance Index of 96/60 and the difficult level is defined as an RPI of 75/90.

Percentile Ranks (PR) are used to describe the subject's standing in comparison to the distribution of scores within the norming sample. However, in the WRMT–R these scores are extended to range from a PR of one-tenth (.01) to a PR of 99.9.

Standard Scores (SS) are expressed as a mean of 100 and a standard deviation of 15, as a T score with a mean of 50 and a standard deviation of 10, as stanine scores, and as normal curve equivalent scores with a mean of 50 and a standard deviation of 21.06.

In the Summary Test Record, the scores are used to complete four profiles and a scores summary. The profiles are an instructional level profile, a diagnostic basic skills profile, a diagnostic comprehension profile, and a percentile rank profile. The summary of scores is used for subtests three through six, the basic skills cluster, the reading comprehension cluster, and the total reading cluster.

Between October 1995 and June 1996, and between September and November 1996, a representative sample of 3,184 students in kindergarten through grade 12 and an additional 245 young adults aged 18 to 22 were tested at 129 sites in four states. The test was renormed using this sample.

Reliability data consists of split-half correlations. The reliability coefficients for each of the subtests ranges from .34 to .98 with median coefficients ranging from .84 to .98.

To establish content validity, it would be necessary to argue that this test represents items from both curriculum and theoretical constructs and processes used in reading. No such data are offered. Concurrent validity is assessed by correlating performance on the WRMT–R with another reading test by the same author. This raises serious questions about the validity of the test.

How Does the *Woodcock Reading Mastery Test-R* Inform Instruction?

The 1998 revision of the Examiner's Manual includes a chapter written by Nancy Mather and Elaine Barnes on the instructional implications of the WRMT–R. The chapter includes seven case studies that inform your interpretation of the tests data. The chapter also offers an excellent overview of the many ways in which the test may be used to inform instruction. These authors suggest that in reviewing test results, you begin by surveying the student's general reading skill development first and then probe for more specific information. First you would examine scores on the Total Reading Cluster and the diagnostic clusters. You then identify the student's strengths and weaknesses on the components of each cluster. Finally, you analyze individual item responses.

The WRMT–R is probably more useful to reading specialists who are thoroughly diagnosing reading difficulties than to classroom teachers who are planning developmental instruction. Luann Dreifuerst, a reading specialist in Wisconsin, uses the Woodcock Reading Mastery Test as one part of the profile she gathers on her students.

Luann selects students for whom she feels that the Woodcock would provide additional information and she also selects sub-tests of the test to administer to individual students. For example, one of the subtests provides an indication of the student's short term memory and the subtest on comprehension is useful for assessing the meaning that children are getting from the text.

Luann uses the information obtained from the Woodcock, with other information from such sources as running records, to plan instruction for individuals and small groups. For example, she might use the information about the student's ability to identify sight words and the phonic strategies that they have to plan for instruction that would focus on recognizing given sight words or specific phonic strategies.

What Are the Advantages of the Woodcock Reading Mastery Tests-R?

The manual is exceptionally well written and complete. The checklist for preparing to administer the test is extremely useful. The administration guidelines are precise. The WRMT–R offers three levels of score interpretation, with each level using increasingly more normative data. The test appears to be well normed.

The Summary Test Record is designed to present the data clearly and in ways that are easily understood and interpreted. The clustering of scores is useful in diagnosis. The very thorough word attack error inventory could be very useful in diagnosis. It is useful to

be able to interpret vocabulary data across four different reading vocabularies.

What Are the Disadvantages of the Woodcock Reading Mastery Tests-R?

The WRMT–R uses some very unusual subtest designs that are not consistent with most other tests of reading ability. This is especially true of the visual-auditory learning subtest which uses rebuses, the word attack subtest that uses nonsense words, and the passage comprehension subtest which uses a modified cloze.

While the use of nonsense words on the word attack subtest may increase the validity of the test by really measuring word attack skill, the practice of using nonsense test items will be troublesome to some teachers and reading specialists. You will need to consider your own views on this practice in judging the test. Some teachers will also be concerned about the degree to which this test fragments the reading process. You may want to use the WRMT–R along with more holistic forms of assessment, rather than using it alone. It would be wise to double-check your interpretations of the WRMT–R with your own careful, professional observations of readers.

The administration of the test can be very time consuming and tedious for some subjects. The subtests that are said to measure "readiness for reading" are likely to be judged inadequate by those teachers and reading specialists who are attuned to the latest information about emergent literacy.

Scoring of the test is tedious. This can be corrected by using ASSIST, the microcomputer software program for scoring.

Where Do I Get More Information About the *Woodcock Reading Mastery Tests–R?*

Cooter, R. B. (1989). Review of the Woodcock Reading Mastery Tests–Revised. In Conoley, J. C., & Kramer, J. J. (Eds.), *The tenth mental measurements yearbook*. Lincoln, NE: University of Nebraska Press.

Jaeger, R. M. (1989). Review of the Woodcock Reading Mastery Tests–Revised. In Conoley, J. C., & Kramer, J. J. (Eds.), *The tenth mental measurements yearbook*. Lincoln, NE: University of Nebraska Press.

Woodcock, R. W. (1998). *Woodcock reading mastery tests–revised examiner's manual*. Circle Pines, MN: American Guidance Service.

Writer Self-Perception Scale

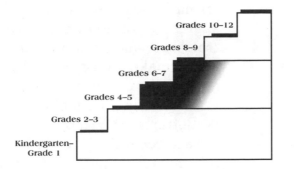

Grades 10–12
Grades 8–9
Grades 6–7
Grades 4–5
Grades 2–3
Kindergarten–Grade 1

Level:

Fourth Grade

through

Sixth Grade

What Is It?

The *Writer Self-Perception Scale* (WSPS) is an instrument to measure how intermediate-grade learners feel about themselves as writers. The scale is based on a theory of self-efficacy which states that a person's judgments of his or her ability to perform an activity effect the way in which the activity is performed. Children who have made positive associations with writing will probably welcome opportunities to write, put more effort into their writing, and demonstrate greater persistence in become better writers.

The authors identify five basic factors that writers take into account when they are determining their ability as writers. These factors are:

- *General Performance* (GPR)—A broad category that includes past success, amount of effort necessary, the need for assistance, patterns of progress, task difficulty, task persistence and belief in the effectiveness of instruction.
- *Specific Progress* (SP)—Deal with explicit dimensions of writing such as focus, clarity, organization, style, and coherence.
- *Observational Comparison* (OC)—How a child perceives his or her writing performance in relation to peers.
- *Social Feedback* (SF)—The child's perception of feedback about writing efforts from teachers, classmates, and family members.
- *Physiological States* (PS)—Internal feeling the child experiences during writing.

The WSPS consists of 38 items. There is one general item, "I think I am a good writer," and 37 items that measure one of each of the five scales described above. Students are asked to indicate their degree of agreement on a five-point scale representing "strongly agree, agree, undecided, disagree, and strongly disagree." The authors suggest that before duplicating the scale (Figure 34) that you remove the factor designators (GPR, SP, OC and so on).

You calculate a raw score for each of the five factors. These scores are then interpreted as "high, average or low." For example, if your fourth grade student had a raw score of 36 on General Progress (GPR) you would compare that on the scoring sheet (Figure 36) with the average fourth grade score of 35. This would indicate that you student's perception of general progress is in the average range compared to the fourth graders in the norming sample. These evaluations were determined through a norming process that included subjects drawn from three large school districts located in south central Pennsylvania, as well as suburban districts in Arkansas, Connecticut, and North Carolina. A total of 964 students in fourth through sixth grade participated in the study.

Reliability of the instrument has been well established through internal consistency coefficients. The construct validity of the instrument is established through linkage to well regarded learning theory and research in the affective domain. The scale has significant concurrent validity with the *Elementary Reading Attitude Survey*.

The *Writer Self-Perception Scale* (Figure 31), the *Writer Self-Perception Scale: Directions for Administration Scoring, and Interpretation* (Figure 32), and the *Writer Self-Perception Scale Scoring Sheet* (Figure 33) are reprinted here with the permission of the authors and the International Reading Association.

How Does the *Writer Self-Perception Scale* Inform Instruction?

You will interpret each of your learner's scores on each of the five scales as either "high, average, or low." You could examine the ratings on each

of you students on this factor to determine the overall perception of general progress as writers. If you found several students whose perception of performance was low, you could launch an aggressive campaign, for example, to "celebrate our work as writers." You might make a large wall chart of the goals children have written in their writing folders under "Things I Want to do Better as a Writer." A composite list drawn from all of the students could become a focal point of your writing celebration. You could highlight each of the goals as it is achieved.

You could administer the scale in the fall and again in the spring to learn how your students' self-perceptions changed over the school year. If these data became part of a portfolio, you could track such progress from year to year.

By carefully examining the overall perceptions on each of the five scales you can set quite specific instructional goals. By focusing on an individual child, you can set very important instructional goals for each of your learners.

What Are the Advantages of the *Writer Self-Perception Scale?*

The scale is well grounded in the theory and research on self-perception and motivation. Knowing a writer's self-perception can provide you with valuable insights in planning instruction. The scale can be easily administered to groups of learners.

What Are the Disadvantages of the *Writer Self-Perception Scale?*

The scale yields only a general indication of a child's self-perception of writ-

Figure 31   The Writer Self-Perception Scale

Listed below are statements about writing. Please read each statement carefully. Then circle the letters that show how much you agree or disagree with the statement. Use the following scale:

SA = Strongly Agree
A   = Agree
U   = Undecided
D   = Disagree
SD = Strongly Disagree

Example: **I think Batman is the greatest super hero.**   SA   A   U   D   SD

If you are *really positive* that Batman is the greatest, circle SA (Strongly Agree).
If you *think* that Batman is good but maybe not great, circle A (Agree).
If you can't *decide* whether or not Batman is the greatest, circle U (Undecided).
If you *think* that Batman is not all that great, circle D (Disagree).
If you are *really positive* that Batman is not the greatest, circle SD (Strongly Disagree).

(OC)	1.	I write better than other kids in my class.	SA A U D SD
(PS)	2.	I like how writing makes me feel inside.	SA A U D SD
(GPR)	3.	Writing is easier for me than it used to be.	SA A U D SD
(OC)	4.	When I write, my organization is better than the other kids in my class.	SA A U D SD
(SF)	5.	People in my family think I am a good writer.	SA A U D SD
(GPR)	6.	I am getting better at writing.	SA A U D SD
(PS)	7.	When I write, I feel calm.	SA A U D SD
(OC)	8.	My writing is more interesting than my classmates' writing.	SA A U D SD
(SF)	9.	My teacher thinks my writing is fine.	SA A U D SD
(SF)	10.	Other kids think I am a good writer.	SA A U D SD
(OC)	11.	My sentences and paragraphs fit together as well as my classmates' sentences and paragraphs.	SA A U D SD
(GPR)	12.	I need less help to write well than I used to.	SA A U D SD
(SF)	13.	People in my family think I write pretty well.	SA A U D SD
(GPR)	14.	I write better now than I could before.	SA A U D SD
(GEN)	15.	I think I am a good writer.	SA A U D SD
(OC)	16.	I put my sentences in a better order than the other kids.	SA A U D SD

(GPR) 17.	My writing has improved.	SA A U D SD
(GPR) 18.	My writing is better than before.	SA A U D SD
(GPR) 19.	It's easier to write well now than it used to be.	SA A U D SD
(GPR) 20.	The organization of my writing has really improved.	SA A U D SD
(OC) 21.	The sentences I use in my writing stick to the topic more than the ones the other kids use.	SA A U D SD
(SPR) 22.	The words I use in my writing are better than the ones I used before.	SA A U D SD
(OC) 23.	I write more often than other kids.	SA A U D SD
(PS) 24.	I am relaxed when I write.	SA A U D SD
(SPR) 25.	My descriptions are more interesting than before.	SA A U D SD
(OC) 26.	The words I use in my writing are better than the ones other kids use.	SA A U D SD
(PS) 27.	I feel comfortable when I write.	SA A U D SD
(SF) 28.	My teacher thinks I am a good water.	SA A U D SD
(SPR) 29.	My sentences stick to the topic better now.	SA A U D SD
(OC) 30.	My writing seems to be more clear than my class-mates' writing.	SA A U D SD
(SPR) 31.	When I write, the sentences and paragraphs fit to-gether better than they used to.	SA A U D SD
(PS) 32.	Writing makes me feel good.	SA A U D SD
(SF) 33.	I can tell that my teacher thinks my writing is fine.	SA A U D SD
(SPR) 34.	The order of my sentences makes better sense now.	SA A U D SD
(PS) 35.	I enjoy writing.	SA A U D SD
(SPR) 36.	My writing is more clear than it used to be.	SA A U D SD
(SF) 37.	My classmates would say I write well.	SA A U D SD
(SPR) 38.	I choose the words I use in my writing more carefully now.	SA A U D SD

Figure 32   The Writer Self-Perception Scale Directions for Administration, Scoring and Interpretation

The Writer Self-Perception Scale (WSPS) provides an estimate of how children feel about themselves as writers. The scale consists of 38 items that assess self-perception along five dimensions of self-efficacy (General Progress, Specific Progress, Observational Comparison, Social Feedback, and Physiological States). Children are asked to indicate how strongly they agree or disagree with each statement using a 5-point scale ranging from Strongly Agree (5) to Strongly Disagree (1). The information yielded by this scale can be used to devise ways of enhancing children's self-esteem in writing and, ideally, to increase their motivation for writing. The following directions explain specifically what you are to do.

Administration

To ensure useful results, the children must (a) understand exactly what they are to do, (b) have sufficient time to complete all items, and (c) respond honestly and thoughtfully. Briefly explain to the children that they are being asked to complete a questionnaire about writing. Emphasize that this is not a test and that there are no right or wrong answers. Tell them that they should be as honest as possible because their responses will be confidential. Ask the children to fill in their names, grade levels, and classrooms as appropriate. Read the directions aloud and work through the example with the students as a group. Discuss the response options and make sure that all children understand the rating scale before moving on. The children should be instructed to raise their hands to ask questions about any words or ideas that are unfamiliar.

The children should then read each item and circle their response to the statement. They should work at their own pace. Remind the children that they should be sure to respond to all items. When all items are completed, the children should stop, put their pencils down, and wait for further instructions. Care should be taken that children who work more slowly are not disturbed by classmates who have already finished.

Scoring

To score the WSPS, enter the following point values for each response on the WSPS scoring sheet (Strongly Agree = 5, Agree = 4, Undecided = 3, Disagree = 2, Strongly Disagree = 1) for each item number under the appropriate scale. Sum each column to obtain a raw score for each of the five specific scales.

Interpretation

Each scale is interpreted in relation to its total possible score. For example, because the WSPS uses a 5-point scale and the General Progress scale consists of 8 items, the highest total score is 40 (8 x 5 = 40). Therefore, a score that would fall approximately at the average or mean score (35) would indicate that the child's perception of her- or himself as a writer falls in the average range with respect to General Progress. Note that each remaining scale has a different possible maximum raw score (Specific Progress = 35, Observational Comparison = 45, Social Feedback = 35, and Physiological States = 30) and should be interpreted accordingly using the high, average, and low designations on the scoring sheet.

Figure 33   The Writer Self-Perception Scale Scoring Sheet

Student name _____

Teacher _____

Grade _____   Date _____

Scoring key: 5 = Strongly Agree (SA)
4 = Agree (A)
3 = Undecided (U)
2 = Disagree (D)
1 = Strongly Disagree (SD)

Scales

General Progress (GPR)	Specific Progress (SPR)	Observational Comparison (OC)	Social Feedback (SF)	Physiological States (PS)
3. _____	22. _____	1. _____	5. _____	2. _____
6. _____	25. _____	4. _____	9. _____	7. _____
12. _____	29. _____	8. _____	10. _____	24. _____
14. _____	31. _____	11. _____	13. _____	27. _____
17. _____	34. _____	16. _____	28. _____	32. _____
18. _____	36. _____	21. _____	33. _____	35. _____
19. _____	38. _____	23. _____	37. _____	
20. _____		26. _____		
		30. _____		

Raw Scores

_____ of 40   _____ of 35   _____ of 45   _____ of 35   _____ of 30

Score interpretation	GPR	SPR	OC	SF	PS
High	39+	34+	37+	32+	28+
Average	35	29	20	27	22
Low	30	24	23	22	16

ing ability and must be used along with your own observations, work samples, and conversations with your learners. Further, like all self-report assessment tools, students may tell you what they think you want to hear rather than what they truly believe. This further increases the importance of you using observations and other sources of data to support or refute information learned from the scale. The number of items for each of the scales is sufficiently low as to suggest that you might place more credibility in an overall evaluation rather than individual scale scores.

Where Do I Get More Information About the *Writer Self-Perception Scale?*

Bottomley, D. M., Henk, W. A., & Melnick, S. A. (1997). Assessing children's views about themselves as writers using the Writer Self-Perception Scale. *The Reading Teacher, 51,* 4, 286–296.

Appendix A
Portraits of Writers

Precon-ventional

At this stage the children play at writing (scribble writing) and make random letters, The children may add these "words" to drawing to build meaning about their pictures. They may tell lengthy stories about their pictures.

Emergent

These children see themselves as writers. They may write their names and some familiar words in a way that others may understand. One or two letters, usually initial or ending consonants, may represent a whole word. They often use letters to label pictures. They will pretend to read their own writing, often elaborating to make a story.

Developing

Students clearly attempt to write with some recognizable letters and perhaps a few familiar words They will use beginning, middle, and ending sounds to make these words. For example, learn might be LRn. They often interchange upper- and lower-case letters. They begin to write noun-verb phrases such as MI DG PLS (My dog plays). Their work looks like writing. For example, the writing goes across the page and begins to include spacing. They are able to read their own writing aloud for at least a short time after writing, but later may not remember what they intended.

Beginning

Students write about immediate experiences that self and others can read. They begin to write recognizable short sentences with some descriptive words. They use some capitals and periods, but not always in the right places. Many letters are formed legibly. Some words are spelled phonetically, and some are correct. (Example: Once apon a tim ther wuz a Huntr be whent hunting evryday.) They often start a story with "Once upon a time" or finish with "The end." Children may revise by adding on.

Expanding

Students often write about their experiences and interests. They begin to consider audience by adapting the tone to suit their purposes. For example, in a Halloween story, word choice, characterization, and plot will be different when written for a kindergartner than for a peer. Pieces contain a beginning, middle, and end which may be elaborated with description and detail. They enjoy reading their stories and are able to offer specific feedback to peers. Their editing skills continue to grow, though are still fairly inconsistent. Students no longer labor over the physical act of writing. Many common words are spelled correctly, however, inconsistencies frequently occur.

Bridging   Students begin to develop and organize their ideas into paragraphs with teacher guidance. Students at this stage are able to write for an increasing number of purposes. This is a time of practice, and the writing is often uneven: the writer may focus on one aspect of the piece, but pay less attention to others. Students are learning that meaning can be made more precise through the use of details, reasons, and examples. Literary devices such as dialogue, similes, and alliteration are added during the revision process (usually with teacher guidance). Students edit their own and their peers' work with greater precision.

Fluent   This is a stage of increasing complexity. The writer has internalized appropriate tone and mood. For example, when given a teacher-directed assignment to write a biographical essay on a leader, the writer would know to use a serious tone. The writer attempts to vary sentence length and complexity. For example, they may start a sentence with an adverbial phrase ("Nervously, the boy sat at his desk, awaiting his turn to speak.") They also use transitions effectively, such as: however, and, but, and or. These writers have internalized a variety of literary devices. Writing is becoming more coherent and organized within paragraphs and in the connection of paragraphs. Revision strategies include providing examples, adding reasons, and deleting in order to clarify. In their editing, they find most of their own basic spelling, grammar, punctuation, and capitalization errors.

Proficient   This level is sophisticated. These writers often deal with abstract and complex issues in their writing. They are prolific and versatile. These writers show great flexibility in moving between teacher-directed and self-selected topics. These children show a willingness to revise and enjoy the art of writing.

Independent   These writers have internalized the writing process and persevere through extensive projects. These analytic writers may have their own distinctive style, but through their evaluation of written material, their style continues to grow.

Portraits of Readers

Preconven-
tional

Preconventional learners display curiosity about books and read-ing. They enjoy listening to stories and have favorites. They also enjoy holding the book and turning pages. They may talk about the story and label and comment on the pictures. They are inter-ested in environmental print such as favorite restaurant signs, traffic signs, and cereal boxes. These children know some letter names, many go through this stage before kindergarten.

Emergent

Emergent learners are curious about reading and see themselves as potential readers. They may role-play themselves as readers. They rely on pictures to tell the story but are beginning to focus on print. During read-aloud, they may chime in with a familiar or predictable word or phrase. Also, after hearing pattern, rhym-ing, or predictable books many times, they may memorize them. They also may enjoy rhyming and playing with words. They will recognize familiar words such as their names or favorite places. They know some letter sounds. Children at this age are highly motivated and may move through this stage rather quickly.

Developing

Developing learners see themselves as readers and read simple word pattern books such as consonant–vowel–consonant word rhyming books. They know most letter sounds and recognize simple words such as: it, dog, cat, and, the, etc. They now merge print and illustrations to build meaning. They can retell the main idea of a story. This is another stage that children may pass through quickly.

Beginning

Beginning learners rely on print more than illustrations to cre-ate meaning. They understand basic punctuation such as periods, exclamations, and question marks. These students can read early-reader books such as *I Can Read* books or Dr. Seuss books. Later on in this stage they will read harder early-reader books such as *Little Bear* or *Frog and Toad* books. During silent reading time, these students may initially browse, but gradually are able to silent read for five minutes or more. They may take a develop-mental leap as they integrate reading strategies (sentence struc-ture, meaning, phonetic clues). They know many words by sight. They are able to retell the beginning, middle, and end of stories. This is an exciting stage, however, it may take significantly longer to move through than earlier stages.

Expanding

This is a practicing and stretching stage. These students may read known and predictable favorites while also stretching into a variety of new materials. They may read beginning chapter books such as the *Polk Street Series*. They may also read non-fiction materials, comics, or magazines, such as *New True Books, Ranger Rick,* or *Garfield*. They now silent read for a longer period (ten minutes or more). They use a variety of reading strategies independently. These students may make connections between reading, writing, and experiences. For example, after hearing the story, *Charlotte's Web,* a child may be inspired to write about a special relationship. These students are also able to retell plot, characters, and events of stories they read or hear. They can recognize different types of books such as non-fiction, fiction, and poetry.

Bridging

This is a connecting stage where readers strengthen their skills by reading longer books that are no longer vocabulary controlled. These students read medium-level chapter books such as *Ramona* books or *James and the Giant Peach*. They may broaden their interests by reading a wide variety of materials such as *World* magazine, *Calvin and Hobbes, EyeWitness*, or *Explorer* books. They are able to silent read for twenty minutes or more. These children may be able to use reference materials to do a simple report. Their increased knowledge of literary elements and genres may allow them to describe a character's growth over time, understand the importance of the setting to a story, and compare and contrast books.

Fluent

This is a level of increased sophistication. These students can deal with issues and topics which are becoming more complex. These students can read most young adult literature such as *Hatchet, Snow Treasure*, and *From the Mixed-Up Files of Mrs. Basil E. Frankweiler.* They select and finish a wide variety of materials independently. These students participate in teacher-guided literary discussions.

Proficient

This level is sophisticated. These are avid readers who independently select challenging material such as the trilogy by Tolkien, *The Westing Game*, and unabridged classics. These readers can move between genres with ease, although they may have established strong preferences. They can become deeply involved in literary discussions. These students will seek out additional information after reading material of interest.

Independent

These prolific readers select material of a complex nature, such as *This Boy's Life, Watership Down,* and *The Martian Chronicles*. These readers evaluate, interpret, and analyze in depth.

Checklists

WRITING CONTINUUM CHECKLIST

Preconventional

			Makes marks other than drawing on paper (scribble writing)
			Primarily relies on pictures to convey meaning
			Sometimes labels and adds "words" to pictures
			Tells about own writing

Emergent

			Sees self as writer
			Copies names and familiar words
			Uses pictures and print to convey meaning
			Pretends to read own writing
			Prints with upper-case letters
			Uses beginning/ending consonants to make words

Developing

			Takes risks with writing
			Begins to read own writing
			Writes names and favorite words
			Writing is from top-bottom, left-right, front-back
			May interchange upper- and lower-case letters
			Begins to use spacing between words
			Uses beginning, middle, and ending sounds to make words
			Begins to write noun-verb phrases

Beginning

			Writes pieces that self and others can read
			Begins to write recognizable short sentences
			Writes about observations and experiences with some descriptive words
			Experiments with capitals and punctuation
			Forms many letters legibly
			Uses phonetic spelling to write independently
			Spells some words correctly
			Begins to revise by adding on

Expanding

			Begins to consider audience
			Writes pieces with beginning, middle, and end
			Revises by adding description and detail
			Listens to peers' writing and offers feedback
			Edits for punctuation and spelling
			Uses capital letters and periods
			Forms letters with ease
			Spells many common words correctly

Bridging

			Begins to write for various purposes
			Begins to organize ideas in logical sequence
			Begins to develop paragraphs
			Begins to revise by adding literary devices
			Develops editing and proofreading skills
			Employs strategies to spell difficult words correctly

Fluent

			Uses appropriate tone and mood for a variety of purposes
			Experiments with complex sentence structure
			Connects paragraphs in logical sequence
			Uses an increased repertoire of literary devices
			Revises for clarity by adding reasons and examples
			Includes deleting in revision strategies
			Edits with greater precision (spelling, grammar, punctuation, capitalization)

Proficient

			Adapts style for a wide range of purposes
			Varies sentence complexity naturally
			Uses literary devices effectively
			Integrates information from a variety of sources to increase power of writing
			Uses sophisticated descriptive language
			Uses many revision strategies effectively

Independent

			Writes cohesive in-depth pieces
			Internalizes writing process
			Analyzes and evaluates written material in-depth
			Perseveres through complex writing projects

READING CONTINUUM CHECKLIST

Preconventional

			Holds book, correctly turns pages
			Chooses books and has favorites
			Shows start/end of book
			Listens and responds to literature
			Knows some letter names
			Interested in environmental print

Emergent

			Pretends to read
			Uses illustrations to tell story
			Participates in reading of familiar books
			Knows some letter sounds
			Recognizes names/words in context
			Memorizes pattern books and familiar books
			Rhymes and plays with words

Developing

			Sees self as reader
			Reads books with word patterns
			Knows most letter sounds
			Retells main idea of text
			Recognizes simple words
			Relies on print and illustrations

Beginning

			Reads early-reader books
			Relies on print more than illustrations
			Uses sentence structure clues
			Uses meaning clues
			Uses phonetic clues
			Retells beginning, middle, and end
			Recognizes names/words by sight
			Begins to read silently
			Understands basic punctuation

Expanding

			Reads beginning chapter books
			Reads and finishes a variety of materials with frequent guidance
			Uses reading strategies appropriately
			Retells plot, characters, and events
			Recognizes different types of books
			Makes connections between reading, writing, and experiences
			Silent reads for short periods

Bridging

			Reads medium level chapter books
			Reads and finishes a variety of materials with guidance
			Reads and understands most new words
			Uses reference materials to locate information with guidance
			Increases knowledge of literary elements and genres
			Silent reads for extended periods

Fluent

			Reads most young adult literature
			Selects, reads, and finishes a wide variety of materials
			Uses reference materials independently
			Understands literary elements and genres
			Begins to interpret deeper meaning in young adult literature w/ frequent guidance
			Participates in guided literary discussions

Proficient

			Reads complex young adult literature
			Moves between many genres with ease
			Integrates non-fiction information to develop a deeper understanding
			Interprets sophisticated meaning in young adult literature with guidance
			Participates in complex literary discussions

Independent

			Voluntarily reads and understands a wide variety of complex and sophisticated materials with ease
			Evaluates, interprets, and analyzes literary elements critically

Appendix B

Key Learning Outcomes for Writing
Dancing with the Pen
Ministry of Education, New Zealand

FORMING INTENTIONS

Choosing Topics

In choosing topics successfully, learners will:

- value first-hand experience and their own knowledge;
- make use of their surroundings, both inside and outside school;
- discuss their ideas freely;
- research their ideas in a variety of ways;
- adapt and make use of their own topics for writing;
- show initiative in selecting their own topics for writing,
- feel confident enough to muse on selecting a topic.

Determining the Audience

In determining audience successfully, learners will:

- have clear goals, and know how these will affect their writing,
- feel that what they will write is valuable and interesting to others;
- expect to respond to, and profit from, others; responses and writings;
- distinguish between public and private writing, and the effects of audience on content clarity, and expression;
- expect to receive help from the teacher, from others' and from examples of writing for different audiences.

Finding Out, Selecting and Ordering Information

In finding out, selecting and ordering information successfully learners will:

- recognize what they know and what they need to know,
- feel ready to seek and find further information,
- feel satisfaction in discovery;
- make use of both spoken and written language in selecting and evaluating information;
- order and focus information for a selected audience;
- make use of appropriate study skills, techniques, and tools.

Handling Appropriate Forms

In handling appropriate forms successfully, learners will:

- know about the characteristics of different genres;
- structure their own writing, within a genre, soundly and effectively;
- recognize differences in voice, register, and style,
- write in a variety of genres, forms, styles, and registers.

COMPOSING AND DRAFTING

Getting It Down On Paper—Revising It As You Go

In Composing and drafting successfully, learners will:

- internalize the information gathered and present it in their own words;
- use revision strategies effectively to improve communication;
- develop their ideas and feelings in a well-formed structure;
- make effective use of technical aids, for example, dictionaries and word processors;
- evaluate the accuracy and effectiveness of what they have written;
- seek and profit from the on-going responses of others;
- recognize and negotiate the time necessary for a particular task.

CORRECTING AND PUBLISHING

Correcting and Proofreading

In correcting and proof-reading successfully, learners will:

- show respect for the reader by applying what they know in correcting text;
- show independence in doing their own proof-reading;
- develop competence in spelling and using surface features.

Publishing

In publishing successfully, learners will:

- be keen to select and publish their work;
- make use of design in the effective presentation of text;
- take the audience into account;
- seek and give responses on their own and others' text layout;
- use a variety of publishing media, forms and styles;
- make good use of available resources in materials and time.

OUTCOMES

Audience Response

In responding to others writing, and profiting from others' responses, learners will:

- readily share their published work with many others both outside the classroom;
- be eager to read the published work of others;
- expect a response to their published writing;
- see the purpose and value of publication and response;
- react positively to others' responses, making appropriate adjustments to their own writing;
- offer constructive criticism with courtesy and understanding.

Key Learning Outcomes for Writing are from *Dancing With the Pen*, first published 1992 by Learning Media, Ministry of Education, Box 3292, Wellington, New Zealand. Used with permission of the Ministry of Education.

Appendix C

Answer each of the following questions according to the following scale:

5 Yes, very well
4 Yes, more than adequately
3 Yes, adequately
2 No, not too well
1 No, poorly
NA Not applicable or can't tell

1. _____ Did the student recall a sufficient number of ideas

2. _____ Did the student recall the ideas accurately?

3. _____ Did the student select the most important details to recall?

4. _____ Did the student understand explicit pronouns and connectives?

5. _____ Did the student infer important implicitly stated information?

6. _____ Did the student include the explicitly stated main points?

7. _____ Did the student create any new summarizing statements?

8. _____ Did the student use the organizational pattern used by the author?

9. _____ Did the student elaborate appropriately?

10. _____ Did the student know how to adjust strategies to the purpose given?

What effective comprehension processes were evident in the students recall?

What comprehension processes were not evident, or seemed to be causing problems?

To what extent was the student's performance as just described affected by each of the following?

1. Limited prior knowledge or vocabulary.

2. Limited motivation or interest.

3. Cultural differences.

4. Decoding problems.

5. Difficulties in the text.

6. Social Context.

7. Discomfort with the task.

8. Other environmental influences.

Glossary

Achievement Test	A test that measures the extent to which students have mastered an area of study or a set of skills.
Analytic Scoring	Assigning a set of scores to predetermined traits in a piece of writing.
Anchors	Actual examples of student writing that are used to judge other writing in analytic or holistic scoring. Sometimes called benchmarks.
Assessment	The practice of collecting information about what learners know and can do. Includes both qualitative and quantitative data used to make judgments about what students know and should learn next.
Benchmarks	Actual samples of student work or descriptions of student performance that are used to judge the quality of work. Usually used in evaluating writing.
Constructed Response	Students are required to respond to a stimulus with a narrowly prescribed written or oral response such as short answer questions or data interpretation.
Constructed Response Items	Require students to produce an answer rather than select an answer from a set of possible answers.
Correlation Coefficient	A measure of the degree of relationship between two variables (sets of subjects, two research items, the performance of a group on two tests). Correlation coefficients (indicated as r) range from -1.00 to 0.00 to +1.00. An r of -1.00 indicates a perfect negative relationship. An r of 0.00 indicates no relationship, and an r of + 1.00 indicates a perfect positive relationship.
Error of Measurement	A statistic that estimates the degree to which the ob served score on a test may differ from the actual performance. The error of measurement is a way to indicate the reliability of a test.
Evaluation	The process of assigning meaning to the data collected on learners. Evaluation may focus on either what the learner can do or what the learner cannot do.

Generalizable	The extent to which a student's performance on an assessment measure can be extended to indicate achievement of a domain of study or a set of skills.
Grade Equivalent Score	Interprets a student's performance in terms of grade level. A grade score of 2.6, for example, would mean a student's performance was like that of a typical second-grader in the sixth month of second grade.
Holistic Scoring	The process of evaluating a piece of writing by assigning one, over-all score to it.
Item Analysis	The process of evaluating individual test items as to the difficulty level and discriminating power of an item.
Local Percentile Rank	Works like the National Percentile Rank except that the comparison group is local rather than national. With this score one can compare student's performance against that of other learners at the same grade level in the school system.
National Percentile Rank	Ranges from 1 to 99 and indicates the percentage of students in the norming group who earned raw scores the same as or lower than a given student's score.
Normal Curve Equivalent	Scores ranging from 1 to 99 with a mean of 50. Normal Curve Equivalent scores can be averaged and are often used to report performance in Title I programs.
Norming Sample	The group of students that was used to determine the norms for a test. The performance of the norming sample becomes the yardstick against which all future performance on the test is judged.
Norms	The statistics which describe the performance of the norming sample on a norm-referenced test.
Norm-Referenced Test	A test that compares the performance of students against the performance of the norming sample of students.
P-Value	The percent of students who answered a test item correctly. This is often used to judge the difficulty of a test item.
Performance-Based Assessment	Students construct their own responses to questions or prompts rather than selecting an answer from predetermined alternatives. Also known as alternative or authentic assessment.

Raw Score

The number of test items correctly answered by a student.

Reliability

The degree to which a test consistently measures what it is supposed to measure. The degree to which a test supports a complete and accurate measurement of a student's performance across time and tasks.

Rubric

A set of rules or criteria to give direction to the scoring of writing pieces.

Scale Score

A standard score that permits comparisons from grade to grade, across time and among different forms of a test.

Standardized Test

A test that is administered, scored and interpreted exactly the same way each time it is administered.

Stanine Scores

Distribute performance on a test over unequal categories ranging from 1 to 9 with the average being 5. Stanine scores permit students and parents to broadly identify areas of strength and weakness in the test scores.

Validity

The degree to which a test measures what it is actually supposed to measure. The degree to which decisions can be based on the quality of a test.

Index

About the Author

Bill Harp is Professor of Language Arts and Literacy in The Graduate School of Education, University of Massachusetts Lowell. There he works with students who are becoming reading specialists at the masters and doctoral levels. His teaching experience ranges from Head Start through sixth grade, and he has been an elementary school principal and director of programs for the gifted and talented.

He is co-author with Jo Ann Brewer of a college text on the teaching of reading entitled *Reading and Writing: Teaching for the Connections* published by Harcourt College Publishers. He and Jo Ann, his wife, are currently working on a new college text entitled *Becoming An Informed Teacher of Reading: Striving Towards Best Practice* to be published by Merrill. Bill also serves as editor of *The Bill Harp Professional Teachers Library*, in imprint of Christopher-Gordon Publishers, Inc.

Bill and Jo Ann enjoy three grandchildren who range in age from six to twelve. Their hope is that these children will grow to love reading and writing as much as their grandparents do.